Hacking Knoppix

Hacking Knoppix

Scott Granneman

Wiley Publishing, Inc.

Hacking Knoppix

Published by
Wiley Publishing, Inc.
10475 Crosspoint Boulevard
Indianapolis, IN 46256
www.wiley.com

ISBN-13: 978-0-7645-9784-8
ISBN-10: 0-7645-9784-1

Manufactured in the United States of America

10 9 8 7 6 5 4 3 2 1

1B/RU/RS/QV/IN

For general information on our other products and services or to obtain technical support, please contact our Customer Care Department within the U.S. at (800) 762-2974, outside the U.S. at (317) 572-3993 or fax (317) 572-4002.

Wiley also publishes its books in a variety of electronic formats. Some content that appears in print may not be available in electronic books.

Library of Congress Cataloging-in-Publication Data

Granneman, Scott.
  Hacking Knoppix / Scott Granneman.
    p. cm.
  Includes index.
  ISBN-13: 978-0-7645-9784-8 (paper/cd-rom)
  ISBN-10: 0-7645-9784-1 (paper/cd-rom)
  1. Linux. 2. Knoppix (Computer file) 3. Operating systems (Computers) I. Title.
  QA76.76.O63G7229 2005
  005.4'32-dc22
                    2005029725

About the Author

Scott Granneman is an author, educator, and consultant. Scott's book on the Firefox web browser, *Don't Click on the Blue E!: Switching to Firefox,* has garnered wide praise. In addition, he is a monthly columnist for SecurityFocus and for *Linux Magazine*, and he blogs professionally on the Open Source Weblog. He is currently an adjunct professor at Washington University in St. Louis, where he teaches a variety of courses about technology, social software, and the Internet. Finally, as a co-owner of WebSanity, Scott helps nonprofits and businesses use the company's Content Management System to take full advantage of the Web's communication, sales, and service opportunities. He's been using Linux for a decade, and swears by it.

Credits

Executive Editor
Carol Long

Acquisitions Editor
Debra Williams Cauley

Development Editor
Maryann Steinhart

Technical Editors
Robert Citek
Jason Luster

Production Editor
William A. Barton

Copy Editor
Luann Rouff

Editorial Manager
Mary Beth Wakefield

Production Manager
Tim Tate

Vice President and Executive Group Publisher
Richard Swadley

Vice President and Publisher
Joseph B. Wikert

Project Coordinator
Michael Kruzil

Graphics and Production Specialists
Lauren Goddard
Stephanie D. Jumper
Barbara Moore
Melanee Prendergast

Quality Control Technicians
John Greenough
Leeann Harney
Jessica Kramer

Media Project Supervisor
Laura Moss

Media Development Specialist
Angela Denny
Kit Malone
Travis Silvers

Proofreading and Indexing
TECHBOOKS Production Services

Cover Design
Anthony Bunyan

Contents at a Glance

Contents

Acknowledgments

Hacking Knoppix has truly been a team effort, and there are a lot of folks to recognize. In particular, I want to acknowledge the hard work, energy, and flat-out brilliance displayed by Klaus Knopper and all of the other hackers, programmers, developers, and users who have contributed in a thousand different ways to the growth of one of the coolest and most innovative technologies available today: Knoppix.

This book couldn't have been written without the help and support of many important individuals. My agent, Laura Lewin, has been helpful in too many ways for me to recount. My main editor at Wiley, Debra Williams Cauley, shepherded this work effectively, efficiently, and with great care and humanity. Thanks, Debra! My technical editor and guru, and all-around great human being, Robert Citek, continues to teach me a tremendous amount about Linux and open source. Jerry Bryan has looked over everything I've written in the last several years and helps make things shine. My wife, Denise, supported me completely during her own tough times and has always given me an example to follow. Finally, my cute little Shih Tzu, Libby, was a boon companion at all times and deserves almost constant belly rubs.

Paul Love, Josh Myer, and Robert Citrek contributed chapters to this book:

Paul Love—CISSP, CISA, CISM, Security+—has been in the IT field for 15 years and is currently a security manager at a financial institution. Paul holds a master of science degree in network security and a bachelor's degree in information systems. He was the lead author of *Beginning Unix*, has co-authored two Linux security books, contributed to multiple Linux/Unix books, and has been the technical editor for more than 10 best-selling Linux and Unix books.

Josh Myer is Linux Administrator for ibiblio at the University of North Carolina-Chapel Hill. He's proficient in multiple programming languages and works in Linux, Windows, Mac OS X, Solaris, SCO Unix, and SCO Xenix operating systems. He has designed in GCC and GNU Make, Microsoft Visual Studio, and Apple development environments, and his experience includes systems administration, clustering, and networking.

Robert Citek has a master of science degree microbiology from the University of California at Riverside, and currently works for Orion Genomics as a bioinformaticist exploring various plant and animal genomes using a number of open-source software tools, including Knoppix. He has worked with Unix since the mid-eighties, and with GNU/Linux since the mid-nineties, both as a hobbyist and as a computational biologist. You can find him on the Knoppix forums at http://knoppix.net.

Alex de Landgraaf, John A. Goebel, and Benjamin Mako Hill also contributed to the writing of this book.

Introduction

Years ago, Bob heard about Linux, and he wanted to give it a whirl. It sounded interesting: open source, free, powerful, stable. So he asked Alice, a friend of his who uses Linux, "Hey, I'm running Windows right now, and I want to keep running it, but how do I try Linux out for myself?"

"Well," she said, "we can either back up your whole hard drive, wipe it, install Linux, let you try it out, and then remove Linux and put Windows back on, along with all your data, or . . ."

"Whoa! I just want to try it out, not turn this into a project! Isn't there an easier way?"

"OK," she said, "we can set up your machine to dual boot Windows and Linux. We'll resize your hard drive partitions—oh, yeah, we need to buy some software to do that, about $50 or so—and then we'll install Linux in a new partition, and then when you turn your box on, you can choose either Windows or Linux. How's that?"

"That sounds like a lot of work too. I just want to play with Linux. I don't want to commit to it. Is there anything else I can do?"

Alice thought for a moment. "No, not really."

Bob walked away, another potential Linux user that remained just that: potential.

There had to be a better way. Soon enough, there was, and there was much rejoicing in Linuxland. That rejoicing has spread over the years, and now more and more computer users— many of them living outside Linuxland in Windowsworld—are discovering that there's a software tool available that enables them to try out Linux painlessly, and do a whole heck of a lot more besides. With this fantastic tool, users can do any of the following:

- Recover precious data from a machine (running Linux or Windows!) that won't boot
- Test the security of a machine, a local area network, or a public server
- Play games, listen to music, view videos, or look at pictures
- Surf the Web, shoot off emails, instant message pals, and download software
- Fix common problems with computers running either Windows or Linux
- Create their own customized version that suits their needs perfectly

Best of all, this tool has all the characteristics of the best that the world of Linux has to offer: it's free, it's awesomely innovative and astoundingly clever, and it's flat out fun. In addition, for those of us who love (and live) to learn, by combining the brainpower of a dedicated organization of volunteers all over the world, there's always something new and exciting to learn about this software.

The name of this tool, of course, is Knoppix.

About This Book

Hacking Knoppix is your guide to the wonderful world of Knoppix. The authors have been using Knoppix for years, in all sorts of various ways, and we all jumped at the chance to share our experiences and hard-won knowledge with you. We hope you find *Hacking Knoppix* interesting, inspiring, and useful.

You don't need to read this book straight through from beginning to end. Instead, feel free to jump around from chapter to chapter and dive into the stuff that interests you first. Just be sure to try out the stuff that's covered. It'll make this book more enjoyable, and you'll learn Knoppix a lot faster and more effectively.

Who Is This Book Written For?

This book is not just for Linux users. Folks who use Windows (in other words, most people) will find that Knoppix is darn handy to keep in their toolkits as well. Many are the Windows machines that I've fixed with nothing more than patience, my trusty Knoppix CD, and a pinch of luck.

This book is aimed at intermediate to advanced computer users. If you've used Linux a bit, the topics will be a bit easier for you, but Linux experience is not absolutely required as long as you keep an open mind and want to learn.

You need access to a computer that can run Knoppix, of course. Right now, this means an Intel-compatible CPU that's at least a 486, a bare minimum of 96MB of RAM, a bootable CD-ROM drive or a boot floppy and standard CD-ROM, a standard SVGA-compatible video card, and a serial, PS/2, or USB mouse.

Those are the official Knoppix recommendations. In reality, here's what I'd try to have: a Pentium III or the AMD equivalent, a decent video card with at least 4MB of VRAM, and 128MB of RAM at the bare minimum—256MB of RAM is better, and 512MB is positively sweet.

How This Book Is Organized

The 12 chapters of this book are divided into four major parts, each focusing on a different topic. Two appendixes round out the volume.

Part I: Navigating the Amazing Knoppix Toolkit

Part I is an introduction to the software tools included with Knoppix. Chapter 1 covers the important apps that any modern computer user is going to look for in an operating system, such as printing, multimedia, burning CDs, and creating documents of all kinds. Chapter 2 moves on to Internet-based software. First you connect to the Net with broadband, wireless, or dial-up, and then you can use programs such as BitTorrent, Firefox, KMail, and Gaim—all fun and awesome. Chapter 3 is about using Knoppix to link to other machines, files, and printers, and enabling others to connect to your Knoppix machine to access selected resources.

Part II: Rescuing and Recovering Systems Using Knoppix

Part II is where you start to put Knoppix to work beyond simply running programs. You begin using Knoppix to fix problems. Chapter 4 uses Knoppix to repair issues common to Linux boxes, and Chapter 5 does the same for Windows. Ever had a problem with GRUB or a partition table, or had an issue with boot.ini or viruses? Then Chapters 4 and 5 will come in handy. Chapter 6 looks at how you can use Knoppix to make your systems and networks more secure by utilizing encryption, testing for vulnerabilities, or sniffing packets, among other cool tricks.

Part III: Knoppix Variants

Knoppix itself has become a building block for other Linux Live CD distros that perform an astonishing variety of tasks. Part III presents the coolest and most useful of those Knoppix variants. Chapter 7 investigates distros that help scientists perform their jobs (if you've ever wanted an easy way to create a super-powerful Linux cluster, this is the chapter for you!). Chapter 8 analyzes four Knoppix-based distros that focus on security. These are some of the most powerful CDs a computer or security pro could have in her toolkit. Check 'em out!

Part IV: Customizing Knoppix and Live CDs

In Part IV, you learn how to create your own Knoppix-based Live CD. This is some really cool stuff! Chapter 9 leads you through various customizations you can make without remastering your distro. Chapter 10 guides you through the intense procedure of changing and remastering Knoppix, and we think you'll be surprised when you discover that it's a detailed, but eminently doable, process. In Chapters 11 and 12, you put what you learned in Chapter 10 to work. Chapter 11 walks you through creating Archix, a distro for kids, and Chapter 12 helps you create a distro called Myppix that is totally focused on you and your specific Linux needs.

Appendixes

The two appendixes provide you with important but auxiliary information about Knoppix. Appendix A goes over the Knoppix boot process with a fine-tooth comb. You may think you know how Linux machines boot, but trust us: Knoppix is different. We guarantee that you'll find techniques in this appendix that you had no idea existed. Appendix B helps you take Knoppix off of the CD it comes on and put it onto your hard drive. If you like Knoppix so much that you want it to become your main OS of choice, Appendix B will help you do so..

README: Some Things You Really Need to Know

Starting with Knoppix 3.8.1, UnionFS—a stackable unification filesystem—was added to the distro. This was an enormous change because at one blush, several longstanding problems installing software on top of a CD-based distro were solved, and many new possibilities became available to Knoppix users. To maximize your use of Knoppix, you need to understand what UnionFS does and how you can use it. This is extremely important, and the authors of *Hacking Knoppix* assume throughout this book that you have read this section.

The knoppix-mkimage Script

The knoppix-mkimage script is amazingly useful. It enables you to save virtually any change you make to Knoppix while you're running it. Think about that for a second. Previously, you couldn't really install new programs on top of Knoppix because the /usr directory was read-only (yes, there were a few hackish ways around that, which you'll see in Chapter 10). You could save changes made to your home directory, but that was about it. Now, thanks to a fantastic new technology called UnionFS, you can basically make any change you want to your running copy of Knoppix, save those changes to a structure that in essence layers on top of the read-only Knoppix, reboot Knoppix, and have all those changes you made automatically restored and available for your use.

With a Knoppix CD and a USB flash drive, you can sit in front of almost any computer and, in a few minutes, find yourself using Knoppix with your settings, configurations, programs, and customizations. That is, if you don't realize it yet, wicked cool!

Note For details about UnionFS and how it works, see "A Stackable Unification File System" at www. fsl.cs.sunysb.edu/project-unionfs.html, *Linux Journal*'s "Kernel Korner—Unionfs: Bringing File-systems Together" at http://linuxjournal.com/article/7714, and "LinuxHints/KnoppixUnionFS" at www.hants.lug.org.uk/cgi-bin/wiki.pl?LinuxHints/KnoppixUnionFS.

To use UnionFS with Knoppix, first run the knoppix-mkimage script by selecting the Knoppix menu → Configure → Create a Persistent KNOPIX Disk Image. An introduction screen (see Figure 1) is displayed with all the details.

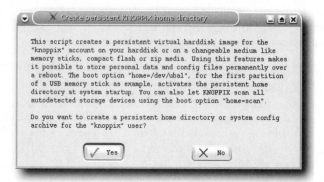

Figure I-1: The knoppix-mkimage introduction screen

Note Don't worry about the title bar of the window, which refers to an older script that created a Knoppix home directory instead of an entire disk image. The Knoppix developers will clean up that bit of legacy code sometime soon.

Familiarize yourself with this overview, and then click Yes. Next, select the writable media you want to use to store your files, as shown in Figure 2.

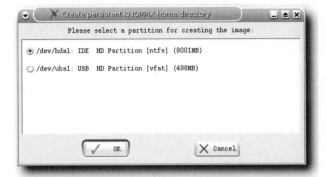

Figure I-2: Where do you want to store your persistent image?

Knoppix automatically detects hard drives, USB flash drives, Zip drives, and other writable media that it can use. A USB flash drive would give you maximum portability. Feel free, though, to use your hard drive if you plan to reboot Knoppix a lot on the machine you're using. If you're going to use your hard drive, don't worry about wiping out everything—you'll be asked in just a moment to select how big you want your disk image to be, so you could even select a partition containing Windows if you wanted.

Next, indicate whether you want to encrypt the disk image you're going to create (see Figure 3).

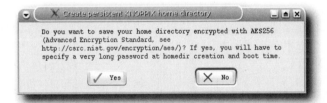

Figure I-3: For maximum security, encrypt your persistent image.

If you're really paranoid, then by all means, choose Yes; just be aware that you're going to have to enter a 20-character password every time you boot. If you're talking the security of important documents, however, this is hardly a burden. If you don't need to worry about securing your disk image, click No.

Then you have a big decision to make: how big should your persistent disk image be (see Figure 4)?

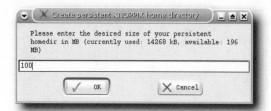

Figure I-4: How big do you want your persistent image to be?

The size you choose here is totally dependent upon how you plan to use Knoppix. If you're going to be using Knoppix on the same desktop machine for quite a period of time, you may want to create a multi-gigabyte disk image. If you're going to store the image on a USB flash drive, you're probably thinking in terms of a few hundred megabytes or so. Just make sure that the device you choose has enough room on it. If you're just starting out with UnionFS and the `knoppix-mkimage` script, that means a minimum of 100MB, which nowadays is chicken feed.

 Make sure that you specify the size of the persistent disk image in MB! A 2GB image, therefore, would be entered as 2000 (or 2048 if you want to be pedantic).

Click OK, and `knoppix-mkimage` does its job. This can take a while, so be patient. If it appears that the script is hung, be patient a bit longer. It's working.

Finally `knoppix-mkimage` finishes, indicating success, as shown in Figure 5.

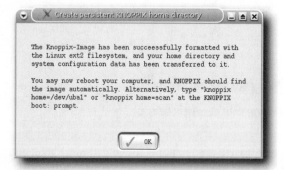

Figure I-5: Your persistent image has been created.

To use your new persistent disk image, you have to use a cheatcode (a special instruction for Knoppix) at boot time. Use `knoppix home=scan` to have Knoppix search for your persistent home directory at boot time. You can specify the location as well; for instance, if you stored the image on your hard drive, you would use `knoppix home=/dev/hda1` to use the persistent disk image on the hda1 partition.

You can also use knoppix-mkimage to save files you add, configuration files you change, and even applications that you download and install using APT, which are discussed in Chapter 10. Thanks to your persistent disk image, the changes you make will be available upon reboot, and you won't have to re-download, re-install, and re-configure Knoppix every time you use the distro.

If you're feeling particularly clever, you can save more than one disk image (see Figure 6).

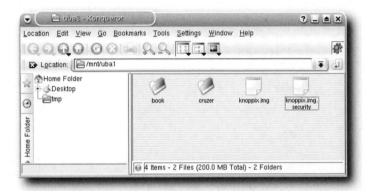

Figure I-6: I like to keep at least a couple of different disk images on my USB flash drive.

Figure 6 shows two images on my USB flash drive: knoppix.img, the current one, and knoppix.img.security, an alternative that's focused on security testing. Normally I use knoppix.img, but if I know I'm going to be doing intensive security work, I change the name of knoppix.img to knoppix.img.normal, and then alter the name of knoppix.img.security to knoppix.img. When I start Knoppix, I simply use knoppix home=scan as usual, but this time the image devoted to security is employed.

When it's time to go back to the normal disk image, I reverse the image renaming process, and I'm good to go. Best of all, you can have as many disk images as you need . . . or will fit onto your media!

As you read the rest of this book, in many places we assume that you're using a persistent disk image, so go ahead right now and get that set up. You'll be glad you did, and it will make your experience with *Hacking Knoppix* more efficient and fun.

Conventions Used in This Book

In this book, you'll find several notification icons—Note, Caution, and Tip—that point out important information. Here's what the three types of icons look like:

Notes provide you with additional information or resources.

A caution indicates that you should use extreme care to avoid a potential disaster.

A tip is advice that can save you time and energy.

Code lines are often longer than what will fit across a page. The symbol ⊃ indicates that the following code line is actually a continuation of the current line. For example,

```
# dpkg-query -W --showformat='${Installed-Size} ${Package}\n' ⊃
   | sort -n
```

is really one line of code when you type it into your editor.

Code, filenames, functions, and so forth within the text of this book appear in a monospace font, while content you will type appears either **bold** or monospaced.

Hacking Precautions

There is no way that just booting Knoppix on a computer can damage that machine. In fact, that's one of the beautiful things about Knoppix: you can boot it, play with it all you want, reboot and take the Knoppix CD out, and your machine remains untouched. However . . .

You still need to be careful with Knoppix, because it is possible—if you know how, and you will be learning how—to delete key system files on your computer, blow up system partitions, and in general render your nice shiny Windows or Linux machine into an unbootable hunk of plastic and silicon that will require either a reinstall or a system rollback (if you're using Windows XP's system restore feature) to work again.

Hey, don't panic! That doesn't mean that Knoppix is dangerous. It just means that it is a powerful tool, and like any powerful tool, you need to treat it with care and respect. Keep your head about you as you read this book and try out the techniques demonstrated for you. A good backup wouldn't hurt either (but then again, it never does).

So have fun with Knoppix, but be careful too. You're about to start learning more about one of the coolest, most innovative, and most powerful software tools available today. Make sure you're responsible—your computer will thank you.

Navigating the Amazing Knoppix Toolkit

Unraveling the Knoppix Toolkit Maze

Linux is famous as an operating system that includes almost everything a software user could ever want right out of the box—and for free. The Knoppix developers had quite a time deciding which of the thousands of packages to include, but they did their homework, made their decisions, and you're the one who benefits. This chapter can't cover everything that comes on the Knoppix disk—that would be a book in itself!—but it does take a look at important apps such as K3b and the GIMP that you'll probably find yourself using at one time or another.

 Note If you don't know how to boot Knoppix, you'll want to learn before you go much further. Head to Appendix A, "Booting Knoppix," for complete instructions. You have to be running Knoppix to really learn from this book.

Beautifying Knoppix

Out of the box, Knoppix has what could be called "uglification issues." It just ain't as pretty and user-friendly as it could be. One of the first things you may want to do when you start up Knoppix is make it look a bit nicer, so that using it won't cause you to constantly grit your teeth at the old, jagged, ugly fonts.

Then, after making your changes, you want to make sure you save your choices so that when you next boot Knoppix, you won't have to reconfigure the appearance of the OS again. That's covered in depth in the Introduction, but if you somehow skipped over it, for now just select Knoppix → Configure → Save Knoppix, choose a hard drive or USB flash drive to save onto, and then choose that source the next time you boot Knoppix.

Replacing System Fonts

The default fonts are definitely ugly. Blech! We think the best solution is to download and install the Microsoft Web fonts, which are attractive and common. However, if you're not using the persistent home directory, you're going to have a problem. You'll be able to install the fonts, but when you restart Knoppix, you'll have to reinstall all the fonts again, because all of your work will have been blown away. With the persistent Knoppix disk image, all of your work is saved, so you can count on your newly installed fonts being there.

To install the Microsoft Web fonts, use KPackage, the KDE software installation tool; it's a front end to Debian's APT (Advanced Package Tool). From the Knoppix menu, choose Utilities ➜ Manage Software in Knoppix to start KPackage. When KPackage opens, select the All tab, as shown in Figure 1-1.

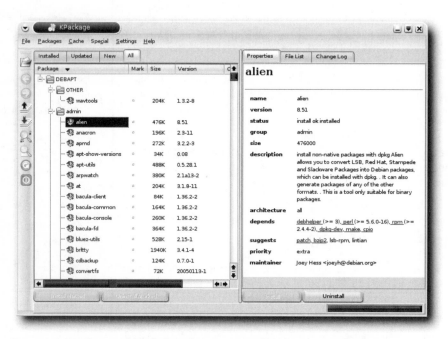

FIGURE 1-1: KPackage makes it relatively easy to install and manage software.

Then follow these steps:

1. In KPackage, select Special ➜ APT:Debian ➜ Update. APT downloads a list of the software available in the APT repositories Knoppix knows about. This can take a few minutes, so just relax.

Tip Don't know what APT is or how to use it? The author of this chapter has prepared "Updating Your Computer with Debian's APT," a presentation for his Linux students that covers the basics, which you can download from www.granneman.com/presentations. (It's available under a Creative Commons license). Alternatively, read the official Debian documentation, APT HOWTO, at www.debian.org/doc/manuals/apt-howto/index.en.html.

2. When the APT update completes, go to the All tab and select File → Find Package. Enter the package name, msttcorefonts, as the search term, and click Find.

3. After KPackage finds the package, close the Find Package window and click the Install button at the bottom of the right pane.

4. An Install window opens. Click the Install button at the bottom. (Yes, this is kind of silly, which is why I prefer to use the command line instead of KPackage for installing software. Using the command line is discussed later in this chapter.) Finally, KPackage begins to actually download and install the software you want onto your system.

5. When it's finished, close KPackage.

Note If you're curious, the Microsoft fonts have been placed into /usr/share/fonts/truetype/ msttcorefonts.

However, you can't start using your newly installed fonts just yet. You need to restart X, and fortunately that's pretty straightforward (unlike using KPackage). From the Knoppix menu, select Logout → End Current Session. After X restarts, you need to log back in, and now you can finally start making intelligent font choices!

Note Remember that if you're not using the persistent Knoppix disk image, when you reboot, you're going to have to repeat this entire process, again and again, in a Sisyphean task that will never end. Set up and use the persistent Knoppix disk image!

Now assign some nice new fonts in appropriate places on your system. Keep in mind that this chapter walks through only the major apps on Knoppix, so you're on your own to change fonts on any other apps you use that aren't covered here.

First, fix KDE itself. From the Knoppix menu, select Control Center, expand Appearance & Themes, and select Fonts. The Fonts Control Center displays, as shown in Figure 1-2.

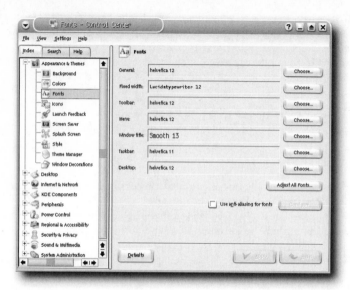

FIGURE 1-2: Changing fonts in the KDE Fonts Control Center

Ugh, what terrible defaults! Lucida typewriter is ugly, Helvetica is so 1960s, and Smooth is anything but. To pick something better, click Adjust All Fonts; then, in the Select Font window, check the box next to Font. Find and choose either Bitstream Vera Sans or Arial (I prefer Bitstream Vera Sans). Notice, however, that the Fixed Width font does not change. To fix that one, click Choose next to Fixed Width and then select Andale Mono, which is a great monospace font. Click Apply at the bottom of the Fonts screen, and you should immediately see your new fonts in action. Close the Control Center.

Next, open the Konqueror file manager (the Personal Files icon on the panel that looks like a house), and select Settings ➔ Configure Konqueror. The Configure window opens, as shown in Figure 1-3.

Once again, Helvetica is the default. Change it to Bitstream Vera Sans or Arial or another font that you like better. Don't click OK yet; while this window is open, you also can fix the fonts Konqueror uses when it's acting as a Web browser.

Tip

Change the value for Height for Icon Text to 10 lines (the default is 1), so that it's easier to read.

Scroll down the left-hand list of icons until you get to Fonts, shown in Figure 1-4.

FIGURE 1-3: Changing the fonts for the Konqueror file manager

FIGURE 1-4: Changing the fonts Konqueror uses when it displays Web pages

Change the fonts on that screen to ones that you like better. The following are our recommendations:

- **Standard font:** Verdana or Bitstream Vera Sans
- **Fixed font:** Andale Mono (if you have it on your system, it's much better than anything in the Courier family)
- **Serif font:** Bitstream Vera Serif or Times New Roman (use Times New Roman only if you must; Bitstream Vera Serif is far easier to read)
- **Sans serif font:** Verdana or Bitstream Vera Sans
- **Cursive font:** Lucida Calligraphy, Lucida Handwriting, and Bradley Hand ITC are great, but none of those is available, so choose Arioso.
- **Fantasy font:** Comic Sans MS isn't bad (you're hardly ever going to need this font), but you can pick anything goofy.

Click OK to make the changes and close this window. You can close Konqueror if you'd like. Now that you've changed your system fonts, move on to program fonts.

Changing Application Fonts

You'll probably find yourself using Mozilla Firefox, KMail, and OpenOffice.org often. You can change their fonts to make these programs more usable, too.

Fixing Firefox Fonts

To set up Firefox's fonts, click the Mozilla icon on the panel (yes, it should be the Firefox icon, but it isn't), and then choose Edit ➔ Preferences, click the General icon, and select Fonts & Colors (see Figure 1-5).

Make these changes:

- **Proportional:** Sans Serif
- **Serif:** Bitstream Vera Serif or Times New Roman
- **Sans serif:** Bitstream Vera Sans or Verdana
- **Monospace:** Andale Mono

Click OK and then OK again to close the Fonts & Colors window. Now isn't that a lot better?

Replacing KMail Fonts

Open KMail from the K menu by selecting Internet ➔ KMail. Choose Settings ➔ Configure KMail, and then click the Appearance icon on the left. You'll see the Fonts tab shown in Figure 1-6.

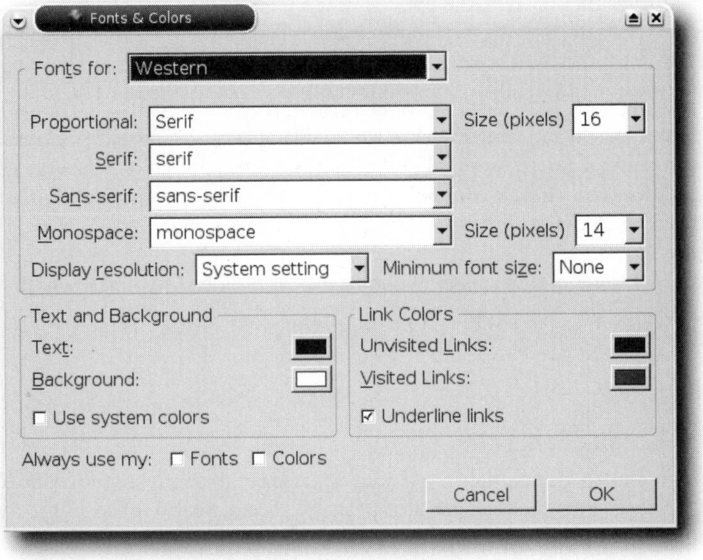

FIGURE 1-5: Changing Firefox's font options

FIGURE 1-6: Change the fonts that KMail uses

If you check the Use Custom Fonts box, the options in the main part of the screen are "ungrayed." Choose an item from the Apply To drop-down list, and select a font for it; then choose another item from the list, make a font choice, and so on, until all of them have been changed. At that point, click OK, and your new font choices will be applied to KMail.

You can choose any fonts you want, of course. We would change everything except Fixed Width font to Bitstream Vera Sans, Verdana, or Arial — basically, something that's pleasant and readable. For Fixed Width font, try Andale Mono if you have it or Bitstream Vera Sans Mono if you don't. Click OK to close KMail's configuration window, and you're good to go.

Note   We recommend changing Composer to Andale Mono to stick to plain text for email, which means a monospaced font.

Switching OpenOffice.org Fonts

Whatever you do, do not open OpenOffice.org (OOo) and expect to configure the fonts. Oh, no. It's not that simple. Instead, from the K menu, select OpenOffice.org 1.1.4 ➜ OpenOffice.org 1.1.4 Printer Administration (see Figure 1-7).

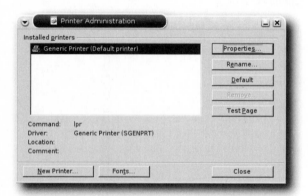

FIGURE 1-7: Isn't it obvious that you should configure fonts when you configure printers? No? We don't think so, either.

Click the Fonts button to open the Fonts window. Then click Add, which opens the Add Fonts window. Click the button labeled "..." in the Source directory area of the window, navigate to /usr/share/fonts/truetype/msttcorefonts, and click Select. Back in the Add Fonts window, check the Create Soft Links Only box, and then click Select All, followed by OK. You are told that many new fonts were added, so click OK to close that window. Click Close to get rid of the Fonts window, and then click Close again to finally exit Printer Administration.

If it's any consolation, this process is much improved in the OpenOffice.org 2.0 release, which is still in beta at the time of this writing. You'll see it in a future release of Knoppix.

To start OOo, click on the program's icon (the one with the birdies) on the panel. After OOo opens (and it'll take a while!), select Tools → Options, click on the + next to Text Document to expand it, and finally select Basic Fonts (Western).

Because you first added all of the Microsoft fonts, OOo (in an effort to achieve maximum compatibility with all the drones using Microsoft Word) changes everything except Heading to Times New Roman, and changes Heading to Arial. Now you're just like the rest of the world.

Setting Up Printers

Once upon a time, an old IT pro was counseling some new IT youngsters gathered around him. He was speaking sagely about keeping your "clients" happy, when someone asked him, "Master, what's the number one thing we can do to keep our computer users from calling us, complaining?" His answer? "Here it is, grasshopper: Make sure they can print. Not being able to print causes angry calls faster than anything else."

Now, that was before the advent of the Internet into popular consciousness, so his answer might be a bit different today, with network access being the new number one concern. Even so, printing would still come in a close second. People get very cranky when they can't print, with good reason: Much as we'd like to believe that we live in the age of the paperless office, experience has proved otherwise.

Fortunately, Knoppix makes it pretty easy to set up printers. Of course, if your printer doesn't work under Linux (Samsung, for example), Knoppix ain't gonna fix that, but if you're trying to use a printer that's supported under Linux, then you should be able to use it with your Knoppix Live CD.

To get started, from the Knoppix menu, choose Configure → Configure printer(s). Knoppix opens the KDE printer configuration tool, shown in Figure 1-8.

KDE's print system uses CUPS (the Common Unix Printing System) by default, and installs several so-called *pseudo printers* by default, including Print to File (PDF), Print to File (PostScript), Send to Fax, and Mail PDF File. All are very cool, and all work well (of course, to fax, you need a working modem).

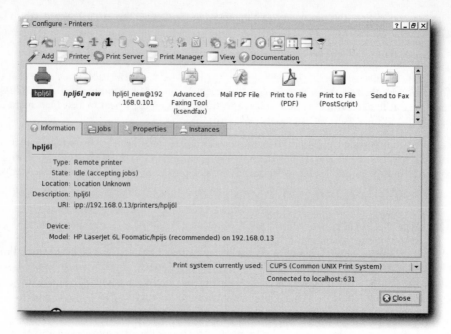

FIGURE 1-8: The KDE (and Knoppix) printer config utility

In addition to pseudo printers, you can add plain ol' real printers as well. To do so, choose Add→ Add Printer/Class. The KDE Printer Wizard opens, and you just walk through the necessary steps to get things set up and working. For example, here's how to connect an HP LaserJet 6L to a Xandros Linux machine shared through Samba:

1. **Introduction:** Click Next.

2. **Backend Selection:** Choose SMB shared printer (Windows). Click Next.

3. **User Identification:** Choose Normal Account and enter a Login and Password for the Xandros box. Click Next.

4. **SMB Printer Settings:** Enter the SMB Workgroup name (MILTON, in this example), the SMB Server name (Cromwell, in this example), and the share name of the Printer (hplj6l, in this example). Click Next.

5. **Printer Model Selection:** Select HP as the Manufacturer and LaserJet 6L as the Model. Click Next.

6. **Driver Selection:** Select HP LaserJet 6L (foomatic + hpijs) [recommended] as the best driver among six options. Click Next.

7. **Printer Test:** Skip until the process has completed because it rarely works for some reason. Click Next.

8. **Banner Selection:** Leave No Banner selected. Click Next.

9. **Printer Quota Settings:** The default (no quota) is fine. Click Next.

10. **Users Access Settings:** The default enables anyone using this Knoppix computer to print, which is fine. Click Next.

11. **General Information:** Name is required, so type in something short that identifies the printer, such as hplj61. Fill in Location and Description if you feel like it. Click Next.

12. **Confirmation:** Look things over. Click Finish.

And now there's a new printer you can use in Knoppix! To test it, select the printer, right-click on it, choose Test Printer, and click Print Test Page. In a moment or two, a test page should appear in your printer.

If the test page is borked and doesn't look right, try changing your driver: Click on the printer to select it, choose the Properties tab in the bottom half of the window, and click the Driver button. Click the Change button, and try a different driver. Lather, rinse, and repeat as needed until your printer works.

Tip

If you can't find your printer in the list of supported devices, or things just aren't working, head to the Linux printing mother lode at LinuxPrinting.org, found, surprisingly enough, at www. linuxprinting.org. If you can't find the info you need at that Website, it's time to get a new printer.

Here's how you can improve printing in Mozilla (and Firefox, if you install that program using Klik). Open Mozilla, go to a page you'd like to print, and select File → Print. Notice that Mozilla prints only to the default printer. If you only have one printer, this isn't a big deal, but if you use a laptop that connects to several printers, this can be a pain. Conversely, look at how KDE applications print. All KDE apps pass along the print request to Kprinter, which, as you've seen, is a really nice front end for printing. You can choose any of the printers you've defined already, or print directly to Postscript or PDF, or print to PDF and have KMail email the resulting PDF, and many other neat options.

In Mozilla's Print dialog box, click the Properties button. In the Printer Properties dialog box, change the Print Command from lpr ${MOZ_PRINTER_NAME:+'-P'}${MOZ_PRINTER_ NAME} to kprinter --stdin. Click OK to close the Printer Properties dialog box, and then click Print to close the Print dialog box. You'll see Mozilla printing, but then Mozilla passes the job along to Kprinter and the KDE Print dialog opens. Make the appropriate choices and click Print. In essence, you're telling Mozilla to pass the print job along to Kprinter, which makes things far handier.

You can pretty much use this trick with any program that doesn't use KDE's print system. Just find where you can specify the printer and enter kprinter --stdin. Test it to make sure things work, and enjoy your slick printing system.

There's one exception (isn't there always?): Adobe Acrobat Reader. To set it up, open Acrobat Reader from the K menu by selecting Multimedia → Viewers → Acrobat Reader. Once it's running, open a PDF (you might need to download one first; to find one, search Google for "file-type:pdf knoppix", which should produce oodles of them) and click Print. In the Printer Command box, enter kprinter without the --stdin. And remember—you only need to do this for non-KDE apps.

Enjoying Multimedia

Multimedia makes computing fun, whether it's music, video, images, or any combination of these. While it's doubtful that you'll ever use Knoppix as a true multimedia box acting as the hub of your digital life, it's still really cool that this Live CD comes with software that you can use to enjoy your multimedia files. Let's walk through the highlights of the software, taking brief looks at some of the best multimedia on any OS, not just Linux.

Listening to Sound

Noise. Notes. Speech. Lines from a movie. Verses from a song. With Knoppix, you can hear it all . . . and change it as well.

Listening to Music with XMMS

Linux users have a huge variety of audio players from which to choose, with more coming out every day, but Knoppix includes an old standby that many people still use and rely upon: XMMS, the X Multimedia System.

Open XMMS from the K menu by selecting Multimedia ➜ XMMS. To use XMMS effectively, you need to be able to see it, and by default the interface is built for folks with perfect eyes who are also looking at the program through powerful electron microscopes. Right-click on a blank area of the program and select Options ➜ DoubleSize. That's much better! Once you master XMMS and its interface, you can go back to the regular size, but for now, use the enlarged view.

Besides the main XMMS window, you really need to display the Playlist Editor window, so click the PL button (or right-click on the program and choose Playlist Editor). The Playlist Editor window opens, docked to XMMS. Resize the playlist by grabbing the bottom right corner and dragging it so that it's bigger. That makes it easier to see the songs that you have queued. Figure 1-9 shows XMMS with a docked Playlist Editor.

FIGURE 1-9: XMMS is simple and effective.

XMMS plays tunes in a wide variety of formats, including MP3, OGG (a patent-free alternative to MP3 — and it sounds better, too!), WAV, and CD audio (in fact, XMMS plays videos in the MPEG format as well). You can add songs to the XMMS playlist by clicking on the +FILE icon, which opens a Load Files dialog box. Navigate to your music, find the files you want to hear, select them, close the dialog, and click the Play button in XMMS. Assuming that your sound card is supported, you should hear your music.

Here's another way to add music to your playlist: Open the Konqueror file manager, navigate to your songs, select the ones you want to hear, and drag them onto the XMMS playlist. Much easier, especially if you always have Konqueror open to manage files.

XMMS isn't a complicated program. If you've ever used any audio player on a computer, you'll probably figure out XMMS pretty quickly. If you get stuck, or you just want to learn more about XMMS, as well as download skins and plug-ins, visit the project's home page at www.xmms.org.

Editing Sound Files with Audacity

Audacity is a free audio recorder and editor that can import digital audio files, manipulate them in an astonishing variety of ways, and then export them. Before you can use Audacity, though, you need a sound file to edit. The sidebar "Converting MP3s to WAVs" explains how you can acquire a sound file.

Once you have a sound file, open Audacity (see Figure 1-10) from the K menu by selecting Multimedia → Audacity.

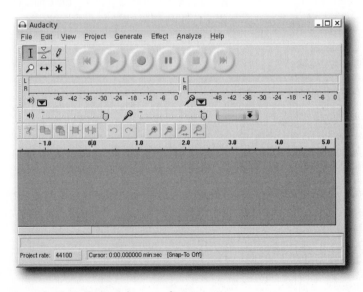

FIGURE 1-10: Audacity, when you first open it

Converting MP3s to WAVs

At IT Conversations (www.itconversations.com), you can listen to streaming audio of interviews and talks by some of the leading thinkers in technology. Streaming audio is cool, but we prefer to have files on our machine for convenience; fortunately, IT Conversations also makes everything available as a download in MP3 format. You can download a bunch of MP3 files, but some of us can't listen to someone talk while we try to write and work!

You can, however, convert the MP3s into CD audio, so you can listen to the interviews and talks while you're driving around in your car (if the CD player in your car handles MP3s, you can skip this section). To convert the MP3s into WAVs, run the following script, which you can name mp32wav and place in your ~/bin directory:

```
for i in *.[mM][pP]3 ; do

  # convert uppercase to lowercase & space to underscore

  name=$(echo $i | tr '[A-Z ]' '[a-z_]')

  # replace .mp3 with .wav

  name=${name//.mp3/.wav}

  # convert mp3 to wav

  mp3-decoder $i --wav $name

done
```

WAV files are a lot bigger than MP3 files, so make sure you have enough space on your hard drive. A rough rule of thumb is that every 1MB of an MP3 will turn into 10MB of a WAV. Knoppix uses your RAM as its "hard drive," and you may quickly use it up if you're not careful. Run df -h to see how much space you have available on your /ramdisk. If you don't have a lot of RAM, check how much is available on one of your "real" hard drives. If you see that you have space on a "real" hard drive, mount it with write access (right-click on the icon on the Knoppix desktop, select Properties, go to the Device tab, uncheck Read only, and mount the drive).

At the end of the process, you should have several WAV files that you could burn to a CD-R/W to listen to in your car (to find out how to burn them, see the "Burning CDs with K3b" section later in this chapter). Keep an eye on your available space, though. When we tried to burn the WAV for Professor Clayton Christensen's "Capturing the Upside" (available from www.itconversations.com/shows/detail135.html), however, it was too big—in fact, at 1 hour and 48 minutes, his talk would take almost two CDs!

Tip

If you get an error message when you first open Audacity informing you `Error Initializing Audio: There was an error initializing the audio i/o layer. You will not be able to play or record audio. Error: Host error`, another program is using your sound card. Are you listening to music with XMMS? Close it! Are your system alert sounds beeping and booping? Turn them off (from the K menu, select Control Center → Sound & Multimedia → System Notifications, check the box next to Apply To All Applications, and click Turn Off All Sounds)! For more help on this issue, see `www.audacityteam.org/wiki/index.pl?LinuxIssues`.

With Audacity running, open your sound file. (We opened `clayton_christensen_-_capturing_the_upside.wav` by selecting File → Open and navigating to the file.) Audacity imports the file — slowly, because it's a big one — and displays it as shown in Figure 1-11.

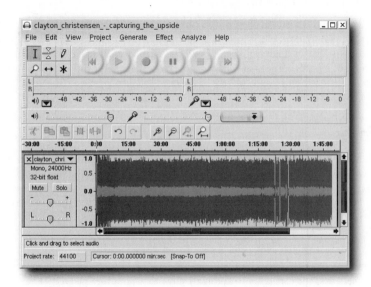

FIGURE 1-11: Audacity with a WAV file, open and ready to edit

The entire file is visible, with the waveform showing the progress of the audio. For this example, we want to break the file roughly in half, say around the first hour mark, at a nice pause (and not just cut Prof. Christensen off in the middle of a sentence). Click somewhere near the hour mark and then click the Play button. When you hear what sounds like a good place to stop, click the Pause button, hold down the Shift key, and press and hold the left arrow key until the cursor gets all the way back to the beginning of the WAV file. (You can use the mouse, although it does have a tendency to slip and you end up cutting off the speaker in the middle of a thought.) Be sure to click the Stop button in Audacity before continuing or you won't be able to use the Edit menu. With the first hour selected, choose Edit → Cut, immediately choose File → New, and, in the new window, choose Edit → Paste.

Tip If the new waveform doesn't look like it did just a few seconds before, that's because Audacity has spread this new one out—if you scroll to the right, you can see the whole file. To return to the previous view, go to View ➤ Fit in Window, and everything is scrunched together again.

To save the new WAV file, select File ➤ Export As WAV, navigate to the location where you want to save the file, and enter an appropriate filename; for this example, that might be `clayton_christensen_-_capturing_the_upside_1.wav` (remember that it was taken from the beginning of the original file, so it's now part one).

Close this file and go back to the original. Once again, select File ➤ Export As WAV, navigate, and save the file as `clayton_christensen_-_capturing_the_upside_2.wav` (because it's the second half of the original file). The original WAV file isn't needed any longer, so you can delete it to reclaim that disk space.

Now there are two files of CD-burnable length; you can burn them both using K3b (discussed later in this chapter) and enjoy Prof. Christensen's brilliant observations in your car during those long road trips. That's just one of the many, many things possible with Audacity. To use the program to the maximum of its capabilities, you really need to investigate Audacity further. You can start with a visit to Audacity's home page at `http://audacity.sourceforge.net`, and then move on to a Google search for "audacity tutorial." You'll find a lot of great stuff.

Viewing Images

Who doesn't like importing and viewing pictures of their friends? And then using software to distort their friends' heads so they look like yumpkin-headed freaks before emailing the results to other friends? Yes, Knoppix makes it all possible. In fact, that's its new motto: "Knoppix: Making Yumpkin-Heads Possible for Years." OK, that part's a silly joke—but the rest is true. Honest!

Using Kuickshow

When it's time to view pictures, you're looking for three things: speed, wide compatibility with a variety of image formats, and the capability to automatically resize an image when it's larger than the monitor. Knoppix comes with Kuickshow (see Figure 1-12), a program that nicely meets those three goals. Open Kuickshow from the K menu by selecting Graphics ➤ Kuickshow:

Theoretically, once Kuickshow is open, you choose File ➤ Open and navigate to the image you want to see, select it, and then view it in Kuickshow. In reality, many folks use the Konqueror file manager to navigate to the image they want, right-click it, and select Open With ➤ Kuickshow. Kuickshow opens, displaying the image. If you want to view other images in the directory, the quickest way is to press PgDn/Page Down on your keyboard to view the next image, and PgUp/Page Up to view the previous image.

There aren't any menus visible in Kuickshow, because it's kind of a bare-bones app. You can, however, make a few changes to the image you're viewing in Kuickshow. To see your options, right-click the image and take a look at the contextual menu (shown in Figure 1-13).

FIGURE 1-12: Kuickshow, open and ready to display pictures

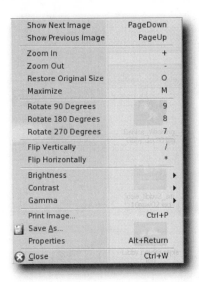

FIGURE 1-13: The Kuickshow contextual menu offers many options.

Everything is pretty self-explanatory in this menu, so it's easy to use. Don't forget that it's available at any time with a simple right-click.

Editing Images with GIMP

Think of the GIMP (the GNU Image Manipulation Program) as an attempt to create an open-source PhotoShop. Now, it's not there yet . . . but it's getting better all the time, and it's probably good enough for the needs of at least 90 percent of users. Certainly, if you're using Knoppix to perform some quick 'n' dirty work, you'll find that the GIMP is probably just right. You'll also find that it's a big, complicated program, worthy of a book on its own. There is no way to cover even a fraction of the GIMP's capabilities here, but we'll point out a couple of things to whet your interest in this fascinating addition to Knoppix.

From the K menu, select Graphics ➔ GIMP Image Editor and then open an image from within the program, right-click an image, and choose Open With. Unfortunately, KDE in Knoppix isn't set to include the GIMP by default in the list of Open With programs, so you need to add it. Here's how: Select Open With ➔ Other. The Open With window appears. Click the + next to Graphics to expand it, and then choose GIMP Image Editor. Before you click OK, check the box next to Remember Application Association for This Type of File if you plan to use the GIMP quite a bit.

GIMP displays an image much like what's shown in Figure 1-14. (This particular image is of Libby, a wonderful dog of one of the authors, back when she was a puppy.)

FIGURE 1-14: The GIMP, ready to edit an image of a really cute little dog

Three windows are open. From left to right, they are the main toolbox, which contains the basic tools you use to work on your images; the image window, containing the picture you're manipulating; and a window containing several panels joined together, including Layers, Channels, Paths, Brushes, Patterns, and Gradients (let's call it the *dialog* window). Notice the menus — the main toolbox has the highest-level menus that govern the image in general, the image window contains all the goodies that enable you to change the image in an almost bewildering variety of ways, while the dialog window lacks menus, which is just fine.

If you know PhotoShop or Fireworks or any other image-manipulation program, then dive into the GIMP and start discovering where it has placed the equivalents to the commands you know. Don't expect to find everything — as mentioned earlier, the GIMP isn't yet up to the capabilities of the proprietary programs, but it's gaining fast.

If your experience with image manipulation is neither deep nor broad), check out the GIMP's Website (`www.gimp.org`) for documentation and just start playing. Jump in with a picture on which you can test techniques and see what happens.

Although most people end up using the GIMP simply to crop and resize images, here's one cool trick that shows you how powerful the program really is. The two most fun menus are Filters and Script-Fu: Filters apply pre-made changes to your picture that alter how it looks, with effects involving light, distortion, and colors; and Script-Fu enables developers to write scripts that perform several actions on a photo, changing it in amazing ways, especially for those of us who don't really know what we're doing. You can access one of our favorites by selecting Script-Fu ➜ Decor ➜ Old Photo. Use the dialog box that appears to make some selections and then click OK. The result is truly cool. Figure 1-15 shows the Script-Fu'd picture of Libby, which looks like it was taken around the turn of the century (not the most recent one).

FIGURE **1-15: That same really cute little dog, circa 1900**

The changes are kind of hard to see in a book with grayscale images, so you just have to try it out for yourself. There are a lot more where that came from — enough to make it possible even for someone who isn't a graphics expert to do some cool things, thanks to a great program, clever programming, and some welcome hand-holding. Acquaint yourself at least a little bit with the GIMP: It's the open-source gold standard for image manipulation.

Note For more information on the GIMP, check out the program's Website at www.gimp.org. Users have written a lot about the GIMP online; search Google and you're sure to find much more information about virtually every aspect of the app.

Manipulating Graphics via the Command Line with ImageMagick

The GIMP is a great program, but it's a GUI app. If you want speed or scriptability, turn to ImageMagick, a command-line program that is amazingly comprehensive and powerful.

Note man imagemagick tells you just about everything you can do with the program. There's a lot there, and it bears your careful reading. For more info, see the program's Website, at www.imagemagick.org.

Let's look at a couple of ways that you can use ImageMagick. It is hoped that these will start to give you some ideas that will inspire you to do far cooler things (if you develop something, share it with us — we're always looking to add new tricks to our toolbox).

Here's an example. In preparing this book, we took a lot of screenshots. We could use KDE's screen capture utility, KSnapshot (available from the K menu by selecting Graphics → More Applications → KSnapshot), but it doesn't save files in TIFF format, which is what our publishers want. So we used ImageMagick and the following six lines, inserted at the bottom of the .bashrc file in /home/knoppix:

```
# take screenshot of chosen window, incl. kde frame
alias window='sleep 3; import -depth 8 -frame window.tif'
# take screenshot of selected area
alias selection='sleep 3; import -depth 8 selection.tif'
# take screenshot of entire screen
alias screenshot='sleep 3; import -depth 8 -window root
screen.tif'
```

Note After adding these lines to .bashrc, don't forget to run source ~/.bashrc so you can immediately begin using your new commands.

The sleep 3 command gives you three seconds to get things set up before the screenshot is taken; if you need more (or less) time, change the number. The import command, part of ImageMagick, does the real work. It grabs an image of the window, a selection of the screen that you specify by clicking and dragging a box, or the entire screen, depending on the name of the file at the end of the command. If you don't want the image to be a TIFF, change the extension to .jpg, .gif, or whatever else you'd like.

Tip We used -depth 8 in the command because if you don't, ImageMagick takes a 16-bit TIFF image, which causes the GIMP and other image programs in Knoppix to complain. If you're not saving the image as a TIFF, remove the depth option.

Here's another way you can use ImageMagick: to convert a lot of images from one format to another. If you have a folder full of TIFFs that you want to convert to JPGs, for example, cd to the directory containing the images and run the following:

```
for i in *.tif ; do convert "$i" "${i%.tif}.jpg" ; rm $i ; done
```

This is a `for` loop that works on every TIFF in the directory. It converts the file from a TIFF to a JPEG, and removes the original TIFF image to keep things neat and clean. Don't want the original file removed? Then get rid of `rm $i ;` and the original TIFF will remain.

If you'll be using this command a lot, turn it into an alias. If you want the freedom to use different image formats on the fly, create an executable file, named `converting` or something like that, in your ~/bin directory, place the following line in the file, and save it:

```
for i in *.$1 ; do convert "$i" "${i%.$1}.$2" ; rm $i ; done
```

Notice that you're including variables now. To use your script, run the following command:

```
$ converting tif jpg
```

`tif` replaces $1, and `jpg` replaces $2 in the script. Want to convert a batch of PNGs to GIFs? Use `converting png gif` instead, and so on.

The final ImageMagick example is one that one of us wrote one night to offer some digital photos on a Website for people to download and use as wallpaper. You can try it too: Gather 50 or so images and begin opening each one in the GIMP, saving the original image in several different common desktop dimensions, including 1024×768, 800×600, and 640×480. You might also want a thumbnail image of about 200×150 so folks could have an idea of the image before they start downloading it. You want the JPEGs to be of the highest quality, except for the thumbnails, which don't need to look as nice.

Manually changing multiple images is boring and tedious, so use the following script, which you can place in a file named `photoresize` in the ~/bin directory:

```
for i in *.jpg ; do
 width=$(identify "$i" | sed -re 's/^.* ([0-9]+)x[0-9]+ . ↵
*$/\1/g' )
 i="${i%.jpg}"
 if test $width -eq 1600 ; then
 for size in 1600x1200 1024x768 800x600 640x480 ; do
 convert "$i.jpg" -resize $size -compress none -quality ↵
    100 "${i}_${size}.jpg"
 done
 size=200x150
 convert "$i.jpg" -resize $size -compress JPEG -quality ↵
    75 "${i}_${size}.jpg"
 fi
done
```

After making it executable with `chmod 744 photoresize`, the script ran perfectly. Most of our images were 1600×1200, but not all. We needed some way to only work with the largest images, and the `identify` command was it. Running `identify sample.jpg` gives you information about the image that looks like this: `sample.jpg JPEG 1600x1200 DirectClass 8-bit 641kb 0.0u 0:01`. Now you know the dimensions, but if you only care about the width, that's where `sed` (stream editor, an old Unix command) comes in.

Basically, `sed` and some regular expression work get the number that corresponds to the width of the original image and write that number to the `width` variable.

Note For more on regular expressions, see Andrew Watt's *Beginning Regular Expressions* at (`www.wrox.com/WileyCDA/WroxTitle/productCd-0764574892.html`).

Now the script performs a test: Does the number in the `width` variable equal 1600? If not, nothing happens, and the image is skipped. If it does match, the oh-so-versatile `convert` command kicks in and changes the dimensions of each image, while also using the highest quality and no compression. Each file is renamed to include the dimensions in the filename to make things clear.

Tip Yes, `convert` can change more than just file types and dimensions. In fact, it can do a whole lot more. `man convert` should be your next stop.

When the whole process is finished, you'll have a nice collection of photographs in a variety of common dimensions, ready for upload to a Website to be shared (under a Creative Commons license!) with anyone. If you'd like to see one of the author's, head to `www.granneman.com/personal/photos/`. Every photo on those pages appears courtesy of ImageMagick.

Watching Video

Digital movies have been getting more and more popular over the last several years as the Internet pipes coming into our homes and businesses have been getting larger and faster. Although ultimately limited in a few key ways, Knoppix enables you to listen to and watch those movies and videos.

Checking Out Video with xine

xine is hardly my favorite video player, for a simple reason: Its UI is pretty bad. Don't get us wrong: The underlying xine video engine is great, but the xine interface is almost baffling in its complexity and lack of clues and feedback. Regardless, that's what Knoppix includes, and so that's what we'll peek at.

Note You can use APT to install other video players with better UIs. In particular, check out mplayer, Kaffeine, or Totem.

Open xine from the K menu by selecting Multimedia → Video → xine media player, but you'll probably use it more often by right-clicking a video file and choosing Open With → xine. Figure 1-16 shows a video file opened in xine.

FIGURE 1-16: Xine, playing Thomas A. Edison's "May Irwin Kiss" (1896)

To control playback, right-click the movie and use the items in the menu. Although xine is pretty simple, it's simply not very pretty to use.

Burning CDs with K3b

Here's a common scenario: Someone's computer won't boot, and he's just got to get his data off that machine. As you'll find out in Chapters 4 and 5, it's really easy to take care of that problem with Knoppix, a NIC, some Ethernet, and a network, but that's not always possible. If the user has a CD-R/W on that machine, though, you can still save his bacon by burning a CD. It's not tremendously hard to burn CD-RWs from the command line, but it's easier to use a nice GUI, and K3b is easily the best CD-burning GUI available for Linux, perhaps even on any platform.

Open K3b from the K menu by selecting Multimedia → K3b. The first time you open it, K3b asks you to confirm your burner's write speeds. It probably defaults to 0, which is obviously of no help, so bump it up to the correct speed and click OK.

Tip

This might be obvious, but K3b won't work unless you have a CD-R/RW device installed on your system, and Knoppix needs to have recognized it. To confirm that K3b sees your CD-R/W, open K3b, select Settings → Configure K3b, and choose the Devices button on the left. Your CD-R/W should be listed. If it isn't, click Add Device and help K3b try to find your burner. If you need broader help getting your CD-R/RW hardware to work, take a look at the CD-Writing HOWTO at www.tldp.org/HOWTO/CD-Writing-HOWTO.html.

Here's something else you need to consider: You can't burn a CD if Knoppix is taking up your only CD-R/W drive! If you have two CD drives, you're set: Boot Knoppix in one and use the other to burn. If you only have one CD-R/W drive, you may need to install Knoppix on your hard drive (see Appendix B) to free your CD drive for the burn (you can uninstall Knoppix after you've checked your new CD).

K3b is divided into two main areas: a file and folder navigation area in the top half of the window and a project view in the bottom half, as shown in Figure 1-17.

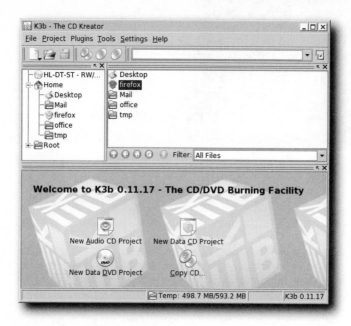

FIGURE 1-17: K3b's main window

K3b makes it very easy to get started by providing buttons for the four most common tasks in the project view. To burn a data CD for backup, choose New Data CD Project. The project view area changes to Current Projects, as shown in Figure 1-18.

Using the top half of the window, navigate to the items you want to burn and begin dragging them into the bottom half of the window. As you add items, the bar at the bottom of the window shows you how much space you've taken up on your CD and how much you have left. Gone over the limit? Just select an item in the project and press your Delete key to remove it from the burn. Once you've correctly specified the items you want to save onto a CD, click the Burn button in the bottom right of the K3b window.

A new window opens up: Data Project. This is an extremely important window because it enables you to tell K3b exactly how you want to burn your CD. You have several options here, and selecting the wrong one can mean the difference between a successful backup and a shiny hunk of plastic.

To lessen the chance that you'll end up with a bad burn, this section covers the key changes you need to make. There's not enough space in the book to cover everything, but K3b has informative built-in help. If you're unsure about an option, just click the What's This button (the one that looks like a question mark) in the upper-right corner of the window, and then select the option in the window about which you'd like more information.

FIGURE 1-18: Creating a Data CD Project in K3b

Setting Burn Speed

The first thing to set is the speed at which you're going to burn your CD. Do this on the Data Project window's Writing tab (see Figure 1-19).

If you leave Speed set to Auto, K3b tries to burn at maximum speed. This may or may not work. Experience has shown that it's a good idea to burn at a slower speed to ensure that the burn is not problematic, no matter what software you use. If you have the time and patience, 4x is slow and steady and almost always works. Granted, it takes about 15 minutes or so to burn a full 700MB disc, but if you do something else while you're burning, it's not a big deal. If you're not that patient, start out fast, test your results, and be prepared to slow things down gradually, testing after each burn until you find the optimum speed for your hardware and your media.

If you leave On the Fly selected, K3b does just that: write the files directly to the CD-R/W without first creating an ISO image. If your hardware is fast enough, this should be no problem. If your hardware is slow, however, or if you're experiencing problems burning, check On the Fly; K3b will first create an ISO image of your data, and then burn that ISO image to disc, a process that takes longer but is more likely to result in a good burn. If you uncheck On the Fly, Remove Image is no longer grayed out; however, you should probably leave Remove Image checked so that K3b erases the ISO it created once it has successfully burned it to disc, thus reclaiming your storage for Knoppix.

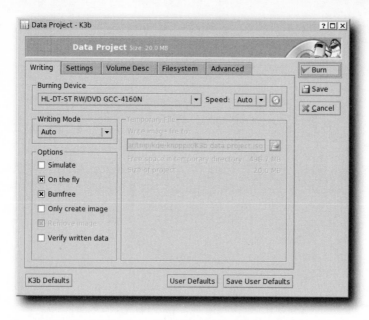

FIGURE 1-19: The Writing tab of the K3b Data Project window

Remember that Knoppix is using your RAM as its hard drive, so you may not be able to write an ISO image unless you have enough RAM to hold it. To find out how much space you've got, run the df -h command in Konsole and note how much free space is available on the /ramdisk row. If you don't have enough room, check how much is available on one of your mounted hard drives. If there's space, mount the hard drive with write access (right-click on the icon on the Knoppix desktop, select Properties, open the Device tab, uncheck Read Only, and mount the drive). One last step: Tell K3b that you want it to use your hard drive to hold the ISO by changing the path for Write Image File To (which is no longer grayed out once you uncheck On the Fly on the Writing tab) so that it points to your newly mounted writable hard drive. Yes, it's a lot of work, but that's what happens when you're using a Live CD.

It's generally a good idea to select Verify Written Data (the final option on the Writing tab), which compares what was burned to the original data, thereby letting you know if something didn't work correctly.

Burning in Sessions

You need to change the settings on the Data Project's Settings tab (see Figure 1-20) only if you plan to add content to your CD over several different burning sessions.

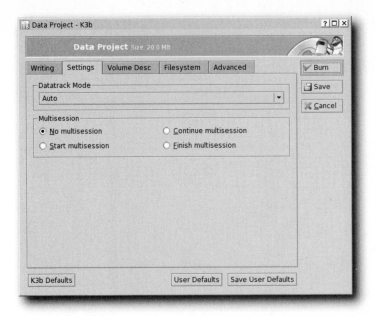

FIGURE 1-20: Setting the kind of session you're using in K3b

Most of the time, you'll probably fill a CD completely, so you want the default: No Multisession. If you're going to use several different sessions, you don't want K3b to "close" the disc until you're finished. To do this correctly, use Start Multisession for the first burn, Continue Multisession for the next burns except the last one, and then complete your CD-R/W with Finish Multisession, which tells K3b that it's all right to close the disc. You'll use the default No Multisession most often, but it's good to know how to create a multiple-session CD if you need one.

Keeping Yourself Informed

The Volume Desc tab is shown in Figure 1-21.

None of the information on the Volume Desc tab prevents a successful burn, but you'll probably want to spend a moment here just so things are organized and clear. In other words, this tab really isn't for the computer—it's for the human user. Fill things out as you see fit.

Understanding Filesystems

The Data Project's Filesystem tab (see Figure 1-22) is very important, especially if you want to make sure that your disc can be used on both Linux and other operating systems. For backups, this is an essential consideration. If you never have to touch a Windows machine, this tab may not be as significant to you, although there are still things here that you will probably want to set.

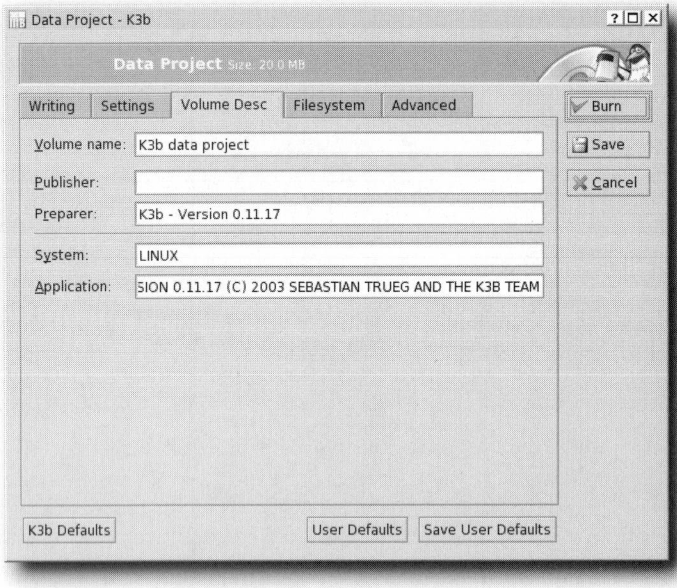

FIGURE 1-21: Describing the disc you're burning in K3b

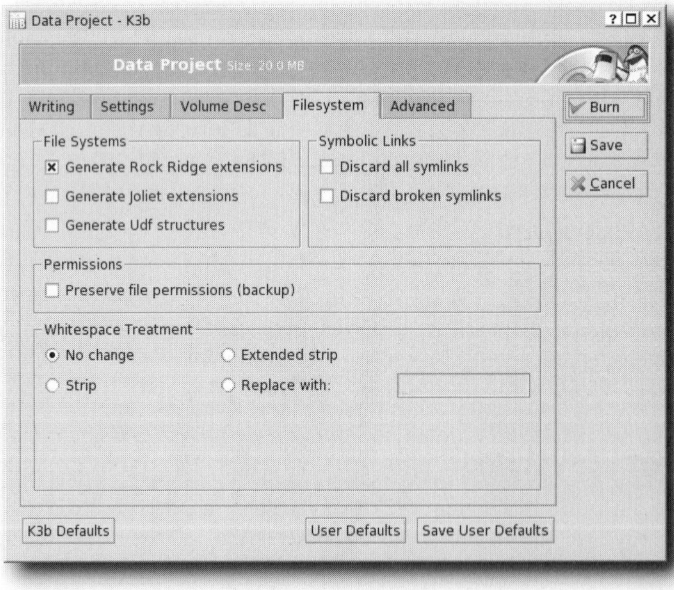

FIGURE 1-22: Tell K3b what kind of filesystem you want to place on your new CD.

Checking the boxes in the File Systems section is key if you're after cross-platform compatibility. There's a wide variety of standards for CDs, and in typical fashion in the computer world, they don't always agree. For instance, when you burn a CD, you can stick to ISO9660 standards, but all filenames must be in all capital letters, and they have to be a maximum of eight characters, plus the period and the extension. DOS, anyone? You can also use the Rock Ridge extensions, which enable UNIX systems (including Linux and Mac OS X) to read CDs that contain files with names of up to 255 characters, as well as support UNIX-like things such as owners, groups, permissions, and symbolic links. However, Windows does not support Rock Ridge (worth $50 billion and with 30,000 employees, Microsoft can't support Rock Ridge?), so don't use it as your only filesystem if you want to access your data on that operating system.

If you want to make sure that Windows users can read the content of your discs, enable Joliet extensions, which support up to 64 characters in filenames (although there's a way around this, as you'll shortly see). Users of Linux and Mac OS X can also read CDs that use Joliet, but Mac OS 9 and earlier will truncate filenames at 31 characters, a major limitation of pre-OS X Macs.

UDF, which stands for Universal Disk Format, is used mainly for DVDs, but CD-R/Ws can also use it. It allows for 127-character filenames, including spaces. The idea is that you can write to CDs and DVDs just like you write to floppies, USB drives, or hard drives: just drag and drop. For UDF to work, though, you need very recent hardware and special drivers if you're using Windows or Mac OS (most Linux distros now include support for UDF-based discs). If you're shooting for wide compatibility, you probably should avoid UDF at this time.

With an understanding of these different filesystems, the options on the Filesystem tab start to make more sense, don't they? If your disc is only going to be used on Linux machines (or Linux and Mac OS X), check Generate Rock Ridge Extensions. If you use Rock Ridge but you don't want symbolic (or "soft") links included on your burn, check Discard All Symlinks. If you are concerned about including soft links, but you want to make sure that you don't accidentally include links to files that aren't included in your burn project, make sure that you check Discard Broken Symlinks.

In addition, remember that if you're using Rock Ridge, you can tell K3b to include information about file permissions along with the burn. To do this, check Preserve File Permissions (Backup). As the name implies, this creates an exact backup of your files — not just the data, but also the meta-information about who owns it and what they can do with it.

If you want to include Windows machines in your burn, check both Generate Rock Ridge Extensions and Generate Joliet Extensions. Your Linux machines will see files of up to 255 characters, while Windows will see files truncated to 64 characters . . . unless you check a box on the next tab, which we'll get to in just a moment.

The options in the Whitespace Treatment area of the window can be useful if you want to get rid of spaces in the filenames on your disc. No change does just that — files that have spaces in their names still do. Nowadays, this isn't really a problem for Linux boxes, so we just usually leave K3b set to that.

Over the years, the standards for burning CDs have morphed in many different directions. Fortunately, most modern hardware and modern operating systems support most of these add-ons and extensions, but it's still a good policy to test all burned CDs on the various CD readers that you plan to use before you rely on those discs! It would be a shame to make backups of your vital data onto CD, intending to transfer the data to a different machine, only to find out after you've repurposed the original box that the different computer can't read your discs. Testing is always worth the time it takes.

Fine-Tuning CD-R/W Filesystems

The Data Project's Advanced tab (see Figure 1-23) enables you to make changes to the basic CD-R/W filesystems.

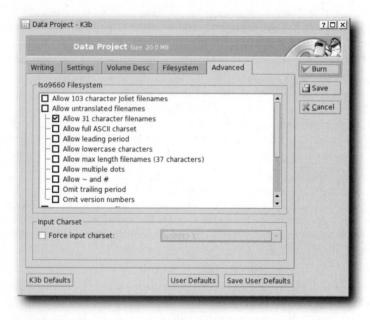

FIGURE 1-23: You can change the basic CD-R/W filesystems in K3b.

Getting beyond the 64-character limit for the Joliet extension was mentioned earlier. Here's how to do it: Check Allow 103 Character Joliet Filenames, and you almost double your allowed filename length on Windows machines. Does this break the official Joliet standard? Yup. Does it appear to work anyway in Windows? Yup, so go for it (but remember to test first). Also remember that you can get up to 255 characters in your filenames using Rock Ridge but only 103 characters using Joliet. Still, for all but the longest of filenames, 103 characters should suffice.

The Allow Untranslated Filenames option has nine sub-options. Checking Allow Untranslated Filenames activates eight of those sub-options — weirdly, you must enable Allow Max Length Filenames (37 Characters) if you want it because that option isn't included by choosing the parent option.

Note In essence, checking either Allow Untranslated Filenames or any of its sub-options breaks the ISO9660 standard. We recommend going ahead and selecting Allow Untranslated Filenames anyway; in for a penny, in for a pound, as they say. Realize that your CD will not play in MS-DOS, but how concerned about that are you? We've burned countless discs with that option on, and we've never had a problem in either Linux or Windows playing those CDs. Your mileage may vary, though.

The Input Charset section enables you to specify the language character set you're using in your filenames. If you don't specify anything, K3b uses the default of ISO-8859-1, which covers Western European languages, such as the one you're using to read this book. If you're using different characters (such as Russian, Asian, or Hebrew, for example) in your filenames, specify the character set you need by checking Force Input Charset and choose from the drop-down menu. If the option you want to use isn't listed (UTF-8 isn't there, for instance), you can manually enter it.

It does take some time to examine all of these options, but if you want to do your burns correctly, you have to know how to use the program.

Ready, Set, Burn

OK, it's time to burn. Click the Burn button in the upper right corner of the window. Depending on the speed of your burner and the speed you've chosen for your burn, you'll shortly be done. While K3b works, it displays a progress bar showing you what it's doing and how far it has progressed. If you get an error, take a look at the info that K3b provides because it can help diagnose the problem.

You can create other kinds of CDs besides simple data disks, but that's probably what you'll use Knoppix for most of the time. The four main tasks are listed in the project area, but check out the Tools menu for other possibilities. Keep in mind that Knoppix comes with most of the software that K3b needs to work its magic, but a few things are missing for space reasons. For example, the transcode package isn't included, so you can't encode audio and video from DVD or AVI files, and you also don't have eMovix, so you won't be able to burn video CDs that will boot and automatically play. (You can add these on your own, however.) Conversely, you *can* create SVCDs (Super Video CDs), believe it or not.

Note The first place to go for information about K3b is the project's home page, at www.k3b.org. There's not a lot there, unfortunately, but you might find something useful, such as the latest news about software releases. However, the mailing list, found at www.sourceforge.net/mailarchive/forum.php?forum_id=1927, is currently averaging a couple of hundred emails a month, so you might be able to find help there, maybe even from Sebastian Trueg, the creator and maintainer of K3b.

If you want to learn more about burning CDs and DVDs, an excellent and up-to-date resource is Andy McFadden's CD-Recordable FAQ, which you can find at www.cdrfaq.org. For Linux-specific information, see the CD-Writing HOWTO at the Linux Documentation Project, www.tldp.org/HOWTO/CD-Writing-HOWTO.html. It's several years old, but still has good stuff in it.

If you want to bypass K3b completely and just use the command line, IBM's developerWorks site has a great tutorial, at www-106.ibm.com/developerworks/linux/library/l-cdburn.html, called Burning CDs on Linux. IBM's site requires free registration, but it's not onerous.

Using Text Editors

Linux is a testament to the continued power and relevance of plain ol' text files. Virtually all configuration information is stored in text files, and many programs are really just scripts in text files. Learn how to edit text files effectively, and you're well on your way to becoming a mighty Linux (and Knoppix) guru!

Editing Configuration Files on the Command Line with vim

Want to start a discussion that will quickly become a debate and eventually escalate into an argument? With all the innocence you can muster, ask a bunch of Linux users, "Which is better? Emacs or vi?" . . . and then step back and watch the fireworks. It's one of the oldest debates in the *nix world, and Knoppix comes down squarely in the middle: It includes both text editors, leaving the choice up to the user.

We believe that vi (actually vim, or "vi improved") is the better of the two editors, and will explore it here. If you want to learn about emacs, there's plenty of information on the Web and in a lot of books. You should still learn vim, though, because while you can't be sure that emacs is on every single *nix machine you'll run into, you *can* be certain that vi (and probably vim) will be installed. Learn vi, and you increase the likelihood that you can fix a machine by changing config files.

Knoppix includes both console- and GUI-based versions of vim. This section covers only the console version, for a couple of reasons. First, if you learn to use vim on the console, moving to the GUI is a piece of cake. Second, the GUI may not always be available, but the console will.

Suppose that you need to edit your `hosts` file so that you can more easily `ssh` to a couple of the boxes on your LAN. Open Konsole (it's the black icon on the panel) and run `cp /etc/hosts` to copy the file to your home directory. Now type `vim hosts` and press Enter, and the newly copied `hosts` file opens (see Figure 1-24).

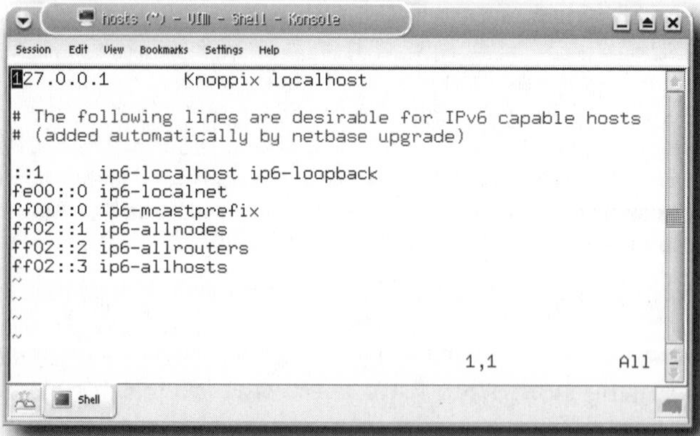

FIGURE 1-24: Editing a copy of the /etc/hosts file with vim.

If you've never used vim (or even emacs) before, you're probably a bit confused at this point. What do you do? Why doesn't anything appear when you start typing? How do you save? Or quit?

The first thing to understand is that vim operates in one of several different modes at a time. When you first open vim, it's in command mode, in which you use your keyboard to move the cursor around, delete information, cut, copy, and paste, and run commands that affect your file (because this is a console app, you can't use your mouse). You want to position the cursor so that you can enter some data. To do so, use the arrow keys on your keyboard (because Knoppix supports them), or use the following key commands:

- h: Moves the cursor one character to the left.

- j: Moves the cursor one character down.

- k: Moves the cursor one character up.

- l: Moves the cursor one character right.

Note   To learn more about vim and all of its commands, just type **vim** on the command line, and then **:help** to enter vim's built-in help system (enter **:q** to get out of help, of course), or look on the Web by searching for "vim tutorial," "vim help," "vim tips," or ".vimrc" if you want to find sample vim config files that people have posted, which can teach you a lot.

Position the cursor at the end of the first line and press **a**. You're now in the insert mode, in which you can insert characters and text into your file. The letter a (append) indicates that you want to append text after the character your cursor is on, while the letter i (for insert) means that you want to begin inserting before the character your cursor is on (again, you can use other commands to signify precisely where you want to begin placing text into the file).

For this example, press Enter so you're on a new line and then enter three new lines into the hosts file, pressing Enter after each one to start the next:

```
192.168.0.10       dante
192.168.0.15       chaucer
192.168.1.20       virgil
```

You know you should save your work often, but you can't do that while you're inserting text. The solution? When you're in insert mode, press Esc to return to command mode. Now enter **:w** (colon, w) to write out (save) the file. To write and immediately quit (exit), use **:wq** (colon, w, q); to quit without saving your work, use **:q!** (colon, q, exclamation point).

For this example, there are a couple of problems in what you just entered, and here's how to fix them. Chaucer is temporarily offline, so it doesn't need to be in the hosts file. You're still in command mode, so maneuver the cursor (using the arrow keys or key commands) until it's somewhere in the Chaucer line. To delete a line, enter **dd** while in command mode; the entire line disappears.

The second problem is a typo in the line about Virgil: The IP address is 192.168.0.20, not 192.168.1.20. That's easy to correct: Position the cursor over the 1, press x to delete just that character, press i to enter insert mode, type a **0**, press Esc to go back into command mode, and finish with **:wq,** which writes the file out and quits vim.

Vim really isn't that difficult to work with—it just takes some getting used to. Once you're comfortable with the basics, it's easy to keep expanding your vim knowledge base, with scripts and macros and regular expressions and all sorts of other fun, powerful stuff. The sooner you can do just a little bit with vim, the sooner you're on your way to using Knoppix more effectively.

Editing Configuration Files Using the GUI Editor Kate

At last count, there were more than 7,000 text editors available for Linux. OK, that's an exaggeration . . . though not much of one. Knoppix includes a few text editors, and they serve their purpose. Probably the easiest-to-use-right-out-of-the-box GUI text editor on the Knoppix disk is Kate. Kate is powerful and officially targeted at developers, although anyone can use it.

From the K menu, select Editors ➔ Kate. Kate opens, as shown in Figure 1-25.

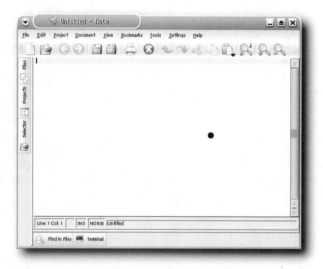

FIGURE 1-25: Kate, the text editor, ready to edit text

If you're reading this book, you've used a text editor sometime in your life, even if it was just Notepad. Kate is very easy to use for simple tasks because it's pretty much like every other text editor in the world, but it contains a lot of special features that make it appropriate for more sophisticated work as well.

There's only space to point out a few of Kate's features here. The best way to learn more about Kate is to go through all the menus, playing with the options and trying things out.

Ever wanted to view different parts of the same file at the same time? Select View ➔ Split Vertical, which enables you to do just that. To return to the single display of a file, select View ➔ Close Current View.

Need to run a command against the file you're working on, but don't want to switch to Konsole? Click the Terminal button at the bottom of the window; a resizable console frame appears, already targeted at the directory in which your file resides. Perfect for a quick `wc -w file.txt` (to find out the number of words in your file) or to run `ifconfig` to grab your machine's IP address and paste it into your file. To close the console, click the Terminal button again.

Finally, do you need to directly open a file on another machine accessible only via SSH, and find that downloading, editing, and uploading it again would be too much trouble? No problem. Kate supports KDE's built-in networking transparency, so select File ➜ Open, and in the Location box enter **fish://username@other.computer.com** (you can use an IP address instead of the domain name, if you want). You may have to accept the machine's SSH key if this is the first time you've connected to it (answer in the affirmative if asked). Enter a password when you're prompted, and boom! You're connected to that machine over a secure connection. Select the file you need, click Open, edit it, save it, close it, and you're done. You just remotely edited a file as though it were sitting right on your machine. Pretty cool, eh?

Note Kate, like any KDE app supporting the built-in libraries providing network transparency, can work with files using a variety of protocols, including FTP, SFTP, SMB, NFS, and WebDAV. For a quick overview of KDE's network transparency, see `www.osdir.com/Article2159.phtml`. For more information on some of these protocols and their usage in Knoppix, take a look at Chapter 3.

Working with Office Software

Like Dilbert, many folks spend their days sitting in offices, working for the Man, trying to earn their daily bread. If you're among them, having Knoppix in your arsenal at least provides you with a cool operating system while you do your time in cubical prison.

Enjoying Interoperability with OpenOffice.org

Office suites are important. In 1984, Apple introduced the first office suite — AppleWorks — a collection of integrated software that enabled users to create text documents, crunch numbers, and work with data (software to give presentations came later). Although it was underpromoted by Apple, and ran only on the Apple II instead of the new Mac, it still proved to be incredibly popular. When Microsoft released Office 95 to coincide with the release of Windows 95, there was no looking back. Now, many people spend most of their workday inside their software office suite.

Microsoft may currently dominate the office suite software market, but things are slowly starting to change. A free, high-quality, open-source office suite has been a long time in coming, and one is finally here: OpenOffice.org (known as OOo to devotees). It runs on Mac OS X, Windows, and Linux; it provides a word processor, spreadsheet, and presentation program; and it exchanges documents with Microsoft's Office suite beautifully. It's an essential tool for any computer user, and it comes with Knoppix.

Unlike some other office suites, OpenOffice.org is not designed to lock in users by forcing them into proprietary data formats. Because it has this philosophy, OOo supports a wide variety of formats, including some that may surprise you.

Most users of OOo know that it reads and writes Microsoft Office formats pretty well. You can open Word, Excel, and PowerPoint files and templates, and it's a pretty sure thing that OOo will display them much like the original Microsoft apps would. In addition, you can save files using Microsoft's Word, Excel, or PowerPoint formats, and most users of those programs should have no problem opening and using your documents. In fact, they'll probably never know that you used something other than a Microsoft program unless you tell them.

OOo actually enables you to save your work in a cornucopia of formats, including the following (listed by application):

- OOo Writer gives you the options of OpenOffice.org 1.0, Microsoft Word 97/2000/XP, Microsoft Word 95, Microsoft Word 6.0, Rich Text Format (RTF), StarWriter, text, and HTML.

- OOo Calc provides OpenOffice.org 1.0, Microsoft Excel 97/2000/XP, Microsoft Excel 95, Microsoft Excel 5.0, Data Interchange Format, dBASE, StarCalc, CSV, and HTML.

- OOo Impress allows for OpenOffice.org 1.0, Microsoft PowerPoint 97/2000/XP, StarDraw, StarImpress, and HTML.

The OpenOffice.org formats are good. They tend to be much smaller in size than their Microsoft counterparts (because they're really just zipped XML-formatted text files); they're open and available to anyone, rather than closed and proprietary; and they're the basis for efforts by the Organization for the Advancement of Structured Information Standards (OASIS) to standardize on a common, open, XML-based format for office suites (predictably, Microsoft has taken a "wait and see" approach to OASIS' goals). However, as with most everything in the open-source world, OOo gives you options and leaves the final decision up to you.

One of the most useful file types that OOo supports is Adobe's PDF. Using OOo 1.1, create a text document and then select File → Export as PDF, or, if you prefer to use the toolbar, click the Export Directly as PDF button, visible in the center of Figure 1-26.

FIGURE 1-26: The OpenOffice.org function toolbar, with the Export Directly as PDF button in the center, between the Edit and Print buttons.

OOo creates excellent PDFs, readable by any Linux, Mac OS X, or Windows user. It really is a fantastic benefit and, as with so many of the really cool things about OOo, it's 100 percent free and built in to the program.

In addition to PDF, OOo now supports a format that may surprise some of you: Macromedia's Flash. Yup, that's right. Macromedia Flash, the cause of so many annoying animated advertisements and useless splash pages on the Web, is now available for export by OOo users — specifically, OOo Impress users. If you create a presentation, select File➔ Export; from the File Format drop-down menu, choose Macromedia Flash (SWF) (`.swf`); and you're done.

Complaints about Flash aside, the capability to export to this format is a pretty useful feature. Flash is widely supported (to the tune of more than 90 percent of Web users, according to Macromedia), and it produces small files that are completely cross-platform. An exported presentation can be placed on a company Website, and users can open it with their Web browsers to view it. If a user clicks on a slide, the next one loads.

OOo is a powerful, deep program, and it's constantly getting better. If you're using Knoppix, however, you're probably not going to use OOo to write your next novel. Instead, you're more likely to recover or quickly edit a few documents. The capability to export those documents in a variety of popular formats is an essential feature of OOo that makes it a key part of your Knoppix toolkit.

Note

The first place to go for information about OOo is, not surprisingly, `www.openoffice.org`. This is the mothership for OOo users, where you can download the program, read the latest OOo news, get some aid if you need it, and contribute to the project if you're so inclined.

The most active online forums for OOo can be accessed at `www.oooforum.org`, an excellent resource.

Another great place to look is `www.openoffice-support.net`, which includes tutorials, descriptions, and HowTo's. The tutorials in particular are quite nice, especially for anyone desiring a lot of screenshots to help in learning the basics of OOo.

Desktop Publishing with Scribus

Scribus is an open-source desktop publishing application that enables you to design, create, and produce documents for publication that contain complex layouts, such as newsletters, brochures, ads, fliers, and even magazines. In addition, because Scribus outputs as PDF (perfect for handing off to your local print shop), you can generate PDFs with advanced features — such as forms and passwords — hitherto only available with the purchase of Adobe's full Acrobat package (which is expensive and does not run on Linux). Scribus brings the full world of desktop publishing (DTP) to Linux and Knoppix — an amazing achievement.

From the K menu, select Office ➔ Scribus. Figure 1-27 shows the Scribus workspace.

Scribus is enormous in capabilities and features, so big that it really needs a book of its own. There's no way to cover the program in any meaningful way here, especially for those who may be new to DTP, so our advice is to just jump in. If you've ever used PageMaker or Quark, you should be right at home in Scribus; if you haven't, Scribus is an excellent program in its own right that you can use to bring yourself up to speed with the world of DTP. Consider it a tremendous bonus that Knoppix makes it easy for anyone to try out this truly amazing program, a harbinger of open source's maturity and growth.

FIGURE 1-27: Scribus, the open-source desktop publishing program

Note

For some excellent overviews of Scribus' capabilities, see www.linuxdevcenter.com/pub/a/ linux/2004/09/02/scribus.html and www.linuxjournal.com/article/7054.

For details on Scribus, go to the program's Website, at www.scribus.net. There's a ton of great information there, including documentation (a lot!), tutorials, a wiki, downloads, and more.

Viewing PDFs with Adobe Acrobat Reader

Linux comes with a wide variety of PDF readers, and Knoppix itself includes KGhostView, GV (GhostView), and Xpdf, in addition to the official one, Adobe's own Acrobat Reader.

You can start Acrobat Reader from the K menu by selecting Multimedia ➜ Viewers ➜ Acrobat Reader, but you'll more commonly click on a PDF you've downloaded, or on a link on a Web page that points to a PDF; and your PDF reader will open, already displaying the file you want to read. Knoppix comes with Adobe's Acrobat Reader as the default app to view PDFs, so you don't need to change anything.

Acrobat Reader supports text selection, which can come in handy if you want to get some text out of a PDF and into another program. To turn this on, click on the text selection icon on the toolbar, shown in the center of Figure 1-28.

FIGURE 1-28: Use the text
selection icon to grab
text out of a PDF.

Note two caveats about text selection, however: First, it won't work in every PDF, only those that
have not "protected" their content (most don't, but some do), and second, sometimes text selection
acts weird. For example, one of us grabbed some text out of a PDF we had created and then pasted
what we'd copied into a text editor. Every instance of the letter "l" was left out! Very weird.

Acrobat Reader is good if you need to quickly read or print a PDF, but if you need to do some
serious work, the command line might be a better option for you. You probably know about the
`ps2pdf` command, which converts PostScript documents into PDFs, but there are others you
should know about as well, and all of them are built into Knoppix:

- `pdf2ps`: Converts a PDF to Postscript, which can sometimes help you get around some
  stupid restrictions that someone put into place with his PDF. Try `pdf2ps`, and then turn
  around and immediately do `ps2pdf`, and you'll often have a usable PDF, sans silly DRM
  restrictions. Here's the syntax:

  ```
  pdf2ps sample.pdf
  ```

- `pdftotext`: Converts a PDF directly to plain text. This works very well. Of course, all
  formatting is lost, but you have the text, which you can now use in any imaginable way.
  Here's the syntax:

  ```
  pdftotext sample.pdf
  ```

- `tiff2pdf`: Converts a TIFF image into a PDF. The TIFF must be an 8-bit image, or
  the command won't work. Here's the syntax:

  ```
  Sample: tiff2pdf sample.tiff > sample.pdf-
  ```

As you can see, there's more than one way to skin a PDF. Go ahead and use Adobe Acrobat
Reader, but keep an eye on KPDF, another PDF viewer with a lot of promise, and don't forget
these really useful commands — they may come in handy at times.

Note

Knoppix is still using the now ancient Adobe Acrobat Reader 4.0, and version 7.0 just came out.
The latest is in fact the greatest, and I'm hoping that it winds up in Knoppix soon.

For a good overview of several PDF readers for Linux, check out LWN's "The Grumpy Editor's
Guide to PDF Viewers," available at `www.lwn.net/Articles/113094`. In particular, KPDF
is going to radically improve once KDE 3.4 comes out, and a later revision of Knoppix includes
that version of KDE, which is great news. KDE.News has the story at `http://dot.
kde.org/1102870587`.

Comparing Two or More Files with Kompare

Kompare is a GUI wrapper for the *diff* program, an ancient (since the 1970s!) UNIX utility that displays the differences between two text files. Here's an example that explains how Kompare — and diff — works. One of us has been working on a poem for a while (more than 12 years), and periodically it is edited. The original file is titled `hoarding_our_lives.txt`; after a few tentative changes, it was saved as `hoarding_our_lives_2.txt`. After reading the second one, it wasn't clear which one was better, but trying to compare the two files was a bit of a pain. Enter Kompare.

Start Kompare from the K menu by selecting Development ➜ Kompare. The Compare Files or Folders window opens, and you're asked to choose your files. Here's our advice: don't do it yet! Instead, choose the diff icon on the left side of the window, enter **/usr/bin/diff** in the Diff Program textbox, and then go back to choosing the files you want to compare by clicking the Files icon. The Source file in this example is `hoarding_our_lives.txt`, and the Destination file is `hoarding_our_lives_2.txt` (you'd choose your own, of course). Then click the Compare button. Kompare opens, looking like what is shown in Figure 1-29.

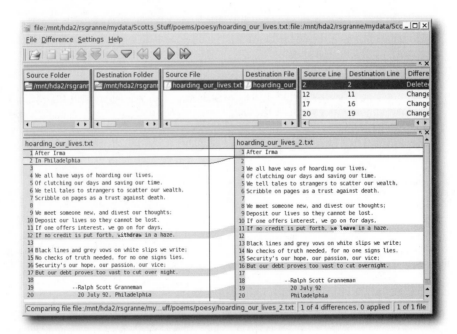

FIGURE 1-29: Kompare compares two files, highlighting the differences.

Kompare is really a neat tool if you want to see the differences between two files. It has highlighted the following differences between the two poem files:

- Line 2 is in file 1 but not in file 2.
- There's one difference between line 12 in file 1 and line 11 in file 2.
- There's one difference between line 17 in file 1 and line 16 in file 2.
- Line 20 in file 1 has been broken into 2 lines in file 2.

After comparing two files, Kompare enables you to decide which changes to accept—in other words, which file is the "correct" one, which will then overwrite the problematic line(s) in the other file. To facilitate this, you can choose Difference → Apply Difference, but that applies changes in only one direction: from left to right. That's not necessarily what you want to do. For example, you might like some things about file 1, and some about file 2. The trick is getting Kompare to work the way you want.

First take care of the stuff in file 1, the one on the left, that you like. For example, you could click on line 12 in file 1 and choose Difference → Apply Difference (or you can press the space-bar on your keyboard). Boom! Immediately the two files have the same line 12. You can do the same for line 20 in file 1.

To arrange it so that file 2 overwrites file 1, you need to change the order in which Kompare displays the files by selecting File → Swap Source with Destination, which switches the display of the two files in Kompare (but not the actual files themselves — `hoarding_our_lives.txt` and `hoarding_our_lives_2.txt` are still in the same folder as before; it's just the way they're shown in Kompare that changes). When you do that, you're first asked to save the two files, so click the Save button. Now you can select line 2 in file 2 (now on the left side of the window) and unify the two files, and then do the same for line 16 in file 2. Select File → Save All, and everything's unified. Whether you're a closet poet or have some other need to compare documents, Kompare will come in handy. You're bound to have plenty of opportunities to use this great tool yourself.

Summary

When you ask most people how they use their computers, besides Internet-related activities (which the next chapter covers), they respond with things such as listening to music, burning CDs, writing documents, looking at pictures, and printing. Knoppix enables users to do all that and more. You might not use Knoppix day in and day out to write your novel, for example, but it truly comes in handy when you need it.

Maximizing Knoppix Internet Tools

The Internet has been central to the growth of Linux — after all, Linus Torvalds could not have marshaled the enthusiasm and work of thousands of people all over the world without it. That's also true for Knoppix. Klaus Knopper is German, but people all over the globe have helped build Knoppix into the exciting, innovative product it is today. This chapter explores the many ways you can combine Knoppix and the Net.

Accessing the Internet

Before you use all the really cool Internet tools that are introduced in the second half of this chapter, you first have to get on the Internet. Most of the time, this isn't a problem: You just boot your computer with the Knoppix CD inserted, and at the end of the boot process, you're connected. Things grow complicated, however, if your hardware isn't recognized or you still can't access broadband.

Connecting via Your Modem

If you're still using dial-up to access the Net, don't despair — you can still use Knoppix. However, the same caveats applicable to modems used with any Linux distro apply to Knoppix: internal modems may or may not work (if it's a WinModem, probably not), external modems are more likely to work. If you're using a laptop, the built-in modem probably is a no-go, but a PCMCIA modem is most likely OK.

In other words, if Knoppix detects your modem, great. Things are looking good, and you should be able to get online. If Knoppix doesn't detect your modem, you have to decide how much time and energy you want to put into getting your modem to work. You can look around on the Knoppix forum, but don't expect very much, frankly. That's why I always keep spare PCI and PCMCIA modems around; I know they work with Linux, and especially Knoppix. Here's the hardware I rely on:

➤ PCI: USRobotics 3CP5610

➤ PCMCIA: USRobotics Megahertz XJ1560

To set up your modem, open the Knoppix menu and select Network/Internet → /dev/modem Connection Setup. You'll be given five options: Serial, USB, IrDA, Bluetooth, and Winmodem. Choose Serial, USB, or Winmodem — whichever matches your hardware — and see whether Knoppix can get your modem working.

Let's assume that Knoppix recognizes your modem. (If it didn't, you'll have checked out PCI or PCMCIA modems and gotten one working yourself.) Now it's time to get connected.

First you have to set up your dial-up account. From the Knoppix menu, choose Network/Internet → Modem Dialer. Once the Modem Dialer window opens, click Configure, which opens the KPPP Configuration window (yes, you're using KPPP, the KDE PPP tool), as shown in Figure 2-1.

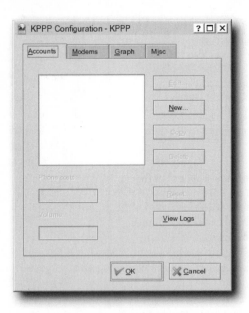

FIGURE 2-1: Configuring your dial-up connection with KPPP

On the Modems tab, select your modem and click Edit. In the Modem window, select the Modem tab and click Query Modem. You should see a string of text go by indicating that Knoppix and KPPP have detected your modem and that it works. This is just an easy way to remove one big item from your troubleshooting list if you find that your modem isn't working.

Return to the Accounts tab and click New. The window that opens asks whether you want to use the Wizard or Manual Setup; if you live in the U.S., don't bother with the wizard, because there's nothing in it for you. Instead, just click the Manual Setup button, which opens the New Account window, shown in Figure 2-2.

FIGURE 2-2: Enter details about your dial-up account.

In the Connection Name field, enter something meaningful to you, such as Earthlink or Panix. Click Add to enter the phone number. Enter only the digits — no spaces, parentheses, or hyphens. That's probably all that you'll have to do in the entire window. If your ISP has given you other stuff to configure, go ahead and do it; otherwise, click OK to close the New Account window, and you're back at the KPPP Configuration window.

To try out your dial-up connection, click OK to close the KPPP Configuration window so you're back at the KPPP window. Enter a Login ID and Password, check Show Log Window so you can tell what the heck is going on (more troubleshooting help), and click Connect. If all is well, the sound of two modems communicating should fill the air, and you are connected eventually. Then you can start enjoying the Internet at 56 Kbps (or worse!) speeds.

Getting Broadband Working

The category of broadband includes DSL, cable, and even ISDN, the original broadband. No matter what you use, you really must have a router/firewall sitting between your network (even if it's only one computer) and the big bad Internet. Don't agonize over this issue: Routers are cheap nowadays (you can get a good Cable/DSL router for $35 or less at Amazon, for example), they're super easy to set up and use, and they do a good job protecting your network. Therefore, no excuses — get one, set it up, and use it.

You'll find that there's an additional benefit as well: virtually every SOHO router/firewall acts as a DHCP server (Dynamic Host Configuration Protocol — for more info, see http://en.wikipedia.org/wiki/DHCP), which means that booting a Knoppix machine on such a network is as smooth as silk. Basically, you start up the computer with the Knoppix disk inserted, allow Knoppix to do its automatic detection thing, and soon enough you're connected to the Internet. It's really, really easy.

If you're not using a router (please go buy a router) and you have a direct ISDN connection, then from the Knoppix menu select Network/Internet → ISDN connection. Make the necessary configurations, and away you go.

If you're not using a router and you have DSL with PPPoE (*please* go buy a router), go to the Knoppix menu and choose Network/Internet → ADSL/PPPOE configuration. Fill in the required data and you should be online. Your first stop will be some online store to buy a router, right?

Cruising Wirelessly

Wireless is wonderful when you can get it and it performs correctly, but it can sometimes be a pain to get it going. If you're using an 802.11b card, you'll probably have few problems because most B cards work with Knoppix. A laptop using Intel's Centrino technology, however, may or may not work even though it's based on 802.11b; it was only recently that Intel released the necessary info to open-source developers so they could get Centrino working with Linux. G cards are a different story. Few work natively in Linux at this time, although that's changing; in the meantime, you can try using the `ndiswrapper` software, which enables you to use Windows drivers to power your G cards under Linux. When `ndiswrapper` works, it's great; when it doesn't, forget it. Drop back to a B card if you can.

Tip

Earlier I noted I always keep both PCI and PCMCIA modems around because I know they work with Linux. I do the same thing with 802.11b. My card of choice is the Lucent Orinoco Gold, which has worked beautifully for me for years. If you can pick one up on eBay, you really should — and the older the card you can get, the better, because wireless card manufacturers keep messing around with their cards' chipsets.

If Knoppix recognizes your card when you boot, you're in wireless heaven. By default, it uses DHCP to get an IP address and all the other needed data for accessing a network. The only hitch may be that the wireless network to which you're attempting to connect uses WEP or WPA to encrypt traffic. If so, you will not connect at first. Instead, from the Knoppix menu select Network/Internet → Wavelan configuration.

A dialog box opens, informing you that you're about to change the parameters of your wireless card: eth0 or eth1, for instance. Click OK. If you want it to work with any wireless access point no matter what the ESSID is, just leave the ESSID text box blank; otherwise, enter the ESSID. Either way, click OK when you're ready to move on.

Next, you're asked for the NWID, or cell identifier. If you need to set the network ID, which helps separate logical networks, enter it, but most of the time you can just leave this blank and click OK.

Set the mode for your card. If you leave it blank, you're choosing Managed; otherwise, enter one of the other listed options (most likely Ad-Hoc if you're not using Managed). Here's what the different modes mean:

- **Managed:** Also known as Infrastructure, in this mode a wireless access point (such as a SOHO wireless router, for example) is used to link a wireless network with a wired one.

- **Ad-Hoc:** If you want to connect two or more wireless machines together without a central hub or switch, use this mode.

- **Master:** Your machine is acting as an access point for other wireless devices.

- **Repeater:** Your machine simply forwards wireless packets.

- **Secondary:** Your machine is either a backup master or a backup repeater.

- **Auto:** Knoppix makes the best choice it can determine, which most likely means Managed.

Make your choice—probably Managed or perhaps Ad-Hoc—and click OK.

Most of you should just leave the Channel Number box empty, which allows Knoppix to automatically select the one it detects. If you know that you're supposed to use a specific channel number—they range from 0 to 16—go ahead and enter it. When this dialog is correct for your network, click OK.

It's best to leave the card frequency box blank, so that it's automatically entered for you, but if you really must enter something, make sure you enter the correct number:

- **802.11a:** 5.15-5.825 GHz, entered as 5.825G, for instance

- **802.11b:** 2.412-2.462 GHz (for the US; other countries vary), entered as 2.412G

- **802.11g:** 2.412-2.462 GHz (for the US; other countries vary), entered as 2.412G

Note To learn more about the exact frequencies your hardware supports, read your vendor's product detail pages, available on the company's Website or included with your wireless card.

Click OK. The next dialog asks for the encryption key—the WEP (Wired Equivalent Privacy) key. If your access point isn't using WEP, leave the box empty; otherwise, enter the 64-bit or 128-bit key. Click OK.

Enter any additional parameters for your wireless card, if you need any (you probably won't have any). Click OK.

Tip All of these dialog boxes are constructing options for the `iwconfig` command, so if you know that command well, you can skip the entire configuration process and just use the command line, with `sudo`.

You're almost finished. The next dialog asks for any additional parameters for `iwspy`, which helps gather wireless statistics. Leave it empty (unless you *really* know what you're doing) and click OK. Then you're asked whether you have any additional parameters for `iwpriv`, which is for settings specific to your particular wireless card driver. Again, leave the text box empty, and click OK. The dialog box closes, you see several settings flash by in the open terminal window, and then — bam! — that window closes, and your wireless card should be working.

Tip If you ever have problems with a working wireless card, make sure your wired connection isn't currently on (run `sudo ifconfig` to see your list of connections). If it is, take down the wired connection (let's say it's eth1) with this command: `sudo ifconfig eth1 down`.

If you have a G card and you have to use `ndiswrapper`, you have another adventure ahead of you. `ndiswrapper` is undeniably cool, but it can be a bear to set up.

Note For the details about `ndiswrapper`, check out the project's home page at `http://ndiswrapper.sourceforge.net`. Even more useful is the project's wiki, at `http://ndiswrapper.sourceforge.net/phpwiki/index.php/`.

Open the Knoppix menu and select Network/Internet → ndiswrapper configuration. The dialog warns you that you're going to need the `.inf` and `.sys` files for your G card's drivers. That is where the fun often begins. If you still have the CD with the original drivers, you're probably not going to tear your hair out. If you don't have that CD, get the necessary driver from the vendor's Website, put it on a USB flash drive or burn it onto a CD, and mount the device onto your Knoppix box. If you can't find the driver, head to the `ndiswrapper` project's Web page that lists supported cards and drivers (`http://ndiswrapper.sourceforge.net/phpwiki/index.php/List`) to try to find the one you need.

The `ndiswrapper` configuration script walks you through the process. You locate your `.inf` and `.sys` files, and set up those drivers. Unfortunately, you must now configure your wireless card by hand, not that it's a big deal. Here's how:

1. Enter the following on the command line:

   ```
   $ sudo iwconfig
   ```

   That verifies that your system recognizes that it has a working wireless NIC.

2. Ensure that your card sees an access point by running the following:

   ```
   $ sudo iwlist eth0 scan
   ```

   The results of this command tell you that your card is working and can interact with your local access point.

3. Assuming that Knoppix saw a wireless card at eth0, the following key commands can be used:

   - `$ sudo iwconfig eth0 essid essidname`: Sets your ESSID. Change `essidname` to the actual name you need to use. To connect to any ESSID, use `any` for `essidname`.

- $ sudo iwconfig eth0 mode modetype: Sets your mode. Substitute mode-type with Managed, Ad-Hoc, and so on.

- $ sudo iwconfig eth0 key restricted wepkey: Sets your WEP encryption key. Replace wepkey with the actual key.

You can, of course, combine all of these on one line, as follows:

```
$ sudo iwconfig eth0 essid home mode Managed key restricted 1234-1234-1234-1234
```

In the end, it all comes down to your time and your circumstances. If you can use a B card that you know works with Knoppix, use it. If you have to use a G card, make sure you have the drivers handy. Finally, practice using ndiswrapper before you find yourself under the gun. ndiswrapper is just a bit tricky, and it would be better for you to have some experience configuring it before you're trying to recover data on a machine that's crashed.

Tip

Knoppix also supports the use of cell phones and even Bluetooth devices for wireless Internet access. If you keep your expectations low, you may just be surprised and happy when it works. To set up your device as a modem, open the Knoppix menu and select Network/Internet ➜ /dev/modem connection setup, and make the necessary choice. After that, use KNOPPIX ➜ Network/Internet ➜ GPRS connection.

Setting a Static Address

DHCP (Dynamic Host Configuration Protocol) is a great technology, and it certainly makes the lives of network admins a lot easier (and, yes, you too are a network admin if you have a home network, even of just two computers, and you manage them), but a dynamic address is not always desirable. For example, what if you're trying to use your Knoppix machine as a server? In cases like that, dynamic addresses are a nuisance, and a static IP address is needed. It isn't hard to set up Knoppix to use a static IP address.

To begin, you need to know what your system is using currently, so enter the following simple, yet incredibly informative, command:

```
$ ifconfig
```

Here are example results from a laptop using a wireless 802.11b card, and you'll probably see something similar:

```
eth0 Link encap:Ethernet HWaddr 00:02:2D:2B:E7:34
 inet addr:192.168.1.5 Bcast:255.255.255.255 Mask:255.255.255.0
 inet6 addr: fe80::202:2dff:fe2b:e734/64 Scope:Link
 UP BROADCAST RUNNING MULTICAST MTU:1500 Metric:1
 RX packets:20209 errors:53 dropped:53 overruns:0 frame:53
 TX packets:15684 errors:12 dropped:0 overruns:0 carrier:0
 collisions:0 txqueuelen:1000
 RX bytes:18936569 (18.0 MiB) TX bytes:3570323 (3.4 MiB)
 Interrupt:3 Base address:0x100
```

```
lo Link encap:Local Loopback
  inet addr:127.0.0.1 Mask:255.0.0.0
  inet6 addr: ::1/128 Scope:Host
  UP LOOPBACK RUNNING MTU:16436 Metric:1
  RX packets:86 errors:0 dropped:0 overruns:0 frame:0
  TX packets:86 errors:0 dropped:0 overruns:0 carrier:0
  collisions:0 txqueuelen:0
  RX bytes:5314 (5.1 KiB) TX bytes:5314 (5.1 KiB)
```

This tells you that the network's DHCP server assigned eth0, the wireless card, the IP address of 192.168.1.5. Before changing the IP to a static address, you first have to make sure that the address isn't in the DHCP pool of assignable addresses, and that requires a question to the network admin. In this example, the DHCP pool ranges from 192.168.1.2 to 192.168.1.50, so anything greater than .50 and less than .255 should be safe. To change the card's IP to a statically assigned address, you'd run the following command:

```
$ sudo ifconfig eth0 inet 192.168.1.100
```

Use the same command to change the network mask or broadcast address. Here's an example:

```
$ sudo ifconfig eth0 netmask 255.255.255.0 broadcast 192.168.1.255
```

Note Yes, you can also hardcode your IP address and other data by opening the Knoppix menu and selecting Network/Internet ➔ Network Card Configuration, but it's faster to just use the command line, and it doesn't hurt to know what the Knoppix config dialog is really doing behind the scenes.

That should get you on the network, but you may not be able to get to www.google.com or your email server. Why not? DNS (Domain Name Server). To configure DNS, you need to edit /etc/resolv.conf. As root, open /etc/resolv.conf with your favorite text editor and add any required DNS addresses. For instance, here's what my resolv.conf file looks like when I'm teaching at Washington University in St. Louis:

```
search artsci.wustl.edu
nameserver 128.252.120.1
nameserver 128.252.135.4
```

The search line isn't really that important, but you need at least one nameserver line, or DNS won't work for you. Ask your network admin what you're supposed to use, and you'll be up and running in no time.

Working on the Internet

Is there anyone left to convince that the Internet has completely revolutionized the way humans acquire and use ICE (information, communication, and entertainment)? We're living in a wondrous time, with new technologies appearing almost daily that enable us to use the Net in exciting ways. Knoppix comes with many of the very best Internet software packages, and those that it doesn't include can easily be added with just a little effort.

Sharing Files with BitTorrent

Knoppix doesn't include any file-sharing apps by default, and that's OK. Most file sharing is focused on music or movies, which isn't super-important when you're in Knoppix. Most file-sharing software is slow and inefficient anyway. BitTorrent (BT for short) is a better way to download and share the ISO images and other large files that you might need to grab when you're running Knoppix.

Most file-sharing software works as follows: You search for a file, and your search is run either against an index of files kept on a central server (the Napster model, which tends to get companies sued into the ground) or against the indexes generated and kept by each individual client computer (the decentralized Gnutella model, which makes it harder for the RIAA and MPAA to track and shut down so-called pirates — copyright infringers — but which also results in really slow searches). Once you've located a file, you download it from the computer that has it, a process that is usually slooooow, even on a fast connection.

BitTorrent is completely different. In essence, BT breaks enormous files into hundreds or even thousands of small pieces. When you begin downloading a file using BT, you're actually downloading those pieces from everyone who has any of those pieces on their computers. As soon as you've downloaded a piece, BT shares it with anyone else trying to acquire the file. Instead of downloading an entire file all at once from one machine, you're downloading pieces of that file from several machines at the same time — and returning the favor by sharing your pieces as well. The result? The more popular the file, the faster the download, sometimes (to quote Mel Brooks' *Spaceballs*) at "ludicrous" speed.

Note

For more information about BitTorrent, read the official BT home page at `http://bitconjurer.org/BitTorrent/`, the Wikipedia article on BT at `http://en.wikipedia.org/wiki/BitTorrent`, or Brian's BitTorrent FAQ and Guide at `www.dessent.net/btfaq/`.

Try out BitTorrent by downloading the latest version of Knoppix using BT. Using your Web browser, head to `http://torrent.unix-ag.uni-kl.de`, the UNIX-AG BitTorrent Tracker, and find the latest version of Knoppix in your language (either EN for English or DE for German). Click the DL link (for download) next to the Knoppix you want, and save the torrent file (a whopping 55KB) to your desktop. And now . . . what? Nothing happens. Where's the ISO image?

Tip

To find other torrent files, use Google. You can find music (especially live "jam band" stuff), software and OS ISOs, movies, and more. Legal? Sure.

Well, remember that Knoppix doesn't come with any file-sharing apps, including BitTorrent, by default. To do anything with that torrent file you just downloaded, you have to install BT. Fortunately, you have APT (discussed in Chapter 1) and the Knoppix persistent disk image, so you can restart Knoppix later and continue to use the BT software you install.

Several different BT software packages are available, including the "real" BitTorrent software packages made by Bram Cohen, the inventor of BT. They're fine, but a BT client called

BitTornado is more fully featured, so get that instead. To do so, enter the following on a command line:

```
# apt-get update && apt-get install bittornado
```

Once BitTornado installs, open it by going to the K menu and selecting Internet ➜ Bittornado Client. A dialog box opens, asking you to choose a torrent file. Aha! That's where the torrent file you downloaded a while back comes in — choose that file, which should be on your desktop, and click OK. You're next asked where you want to save the actual torrent — the large file — that you're downloading. The Knoppix ISO image is around 700MB, so you do *not* want to save that onto your Knoppix desktop, unless you have at least 1GB of RAM. Instead, you should mount a partition of your hard drive with writing turned on (right-click on the partition icon on the desktop, choose Properties, select the Device tab, uncheck Read Only, click OK, and then click on the icon to mount it), and use that to store the download. Once you have chosen a directory on your hard drive, click OK, and BitTornado springs into action, downloading — and uploading — the Knoppix ISO. Figure 2-3 shows the program at work (on a home DSL connection).

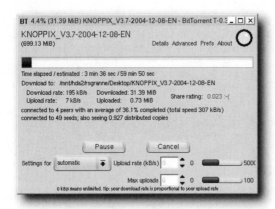

FIGURE 2-3: BitTornado downloading a Knoppix ISO

The screen in the figure shows that 31MB of the ISO have already downloaded, at 196 Kbps, which is pretty darn good. Notice that nearly 1MB of that same ISO have already been shared, a number that increases as long as the BT window is open (that's why it's considered good practice to keep your BT window open after your download is complete, so that others can continue to benefit).

Click the Details and Advanced links in the top right corner of the window to find out a lot more about your download. Play around with those links, and with Preferences as well. The more you learn about BitTorrent, and BitTornado, the more effectively you will to use this powerful software. Already, it is estimated that BT is responsible for 35 percent of all traffic on the Internet (not Peer2Peer traffic — *all* traffic). With its amazing capabilities, this software and those who use it have a very bright future.

Tip

If you want to install and use the original BT client, use `apt-get install bittorrent-gui`. Another fantastic BT client is Azureus, which you can download and install with `apt-get install azureus`.

Browsing the Web with Mozilla Firefox

Knoppix used to include the full Mozilla suite of Web browser, email program, and Web page composer, but it dropped the suite with version 3.8 and instead included Mozilla Firefox, which is a Web browser only. That was a great move. Firefox has the buzz, the extensions and other goodies, and it's a faster, more svelte program.

If you're reading this, you've probably used Firefox before, and you probably know how to use a Web browser. I'm not going to conduct Web Browsing 101 here; instead, let's look at three really cool things that you can do with Firefox.

Improving Your Home Page

When I used to start Firefox, I found that I'd open the same three tabs every time: Gmail, Bloglines, and The Open Source Weblog. I finally realized that what I was doing was inefficient. So I went to Edit→ Preferences, selected General, and for Home Page I entered the following, clicking OK when I finished:

`gmail.google.com|www.bloglines.com/myblogs|opensource.weblogsinc.com`

Now when I open Firefox, it automatically opens those three sites in tabs, ready for me to view. If I click the Home button, those sites appear. Try it out yourself: Determine which sites you return to repeatedly and enter their URLs into the Home Page text box, separating them with the pipe symbol (the | right above the Enter key on most keyboards). Changing your home page into your key home pages makes things more efficient and useful because those presumably are the sites in which you do most of your work.

Installing Extensions

One of the absolute coolest things about Firefox is the hundreds of free extensions that extend the browser in almost infinite ways. You can install new extensions by selecting Tools→ Extensions and clicking Get More Extensions, which opens a new Firefox window pointing to `https://addons.update.mozilla.org/extensions/`. From there, find the extension you want and click Install Now. Restart Firefox to load the extension after it has been downloaded and installed.

The official Mozilla Update site doesn't have every extension—you can find a lot of great ones there, but there are essential extensions on other sites as well. The only thing you need to be aware of is that you can't just install Firefox extensions from any old site. For security's sake, Firefox starts with a whitelist of safe sites from which you can install software; when you try to install extensions from nonwhitelisted sites, Firefox opens an alert bar at the top of the window warning you that the site has been blocked. To add that site to your whitelist, click the Edit Options button on the right of the alert bar, and when the Allowed Sites window opens, click Allow and then OK. Click on the link to install the extension again, and this time Firefox does it without complaint.

Recommended Extensions

I keep an updated list of my installed Firefox extensions on my Website (`http://granneman.com/go/extensions/`), and If you want to see what I'm using right now, check it out. For now, I recommend the following as indispensable:

- Adblock: Look for this in the Miscellaneous section at Mozilla Update. Annoyed by ads on Websites? Just right-click an ad, select Adblock Image, and say bye-bye to that bothersome ad. You can also use regular expressions to block all ads from a certain domain or directory, or matching a particular pattern. You can import the Adblock lists other folks have created; search Google for "adblock import filter list" and try out the ones you find.

- Jybe: `http://jybe.com/download/register.aspx`. Jybe enables you, and anyone else who installs Jybe (IE for Windows, or Firefox on Linux, Mac OS, or Windows), to collaboratively view Web pages in real time and text chat about what you're seeing. Perfect for demos, work sessions, troubleshooting, or long-distance tech support.

- miniT: Look for this in the Tabbed Browsing section at Mozilla Update. With this extension installed, you can drag your tabs to reposition them in any order you'd like. As you drag a tab, a tiny arrow appears, making it clear where your tab is going to go.

- SessionSaver: Look for this in the Tabbed Browsing section at Mozilla Update. If you've ever suffered a Firefox crash and lost all of the Websites you had loaded in your tabs, you'll want SessionSaver. Load this extension and forget about it. Firefox crash? Restart Firefox, and everything is restored: tabs, histories, cookies, everything. Close Firefox with a series of tabs open? Restart Firefox, and they reappear. Awesome.

There are, of course, many more extensions— you can see my full list at my Website and look around Mozilla Update and elsewhere. There's an amazing amount of innovation going on in the area of Firefox extensions, so you're sure to find something wonderful.

Focusing Your Searches

Firefox comes with a lot of neat search tools built in, both obvious (the search box in the upper right corner) and not so obvious (press Ctrl+F to open the search bar at the bottom of the window, or highlight a word or phrase and right-click it to search the Web using your selection). With a little extra effort, you can soup up Firefox and turn it into a lean, mean searchin' machine.

First of all, install a few search toolbars. Try all of them, uninstall the ones you don't like, and keep the one or two that you find particularly useful. Take a look at the Googlebar (`http://googlebar.mozdev.org`), the Clusty toolbar for Firefox (`http://clusty.com/toolbar/firefox`), the A9 toolbar (`http://toolbar.a9.com`), and the Yahoo! toolbar (`http://companion.yahoo.com/firefox`). All have nice features, and all do a good job. Or, just install the Groowe Search toolbar (`http://www.groowe.com`), which has all of them and more!

Next, find a Website that you search often. For example, at AllMusic (`http://allmusic.com,`), you can use the site's Search box to look up a band, an album, or a song. After the hundredth time, though, you'll wonder whether there's an easier way, and there is. Right-click in the Search box. From the options that appear, choose Add a Keyword for this Search, as shown in Figure 2-4.

FIGURE 2-4: Right-click in a site's Search box to add a search keyword.

A new window opens: Add Bookmark. To use this window effectively, click the little arrow button on the far right; when you do, the Bookmarks folder structure is revealed, as shown in Figure 2-5.

FIGURE 2-5: Add the details for your new search keyword.

You're basically adding a new search to Firefox. Select Bookmarks from the list of folders, click New Folder, and give the new folder a name, such as "Search" (clever, eh?). Now you need to name the new search you're creating. Because it's going to search AllMusic, how about entering "allmusic" in the Name textbox? Finally, and this is the biggie, you need to put something in the Keyword textbox. This is the term you're actually going to use to search AllMusic in the future, so the word (and it must be a word — no spaces allowed) should be easy to remember, descriptive, and short — "music" is a good one for this example. When everything has been selected and entered, click Add.

Now try the new search term. In the Location bar of Firefox—where the URL is usually displayed—type the following and then press Enter:

```
music clash
```

AllMusic loads in Firefox, displaying a Web page about the greatest rock 'n' roll band of all time. To try it again, with the second greatest band of all time, use this, again in the Location bar of Firefox, *not* the Search box on the AllMusic Web page:

```
music rolling stones
```

Is that cool or what? Now it doesn't matter what Web page you're on—just clear the Firefox Location bar and enter `music bandname`, click Enter, and AllMusic loads with a biography, discography, and far more about that band.

Try it with any Website's Search box. Pretty soon you'll have all your custom searches defined, saving you time and making it easy to find the information you want, when you want it.

Firefox is a fabulous piece of software, and you'll enjoy exploring its features. It's going to be with us a long time, whether or not Knoppix includes it by default.

Reading and Sending Email with KMail

If you're an email addict like so many of us, you have little self-control when it comes to checking your email. That means that a good email program is key. You want something that's attractive, powerful, and easy to use. Fortunately, Knoppix includes KMail, a favorite open-source email app (you can also find KMail as part of the Kontact PIM, accessible from the K menu: select ➜ Office ➜ Kontact).

To start the program, open the K menu and select ➜ Internet ➜ KMail. A window similar to the one shown in Figure 2-6 opens.

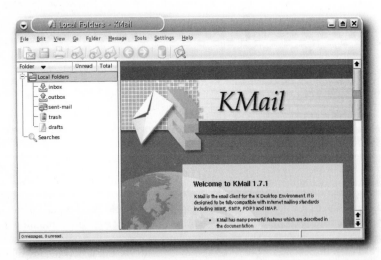

FIGURE 2-6: KMail is open, but you have to configure it before you can use it.

Note If the KMail shown in Figure 2-6 looks a bit different from yours, that's probably because the fonts have been configured using the advice given in Chapter 1. Changing the fonts in KMail makes it far more pleasant to use.

Configuring KMail

After opening KMail, you have to configure it. Select Settings → Configure Kmail to display the window shown in Figure 2-7.

FIGURE 2-7: KMail's Configure window

This chapter can't possibly cover all of KMail's settings, but you'll explore the most important ones, beginning with the Manage Identities screen shown in Figure 2-7. You enter data here, or KMail won't work correctly. Make sure the default identity is selected, and then click Modify. On the General tab, enter the appropriate information for Your Name and Email Address. You can click OK to close the window now, but if you want, go ahead and configure the Cryptography tab (if you have a GPG key set up, which is discussed in Chapter 6), or change the Reply-To address on the Advanced tab, or check Enable signature on the Signature tab, and then enter your usual sig into the box. When everything is just so, click OK to close the Manage Identity window.

Note For more info about KMail, check out its Website (`http://kmail.kde.org`), especially the extensive Documentation section and the excellent FAQ.

Now move on to the second vitally important screen: Network. The first tab, Sending, enables you to specify your SMTP server. By default, Knoppix includes Sendmail, but the vast majority of you will never, ever need that entry (if you *do* need it, you'll know it, and you'll know what to do), so go ahead and select it, and then click Remove to get rid of it. Once that's done, click Add; the Add Transport window appears. Choose SMTP and click OK. The Add Transport window changes into the one shown in Figure 2-8.

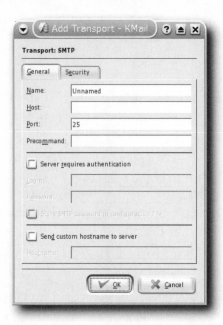

FIGURE 2-8: Adding an SMTP server to KMail

Enter your SMTP details (which are unique to every reader). If you have a Gmail account from Google (and they're free, so why don't you?), you can configure KMail to use Gmail as a powerful, free, easy SMTP server, which vastly simplifies everything. Here's how to do it:

1. In the Name box, use (no surprise!) gmail.

2. In the Host box, enter smtp.gmail.com.

3. Check the Server Requires Authentication option.

4. Enter your full Gmail address (username@gmail.com) in the Login box, and your Gmail password in the Password box.

5. Go to the Security tab — you must do this with Gmail, or things will not work. Under Encryption, choose SSL, and for Authentication Method, select PLAIN. Click OK.

You can now send email using Gmail. Easy, convenient, and it works perfectly.

Tip   If you don't have a Gmail account, get one at http://gmail.google.com. Accounts are free, you get a full gigabyte of storage, and it has the coolest Web mail interface.

You're halfway done; you've taken care of the sending part. Now you need to receive email. Go to the Receiving tab and click the Add button. Figure 2-9 shows the small Add Acc window that opens. Choose the kind of email account you have.

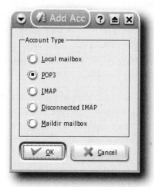

FIGURE 2-9: Tell KMail which kind of email account you use.

You've got five options. Here's what each one means:

- **Local mailbox:** Use this if you have local email stored in the widespread mbox format, in which each folder's messages are stored, concatenated, in a single file. mbox probably should be avoided because one damaged email message can corrupt an entire mbox file containing hundreds or even thousands of messages.

- **POP3:** Post Office Protocol 3, which is what most people use. With POP3, you download your email from your server whenever you check it (yes, you can leave copies on your server, but this is not the correct way to use POP3, and it creates a mess, with copies of email on this machine and that machine).

- **IMAP:** Internet Message Access Protocol, which is what more people should use, especially those who access email from more than one machine. Unlike POP3, IMAP stores email on the server. When you check your mail, only the headers are downloaded; when you view an individual message, the content is downloaded so you can see it. Delete an email, and it is deleted on the server. With IMAP, you always see the same email, no matter which machine you're using to view your mail.

- **Disconnected IMAP:** The same as IMAP, except that a copy of each message is downloaded onto your machine so that you can view, move, and delete messages while you're offline; when you reconnect, your changes are synchronized with the email store on the server. Disconnected IMAP is faster than regular IMAP and enables you to work with email when you aren't connected to the Net.

- **Maildir mailbox:** The successor to mbox, in which each email is stored in a separate file. If you have local emails that have been saved using maildir, this is your choice.

Note For more information about the various email protocols, read Wikipedia's articles at http://en.wikipedia.org/wiki/Simple_Mail_Transfer_Protocol, http://en.wikipedia.org/wiki/POP3, and http://en.wikipedia.org/wiki/IMAP.

The default order is a bit confusing: If you have a collection of old emails saved on your hard drive and you want to read them, choose either Local mailbox or Maildir mailbox. If you want to connect to your email server and read your mail, choose POP3, IMAP, or Disconnected IMAP. If you've set up an email account before, you should have no problems setting up one with KMail. It's all pretty standard. Click OK when everything is correct.

Now move on to Appearance (select from the left panel). On the Layout tab's Message Structure Viewer section, select the radio button next to Show Never. The message structure is a waste of screen real estate, and you're just getting rid of it. On the Headers tab, check the box next to Display Message Sizes—why this box isn't checked by default is unknown. Who doesn't want to know the size of a particular email message?

That's it for configuring KMail; click OK to close the Configure window. KMail immediately connects to the accounts you set up, so you can begin downloading and reading your email. If you want to, you can right-click on the Unread and Total columns in the left message list pane and remove those two columns. Some folks find them unnecessary, but you may want to leave them alone.

Getting the Most Out of KMail

Using KMail couldn't be simpler because all the main functions are on the toolbar. If you're not sure what a particular icon does, hold your mouse over it for a second or two, and a tooltip appears with the name of the icon. For even more functionality, check out the menus. This section provides you with a couple of cool tips about your address book.

When you compose a new message, KMail uses auto-completion to finish names and email addresses after you type the first few letters, but only if you've populated KAddressBook (open the K menu and select Office ➔ Address Manager). By default, KAddressBook stores those addresses in a single file—std.vcf—usually located at ~/.kde/share/apps/kabc/.

If you're using Knoppix on a machine that already has an std.vcf file on it that you want to use, it's easy to do so. Open KAddressBook and look for an Address Books section in the bottom left pane of the program; if you don't see it, select Settings ➔ Show Extension Bar ➔ Address Books, and it will appear. Select the default address book, called resource-name in Knoppix, and click Edit. The Resource Configuration window opens (see Figure 2-10).

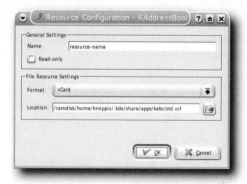

FIGURE 2-10: Point KAddressBook to another address book file.

Change the name from resource-name to something a bit more informative, like hard_drive_ address_book or the like. Leave Format set to vCard, and click the Open File dialog icon button to the right of the Location text box. Navigate to `/mnt/hda2/home/rsgranne/.kde/ share/apps/kabc/std.vcf` (or the equivalent on your system), click OK, and your usual addresses are available. Sweet!

Caution

For this technique to work, you must first mount the hard drive containing your home directory using the icons on the Knoppix desktop. If you want to be able to write to, as well as read, the `std.vcf` file, mount the drive with Read-Only turned off. (Remember how to do that? Right-click on the drive's icon on the desktop, choose Properties, select the Device tab, uncheck Read Only, and click OK to close the Properties window.)

There's another way to auto-populate your address book, but it works only if you use IMAP for your email. (If you're an IMAP junkie, you'll prefer this method). Basically, you store your addresses in a folder on your IMAP server, and then you tell KAddressBook to use that folder as your address book. It sounds kind of crazy, but it works. Here's how to do it:

1. In KMail, right-click on a folder in the list on the left side of the window and choose New Subfolder. Give it a name like "groupware" or something that indicates to you that you're storing more than mail in it. Click OK to create the folder.

2. Select Check Mail to Synchronize Everything.

3. Select Settings → Configure KMail, click the Misc button on the left side of the Configure window, and select the Groupware tab. Check the box next to Enable IMAP Resource Functionality, and then take a look at Resource Folders Are Subfolders Of, which should contain a list of all the IMAP folders on your server. From the list, choose the folder you created in step 1 (`groupware` is the example filename).

4. Definitely uncheck Hide Groupware Folders because otherwise your address book will not be populated.

5. Open KAddressBook. In the Address Books area of the window, click Add. The Add Address Book window opens; choose IMAP and click OK. Now when you add a new contact, it's stored in the groupware/Contacts folder in your IMAP folder structure. You can access your address book from anywhere in the world, at any time!

Tip When you finish adding the IMAP resource, select Settings → Show Extension Bar and choose None so that the Address Books area disappears. There's just no reason for it to sit there taking up space.

If you had contacts stored using IMAP, your address book is immediately populated with a list of all those contacts. Anytime you use Knoppix on a new machine, and it doesn't matter whose machine it is, you always have access to all of your names, numbers, and addresses. Pretty cool, eh?

Instant Messaging with Buddies Using Gaim

Instant messaging has been increasing in popularity over the last several years as it has spread from consumers to business. In fact, many now rely on IM more than email. As one of the key net apps, IM is part of Knoppix in the guise of *Gaim,* which is actually a GNOME IM program that runs perfectly under KDE (as the vast majority of GNOME apps do). Gaim is cool because it supports all of the major IM protocols, including AIM, ICQ, Jabber, MSN Messenger, and Yahoo!, as well as IRC (although it's a bit clumsy) and some others. That's right — with just one program you can IM all your pals, no matter what they're using.

To start Gaim, open the K menu and select Internet → Gaim Internet Messenger. To use Gaim, you need to connect to your IM accounts; Gaim immediately opens the Accounts window so you can authenticate with your existing accounts.

Sign Up for IM Accounts

If you don't have an account with any IM service yet, visit the Websites of the major IM networks and sign up:

- AOL Instant Messenger (AIM): `https://my.screenname.aol.com/_cqr/registration/initRegistration.psp`

- Gadu-Gadu: Register from within Gaim

- ICQ: `www.icq.com/register/`

- Jabber: Register from within Gaim

- MSN Messenger: `https://register.passport.net`

- Yahoo! Messenger: `http://edit.yahoo.com/config/eval_register?new=1`

Click the Add button in the Accounts window to open the Add Account window, shown in Figure 2-11.

FIGURE 2-11: Add IM accounts to Gaim.

Use the Protocol drop-down menu to choose an IM service that you want to use. Fill in the necessary information on the screen, check Remember Password and Auto-Login if you're feeling lazy (not a bad thing!), and click Save when you're done. If you want to connect to any other services, repeat the entire process until you're set up with everything you need.

Now you can start using Gaim. Connect to your registered IM services in the Accounts window by checking the box in the Online column for each IM network you want to join (if you chose Auto-Login, you won't have to do that next time you fire up Gaim). As you connect to each network, the icons representing your IM services will change from gray to color, letting you know that you're successful. Once you're connected, close the Accounts window and focus on the Buddy List window, pictured in Figure 2-12.

FIGURE 2-12: Only a few buddies are online in this example.

If you already have buddies on any of your services, they should show up once you connect. To begin IMing, just right-click on a buddy and choose from the list of options, or click the IM button at the bottom of the window. Keep in mind that the options vary depending on what each service offers. Send a single message, start a chat session, or send a file — it's all possible with Gaim.

To add a new buddy, select Buddies → Add Buddy. The Add Buddy window opens, and you supply just two key pieces of data: Screen Name and Account. Make sure you choose the correct account — if you say MyFriendJuan uses Yahoo!, but he actually uses Jabber, you and Juan will not be IMing any time soon.

Gaim is a mature IM client that does what Internet technologies are supposed to do: make it easy to communicate while reducing the number of programs you have to run on your computer. Thanks to Gaim, you can talk to friends and associates who use Yahoo!, MSN, or AIM without having three or more different IM apps open at the same time. Now that's convenient!

Summary

First you have to get on the Internet, and then you can begin working (and playing) on it. There are many different ways to access that eighth wonder of the world known as the Net, and Knoppix supports all of them. Even better, Knoppix makes it easy to utilize just about any of the many functions people have created for communicating over the Net. With Knoppix in your computing toolkit, that friend of yours living across the world and the family member sitting across town are never more than a couple of clicks away.

Connecting to Other Machines and Resources

One telephone all by itself is a fashion accessory; however, a telephone connected to a telecommunications network can be a lifesaver. In the same way, a computer sitting alone is certainly useful, but when you connect it to a network of other computers, magic happens. You can transfer data, access resources all over the world (or simply in the next room), print to machines not directly connected to your machine, control other computers, and even make Web pages available to anyone in the world. In many ways, the computing revolution over the last decade has really been about networking, and Knoppix makes the fruits of that revolution fully available to its users. Want to make resources on your box available to others using Knoppix? No problem. Want to use Knoppix to access network resources on other boxes? Even easier.

Understanding Remote Control

Sometimes you're sitting in front of one computer, but you really need to see what's happening on another. Maybe you're configuring one as a server and you need to test the other one as a client, or perhaps you're trying to help family members in another city solve a particularly knotty issue, and things would proceed far more smoothly if you could just see exactly what they're viewing. Knoppix makes remote control possible with two different, complementary apps: VNC and FreeNX.

Controlling Another Computer with Remote Desktop Connection

VNC is a free, versatile, multi-platform remote-control server and client that every computer user should have in his or her toolkit. First developed by researchers at the Olivetti & Oracle Research Lab, it was released under the GPL and made available to the world. VNC has received great acclaim because of its power and flexibility. It runs natively on Linux and other varieties of *nix, Windows and PocketPC, Mac OS, Palm OS, OS/2, and, best of all, virtually any machine that can run the alternative Java-based client software. Furthermore, clients running VNC on one OS can access and control any other OS running the server version of VNC. With VNC, you have powerful, free remote control at your fingertips.

Note For more about VNC, read the Wikipedia article at `http://en.wikipedia.org/ wiki/Vnc`.

Knoppix doesn't come with a VNC client, but don't panic. Instead of a single-purpose VNC client, Knoppix comes with Remote Desktop Connection, which enables you to connect to both VNC servers and Windows servers running Remote Desktop Protocol (RDC). RDC is good software, and it comes with better features than most of the VNC clients, so this is a good move on the part of Knoppix.

Note Although this section focuses on VNC, you can use Remote Desktop Connection to connect to a Windows machine running RDP as well. Just enter `rdp:/` in front of the IP address or domain name when you connect.

To start RDC via the GUI, open the K menu and select Internet ➔ Remote Desktop Connection, or enter `krdc -caption %c %i %m` on the command line. The Remote Desktop Connection dialog opens (see Figure 3-1).

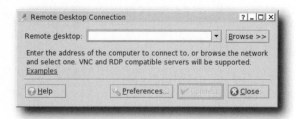

FIGURE 3-1: **Connect to other machines running VNC or RDP with Remote Desktop Connection.**

This example connects to a VNC server, so enter the IP address or domain name in the Remote Desktop box, followed by a colon and the number of the VNC screen (probably 0, but if not, start incrementing by 1 until you hit the right number), and click the Connect button (to connect to a machine running VNC on my LAN, for instance, I enter `192.168.0.13:0` or `chaucer:0` and click Connect). A second screen prompts you to choose your connection speed so that RDC can act accordingly.

RDC presents its options in a very clear fashion, so just pick the connection type appropriate to your network, click OK, enter the VNC server password in the resulting dialog box, click OK, and in a few seconds you're viewing another machine as though you were sitting right in front of it. You can do pretty much anything you want on the remote machine, within reason. Programs that involve a lot of screen redraws — such as games — are out of the question; I can't hear sounds played on Chaucer, and I can't transfer files back and forth between machines using VNC and RDC (for that, use FTP, SSH, or SMB, discussed later in this chapter). Within those limitations, however, you can still run an enormous gamut of programs, make configurations, and check up on what the remote machine is doing, all of which are invaluable tasks.

After RDC is open and running, you'll notice some controls (see Figure 3-2) at the top center of the window.

FIGURE 3-2: Controls at the top
of the RDC window

Hold your mouse over any of those controls for a second or two and a tooltip appears, providing its name. Most of these controls are pretty explanatory, but the following two might come in particularly handy:

- **Autohide on/off (the pushpin):** By default, the controls are always visible, so they can block your view of items at the top of the screen. This control toggles between autohide on, in which case the controls hide until you move your mouse to the top of the screen, and autohide off, the default.

- **Advanced options (the wrench):** This actually contains two sub-options: View Only, which prevents your mouse from doing anything (good for watching demonstrations), and Always Show Local Cursor, which enables you to see both the cursor on the machine you've connected to and the cursor on your client machine.

Remote Desktop Connection is a powerful tool that is extremely helpful when you want to connect to a server running VNC or Remote Desktop Protocol, so make sure you get some practice using it.

Note

For the latest KDE manual for Remote Desktop Connection, check out `http://docs.kde.org/en/3.3/kdenetwork/krdc/index.html`.

Exploring FreeNX

NoMachine (a division of Medialogic) created NoMachine NX, "a Terminal Server and remote access solution" based on the X Window protocol, but containing several improvements, including hyper-efficient compression (100:1 at the highest levels) and smart caching. In addition, NX can convert RDP (Remote Desktop Protocol, used by Microsoft Windows Terminal Services and Citrix MetaFrame) and RFB (Remote Frame Buffer, used by VNC) to NX, greatly improving the efficiency of those two protocols as well.

Note

For more information about NoMachine and its NX software, head over to `http://nomachine.com`.

From a security perspective, NX has much to recommend it. It uses SSH (and the SSH daemon and its port) so that usernames and passwords are encrypted when connecting for the initial authentication. After you've passed that gauntlet and logged in, you can continue to use SSH so that all further traffic is also encrypted. If you're on your LAN and behind a firewall, you can disable session encryption for improved speed, especially with older hardware (we recommend continuing to use SSH unless you're using really old machines with slow CPUs, just to be as secure as possible).

NoMachine made its core technologies available under the GPL, and the result is FreeNX, a completely free implementation of the NX server and client. NoMachine completely supports the efforts of the FreeNX team by helping to ensure that both the free and commercial software remain in sync, which is to be commended.

Note

An interview with two of the KDE developers who brought FreeNX to KDE can be found at `www.osnews.com/printer.php?news_id=8139`. Incredibly, FreeNX is actually just a BASH shell script—several hundred lines of a BASH script, but a BASH script nonetheless!

What kinds of machines can support the FreeNX server? For each KDE user session, you're looking at about 40MB of RAM and around 100MHz of your CPU, which ain't bad. With a good, fast machine, say around 3GHz with 1GB of RAM, you could support 25 parallel sessions or so. Again, that's not bad!

The net result of FreeNX: very fast, secure connections to other machines—and free to boot!

Setting Up FreeNX

To start the FreeNX server, select Knoppix ➜ Services ➜ Start NX Server. A dialog box opens, warning you that a new user named nxuser will be created who can access the FreeNX server. Go ahead and click OK. Another dialog box opens, prompting you to create a password for the new nxuser. To keep things simple for now, use `nxuser` as the password as well, and then click OK.

Caution

Do not use `nxuser` as the password on your machine! Create a good password that will protect your machine and your data. For help in creating a good password, read the SecurityFocus column titled "Pass the Chocolate," available at `www.securityfocus.com/columnists/245`.

FreeNX generates encryption keys so that all communications sent using its protocols are safe from packet sniffers; it spawns a shell window in which you can watch the process.

Meanwhile, another dialog box opens, informing you that it's now possible to log in using the newly created nxuser account. Note that you can log in as any user already on the system, so the user knoppix—who has no password set by default, remember—can also log in. When you click OK to close the dialog box, the shell window spawned by FreeNX also disappears, and FreeNX is up and running.

Command-Line Controls for FreeNX Server

It's pretty easy to change the FreeNX server by using the command line. Once you're running as root (just type `su -` on the command line, press Enter, and you're running as the superuser), you can enter any of the commands following to make alterations:

- `nxserver -listuser`: Displays a list of FreeNX users, which could be very helpful if you want to verify just who can log in to your machine

- `nxserver -adduser username`: Adds a new user, which you probably won't need to do because nxuser is sufficient

- `nxserver -deluser username`: Deletes a user

- `nxserver -passwd username`: Prompts you for a new password for the specified user, which again probably won't need to be done, assuming you picked an adequate password for nxuser when you were originally prompted

- `nxserver -status`: Is FreeNX server running? Find out with this command.

- `nxserver -start`: Starts the FreeNX server if it's not running

- `nxserver -stop`: Stops the FreeNX server if it is running

- `nxserver -restart`: If the FreeNX server is running, restart it; if it's not running, start it. Be forewarned: Anyone connected to your FreeNX server when you run this command is going to be rudely disconnected, unless you use the next command.

- `nxserver -broadcast message`: Sends your *message* to all logged-in users, which you should do before restarting the server

For the full list of possible options, just type **nxserver** on the command line as root and press Enter.

Understanding FTP

FTP (File Transfer Protocol) is one of the oldest protocols still in use on the Net. First proposed in RFC 114 in April 1971 (still available at www.ietf.org/rfc/rfc114.txt), FTP is used millions of times every day, even by people who have no idea that the file they're downloading with their Web browser is arriving on their computer courtesy of a technology that is more than 30 years old.

Unfortunately, FTP has one big problem: security. Because it's so old, FTP simply wasn't designed with security in mind. Consequently, usernames and passwords, as well as all subsequent traffic, is sent in the clear, making it trivially easy for anyone sniffing packets to find out your sensitive information. Knoppix doesn't come with FTP server software, and that's OK: You should use SSH and SFTP, which encrypts all traffic, anyway. However, Knoppix does come with FTP client software, which may come in handy if you have to connect to a server that doesn't support SFTP (in which case, email that server admin and complain — politely! — and ask him to dump FTP and put SFTP in its place), or if you want to connect to an FTP server that is on your LAN and safely behind your firewall.

If you select the K menu → Internet and start looking around for an FTP client, you're going to come up short — if you're looking for a program with the letters "FTP" in its title. Knoppix actually contains an excellent FTP program in an unexpected place: Konqueror, the file manager/ Web browser/FTP client/a million other things.

Suppose you want to use FTP to grab a Knoppix ISO. To start FTPing with Konqueror, click the Personal Files icon (the one that looks like an orange-roofed house) on the KDE panel. Konqueror opens in file manager mode, but you change that immediately by typing **ftp:// ftp.knoppix.nl** in the Location bar and pressing Enter. In a few seconds, you see the window shown in Figure 3-3.

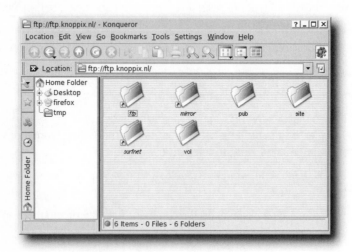

FIGURE 3-3: Konqueror makes a great FTP client.

Click pub to go into that directory, select knoppix, and you're finally at ftp.knoppix.nl/ pub/knoppix. If you'd known that URL, you could have entered that originally and gone directly there. If you know that this is a URL you'll be returning to in the future, bookmark it now by selecting Bookmarks → Add Bookmark. Just remember that your bookmark will disappear when you reboot your machine unless you follow the instructions in the introduction to this book and either create a persistent home directory or save your configuration.

To download a file, just grab it and drag it onto your Desktop, or into any other folder that you can see in the navigation panel on the left side of the Konqueror window. If you don't want to drag and drop, right-click on the file, choose Copy To, and then navigate to and click on the folder into which you want to place it. Yes, Konqueror treats the remote file just like it's a local file, which is the source of this program's power and ease of use — you can grab several files at a time and download all of them at once, if you desire.

Of course, you can go in the other direction just as easily: To upload a file, simply drag it from your Desktop, or anywhere else, drop it in your Konqueror window, and your upload begins. Again, you can grab multiple files at the same time if you really want to make things quick.

It might not have been obvious to you before, but Konqueror does the job and is actually a great FTP program. Try it and you'll see.

Exploring SSH and Its Descendants

As discussed earlier, FTP is insecure because it doesn't protect your traffic during authentication or transmission of data. The same problem is inherent in Telnet, which is used to log in to other machines and run commands. First described in RFC 854 in May 1983 (and still available at `www.ietf.org/rfc/rfc854.txt`), Telnet is another of those protocols that were never built with security in mind. My advice? Never use Telnet. Avoid it completely, because it is simply too dangerous and unsafe. Instead, use SSH.

SSH (secure shell) was first written by Tatu Ylönen of Finland in 1995 as a replacement for Telnet (as well as rlogin and rsh, two other incredibly insecure programs), although the version you're now using with Knoppix is quite separate from Ylönen's now proprietary implementation. SSH is really an amazing program, one that should be a centerpiece of your Knoppix toolkit. With SSH, you can connect to other machines and run commands, transfer files securely, and much more. It's one of those programs about which you can always learn something new.

Ensuring SSH Is On for Secure Connections

In order for you or others to connect to your Knoppix machine via SSH, you need to enable the SSH daemon. Klaus and the other Knoppix developers have made this drop-dead simple: Just open the Knoppix menu and select Services → Start SSH Server. You'll be prompted to assign a password to the user knoppix, so go ahead and enter a good one (you won't see what you're typing as a security measure). After Knoppix accepts your password, press Enter to close the window. The SSH daemon is now running and capable of accepting logins from the user knoppix.

To enable new SSH users, simply add new system users using the `adduser` command on the command line, or with KUser, available at K → System → KUser. Enter the root password (from the Knoppix menu select Root Shell, enter `passwd`, and then type a new password for root), go to User → Add, and give your new user access. Once someone is a system user, she can SSH into your computer and get to work.

Using SSH

To SSH into another box, just open up Konsole (the Terminal Program icon on the panel), type **ssh username@machine**, and press Enter. For example, if I were user `scott` on machine `work.wiley.com`, you could enter `ssh scott@work.wiley.com`. SSH prompts you for a password; type it in, press Enter, and you're in.

If you don't know how to use the command line, you're pretty much stuck at this point. On the other hand, if you know how to navigate using cd and related commands, and how to run programs and work with data using terminal-based editors such as vi, this is your playground.

Using SFTP

If you have to transfer files back and forth, use SFTP instead of FTP, for no other reason than security. Unlike FTP, which sends your name, password, and all data in the clear so that anyone grabbing traffic (which is discussed in Chapter 6) can listen in, SFTP travels over SSH to encrypt everything, which is what you want.

You can use SFTP on the command line if you'd like. If you know your command-line FTP commands, you'll be right at home, because virtually everything is the same. To connect using the command line, just type sftp username@machine in Konsole and press Enter (using the example from the preceding section, you'd enter sftp scott@work.wiley.com). Put in a password when you're prompted, and you're ready to go. If you need to brush up on the commands you can use, try entering help and take a gander at the resulting list.

If you'd prefer to use a GUI — which can definitely be easier in many situations — then you're back to your good friend Konqueror, which does SFTP as well as FTP. Everything is exactly the same, except that you use sftp:// instead of ftp:// in the Location bar. This does *not* mean that you can just change the ftp to sftp for any old site and have things work. In fact, that fails the vast majority of the time because most servers that use FTP do not necessarily use SFTP.

So how would you use Konqueror to connect to a server that supports SFTP? Open Konqueror, put your server's address (something like sftp://work.sftpserver.com) in the Location bar, and press Enter. You should next see a warning dialog similar to the one shown in Figure 3-4.

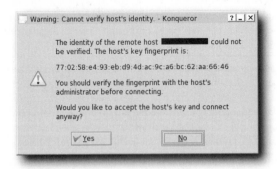

FIGURE 3-4: You have to accept a machine's key the first time you connect to it.

Remember that all traffic sent over SSH is encrypted. To make the encryption possible, keys are exchanged between your computer and the server to which you're connecting. This warning is SSH's way of telling you that it has no way of knowing if the server's key is valid, so it's asking you to validate the key for it. If you know that the key is valid — if, in other words, you're positive that you're not the victim of a man-in-the-middle attack — go ahead and click Yes to add the key to the list found at `~/.ssh/known_hosts` (if the key changes on the server because the OS is reinstalled, for instance, you'll need to find the appropriate line in `known_hosts`, delete it, and reconnect to the server to re-accept and re-enter the key).

After the key is added, you're prompted for a username and password. Go ahead and enter it, and a few seconds later you should see the contents of the SFTP server.

Note Want to know more about man-in-the-middle attacks? Check out Wikipedia's article on the subject, at `http://en.wikipedia.org/wiki/Man_in_the_middle_attack`.

Download and upload files with SFTP in the same way you do so with FTP: just drag and drop, or right-click and choose Copy To. If this is an SFTP site you plan to use several times while you're running Knoppix, go ahead and bookmark it for easy access later.

Be safe: Whenever you have a choice, use SFTP instead of FTP.

Note I use SFTP even at home on my own internal network, partly because I'm paranoid, and partly because I'm so used it now that it's just automatic. It's a good idea to develop the same habit.

Using SCP

If you're a command-line junkie and you're in a hurry, SCP (secure copy) is a great way to quickly copy a file from one machine to another using SSH. SCP basically follows this pattern: `scp user@host1:file1 user@host2:file2`. You can leave out the `user@host`, however, if one of the files you're working with is local, as you'll see in a moment.

For example, suppose you want to use `scp` to copy `me.jpg` from the directory you're currently in to your Website on another machine (called work.wiley.com). Type the following on the command line and press Enter:

```
$ scp me.jpg username@work.wiley.com:/var/www/mywebsite/images
```

You'll be prompted for a password, and, a moment later, `me.jpg` will be available on your Website for viewers around the world.

You've got several JPEGs you want to transfer? Simple!

```
$ scp *.jpg username@work.wiley.com:/var/www/mywebsite/images
```

To copy all the JPEGs on your server to your current machine, but to a different directory than your current one, type this:

```
$ scp username@work.wily.com:/var/www/mywebsite/images ~/pix/website
```

scp can come in quite handy when you want to securely copy files between machines. However, it gets tiresome having to type scp commands if you have a lot of different things to move around. When that happens, you may want to use SFTP, or turn to protocols such as SMB or NFS.

Note Only the basics of SCP are covered here. To learn more, man scp is quite helpful, or search Google for "scp tutorial."

Sharing Files and Printers

To paraphrase the great poet and priest John Donne, no computer is an island, entire of itself. In other words, you can't store every single file you need on your hard drive, and you can't directly connect every printer you need to use to your PC. Instead, you need to access files and printers on other machines, and you might want to make files and printers on your machine available to others. In the Linux world, there are two main protocols used for just such sharing: Samba, the open-source implementation of Microsoft's SMB/CIFS (Server Message Block/Common Internet File System) protocol, and NFS, the open standard Network File System first developed by Sun. Both work well, and support for both is built into Knoppix.

Starting and Configuring Samba

The roots of SMB (Microsoft renamed SMB to CIFS a few years ago, but the name of the Linux implementation is SaMBa — get it?) go back a long way. For the purpose of this discussion, the Samba project began life when a brilliant Australian programmer named Andrew Tridgell reverse-engineered the SMB protocol, implemented it for UNIX, and published his code in 1992. Since then, the Samba project has grown into one of the great open-source success stories.

Note For more information about Samba, visit the Samba project home page at www.samba.org, or read about it at Wikipedia, at http://en.wikipedia.org/wiki/Samba_software.

To start Samba, select Knoppix → Services → Start Samba Server. Enter a password for the user knoppix, and then re-enter the password for verification. Click Yes to export all hard drives so they can be mounted, read, and written to from remote machines. (Normally this would not be a good idea, and if you're going to leave Knoppix running for a while on your machine, you probably shouldn't do this. You definitely shouldn't do this if your Knoppix machine is connected to the Net without a firewall — but you wouldn't do that, would you?)

Samba is now running on your computer. Any machine that supports the SMB/CIFS protocol can now connect to your Knoppix box. This means Linux, of course, but it also means Mac OS X and Windows, which gives you an excellent range of possibilities.

To test that Samba is running correctly, open up Konqueror in Knoppix and type `smb://` `127.0.0.1/` in the Location bar. A list of shares, including partitions and hard drives, is displayed. Click on one of them, and you are prompted for a username and password. Use `knoppix` for the username, and the password is whatever you entered earlier.

You can also test via the command line. As you, not root, enter the following:

```
$ smbclient -L 127.0.0.1
```

When you're asked for a password, just press Enter without entering one. You should see a list of all shares, but this is the list that any anonymous user will see. Don't panic — anonymous users can't actually connect to your folders and files. To prove this to yourself, enter the following on the command line:

```
$ smbclient //127.0.0.1/hda1
```

When prompted for a password, press Enter, just like an anonymous user would. You'll see the following error message:

```
Anonymous login successful
Domain=[WORKGROUP] OS=[Unix] Server=[Samba 3.0.9-Debian]
tree connect failed: NT_STATUS_ACCESS_DENIED
```

At first, things look bad — the anonymous login is successful. But it's OK — although Mr. Anonymous can log in, he can't see, read, or write anything.

Now try it as the approved user knoppix. Enter the following on the command line:

```
$ smbclient //127.0.0.1/hda1 -U knoppix
```

When prompted for a password, enter the password you created earlier. This time, you should be in like Flynn, with an FTP-like prompt, like this:

```
Domain=[KNOPPIX] OS=[Unix] Server=[Samba 3.0.9-Debian]
smb: \>
```

Most of the ftp commands you know should work here as well, including `ls`, `cd`, `get`, `put`, `mget`, `mput`, and `mkdir`. However, `smbclient` has a few commands available that ftp does not: `chown`, `chmod`, `symlink`, `hardlink`, `rd`, and `tar`, for example. (`tar` is definitely one to check out, as you can use it to create tar backups of files and folders on a Samba share.) To see the full list of commands, just type `help` and press Enter.

Note For more information about `smbclient`, type `man smbclient` on the command line.

Remember that, by default, Knoppix does things the easy way and shares everything on the hard drive. If you're going to have Knoppix running for a while, you should either edit the `smb.conf` file to only share appropriate items or turn Samba off when you don't need it by entering `sudo /etc/init.d/samba stop` on the command line. To turn it back on, just use `sudo /etc/init.d/samba start`, and away you go.

Accessing Files and Printers with Samba

As you just learned, `smbclient` is a great way to verify that Samba is running on your Knoppix computer. The real purpose of `smbclient`, though, is to actually connect to a machine running Samba and work with files. You can certainly use it, but it gets a little tedious having to type commands all the time. Fortunately, Knoppix — and KDE — includes a great GUI tool that you can use to browse Samba shares: Konqueror.

 Note This chapter examines accessing files and folders shared via Samba. For connecting to Samba-shared printers, see Chapter 1.

That's right! Konqueror, the file manager that does everything, is not just a great FTP and SFTP browser, but a great Samba browser as well!

To connect to a Samba share on another machine — one that's running Windows, say — open Konqueror by selecting the Personal Files icon on the panel, simply type `smb:/` in the Location bar, and press Enter. Depending on the size of your network, you'll soon see a list of all the Samba workgroups that Konqueror can find. Figure 3-5, for example, shows that Konqueror has found the author's workgroup, Milton.

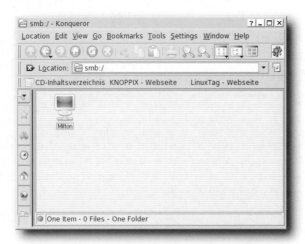

FIGURE 3-5: Konqueror finds your Samba workgroups.

To open a workgroup, click on its icon, and a list of all the machines in that workgroup is displayed, as shown in Figure 3-6.

FIGURE 3-6: Konqueror displays the machines in a selected
Samba workgroup.

See a machine you want to browse? Click it, and after a bit Konqueror shows you the list of
shares available on that computer (see Figure 3-7).

FIGURE 3-7: Konqueror displays the Samba shares in a
selected machine.

Keep in mind that you're seeing shares, not necessarily partitions or drives. A share can consist of an entire partition or drive (although generally that's not a good idea), but it doesn't have to be. You can share a subfolder waaaay down in your directory hierarchy by using Samba; for example, to view some OGGs and MP3s, you might click on the `music` share.

Immediately you're prompted for a username and password, which happens anytime you try to connect to a protected share. Keep in mind that you must enter a Samba username and password, which may not be the same as your login username and password on the box—it depends on how you set up Samba on that computer. If it's a Windows or Mac OS X machine to which you're connecting, it's a login name and password; if it's a Linux box, then login names may not be the same as Samba names. You just have to know how the computer to which you're trying to connect is set up.

Note A few years ago, Konqueror asked you over and over again to enter your username and password—every time you entered a new subfolder, in fact. It was enough to drive you insane. Thankfully, KDE has removed this annoyance. Now you are asked once for a share, and that's it.

Once you've logged in correctly, you get what you came for: the files and folders that you want to access. In my case, that would be rock 'n' roll OGGs and MP3s (all legal). At this point, I might think it's time to play some music—some Smiths, perhaps. I'd click `Rock_Alternative_All_Time_Greats` (yes, I am compulsively organized when it comes to my music collection), click `Smiths`, and then click `Smiths_-_Hatful_of_Hollow_-_01_-_William,_It_Was_Really_Nothing.mp3` and . . . what's this? The file appears in XMMS (the default MP3 player), but there's no sound. Yet music stored locally on the Knoppix machine plays just fine. What's going on?

The problem is that the "music" share that's connected to isn't actually mounted, so XMMS can't play the songs on that share. Right-clicking on `William,_It_Was_Really_Nothing.mp3` and choosing to open it with xine, it plays—after the file is first downloaded onto the machine. That's OK for a single tune, but for an album, or a large video, or anything else, downloading every single file before listening to it, or watching it, is quickly going to grow tedious. To solve that issue, you need to actually mount the Samba share on the other machine to your Knoppix box, so that Knoppix treats the file like it's on the local hard drive.

If you know how to use `smbmount` on the command line, this is your time to shine. Just enter `smbmount` and the appropriate options, and you're set. If you don't know `smbmount`, or you want to learn how to utilize it, start by using LinNeighborhood, included with Knoppix.

To access LinNeighborhood, open the K menu and select Internet ➜ More Applications ➜ LinNeighborhood. The program opens, but before you can begin using it, you need to change a few settings. To start with, choose Edit ➜ Preferences, which opens to the Scan tab shown in Figure 3-8.

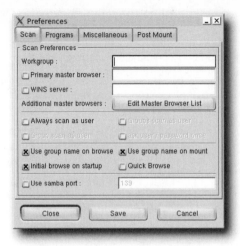

FIGURE 3-8: Setting scan preferences in
LinNeighborhood

On the tab, enter the name of the SMB workgroup that you want to examine in the Workgroup text box. This example will use MILTON (you don't have to use all caps — that's just how Windows does it). Then check the box next to Always Scan As User, which prompts you to enter a username and password at the appropriate time.

Alternatively, you could go to the Miscellaneous tab (see Figure 3-9) and, in the Default User text box, enter the SMB username you use to log in to the SMB shares on your network.

FIGURE 3-9: Tell LinNeighborhood to remember
your Samba username and password.

If you're not feeling paranoid, go ahead and enter the SMB password you use in the Save Default Password text box, and then check the box in front of it.

Note   Keep in mind that if you're connecting to another Knoppix box, the default user is knoppix, with an SMB password that you set when you turned on the SMB server.

After you have your preferences set, click the Save button, and then the Close button. Back in the main LinNeighborhood window, choose Options → Browse Entire Network. A window similar to the one shown in Figure 3-10 opens, asking you to enter a username and password (yes, you did just enter them, and now you have to do it again—weird, eh?).

FIGURE 3-10: Before browsing, you have to enter the username and password again.

Check the Browse as User box, enter a username and password, and click OK. That window closes, and a list of workgroups and machines appears in LinNeighborhood, similar to what is shown in Figure 3-11 (if the list doesn't appear after a reasonable time, double-click the Knoppix icon at the top of the window—the one with the penguin head next to it—and that should display the list).

To mount the music share found on Dante, double-click on Dante. Again you're asked for a username and password, but fortunately these are already filled in for you (if you used the Miscellaneous tab discussed earlier), so all you have to do is click OK. Dante expands to reveal all the shares, including printers, that are available, as shown in Figure 3-12.

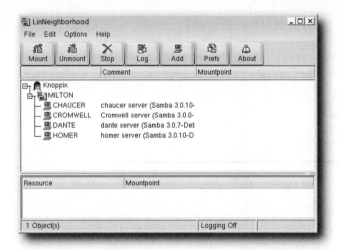

FIGURE 3-11: LinNeighborhood displays a list of machines in a workgroup.

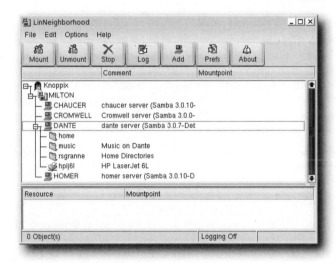

FIGURE 3-12: LinNeighborhood displays a list of Samba shares on a machine.

Double-click the music share, and the Mount Dialog window opens (see Figure 3-13).

FIGURE 3-13: Tell LinNeighborhood exactly
how you want to mount a Samba share.

You shouldn't have to enter anything in this window, unless you're unhappy with the defaults.
By default, LinNeighborhood will create the necessary directories and then, in this example,
mount the music share on Dante at `/home/knoppix/mnt/DANTE/rsgranne/`, which is
probably just fine. If you want the mount point to be somewhere else, though, go ahead and
enter the path. If the SMB User or SMB Password isn't correct, change it. Once you've got
everything the way you like it, click the Mount button to close the Mount Dialog window and
return to the LinNeighborhood window.

You can tell that LinNeighborhood has mounted the Samba share, thanks to the open folder
icon and the path under the Mountpoint column. To test the new mount, open Konqueror
(the Personal Files icon on the panel) and click on the `mnt` directory, the name of the machine
to which you're connecting (`DANTE` in my case), the name of the share (music), `Rock_`
`Alternative_All_Time_Greats`, `Smiths`, and finally `Smiths_-_Hatful_of_`
`Hollow_-_01_-_William,_It_Was_Really_Nothing.mp3`. Almost immediately I hear
Johnny Marr's guitar and Morrissey's croon (you'll hear whatever music file you selected).
Excellent! Create a playlist in XMMS, or just click on individual songs in Konqueror, or even
watch movies; it's all easy, seamless, and quick once you've mounted that Samba share to your
filesystem.

However, you're not done. Remember that you can use LinNeighborhood to help learn the syntax
of `smbmount`? Here's how: In LinNeighborhood, select Options ➔ Export Mountscript. You're
asked where you want to save the file, which by default is named `mountscript`. Because you're
just learning, any old place is fine, so why not the Desktop?

Tip Normally, if you were going to use that file again to mount Samba shares, you'd create a `bin` directory and place it in there, and then run `chmod 744 mountscript` to make it executable. If that sounds useful to you, be sure to read Chapters 10–12, which discuss remastering Knoppix.

Open `mountscript` with your favorite text editor and take a look at it. It's just a bash shell script that calls `smbmount` with the appropriate options. With that script as a template, you can easily add more lines that will mount other SMB shares. If you're feeling really ambitious, you can arrange for that script to run when you boot, automatically mounting several SMB shares onto your local filesystem, saving time and making things simple and easy.

Tip For the full skinny, try `man smbmount`. Here's a hint: If you're going to use `smbmount`, look at the credentials option for better security.

Sharing and Accessing Files with NFS

NFS is actually older than the SMB protocol, but it does far less. SMB enables you to share files and folders as well as printers, whereas NFS only shares files and folders. In terms of security, SMB is better in many ways because it enables you to control access to shares by usernames ("Are you steveb? Then you cannot access the `finance` directory, no matter what machine you're on."), while NFS only controls shares by machine ("Are you coming from the machine named Dante? You are? Great—then no matter who you actually are on that machine, you've got access to the `finance` directory!"). SMB is built in to Windows, obviously, but it's very well supported on Mac OS X and Linux, whereas NFS is primarily a UNIX protocol—you can find support for NFS on Windows, but it just isn't widely used. Nevertheless, if you're looking to easily share files between Linux machines, NFS is quick, easy, and efficient.

To get started with NFS, you need to detail your NFS shares. Suppose you want to make the `/tmp` directory on the Knoppix machine Homer available to the non-Knoppix Linux machine Dante, for example. First you need to ensure that Homer and Dante know each other's IP address. Do that by editing their `/etc/hosts` files. For instance, if Dante's IP address on your LAN is 192.168.0.105 and Homer's is 192.168.0.110, then you add `192.168.0.105 dante` to Homer's `/etc/hosts` file and `192.168.0.110 homer` to Dante's `/etc/hosts` file. Once that task is complete (no reboots required—this is Linux!), the two machines can find each other on your network.

Then open `/etc/exports` on Homer with a text editor (you need to be root, so `sudo vim /etc/exports` if you're using the command line, or `sudo kwrite` if you want to start a GUI text editor as root), and add the following line:

```
/tmp dante(rw,sync)
```

Caution You must be very careful when you're entering the line in the exports file. Notice that there is no space after the machine name and before the parenthesis, and that there is no space after the comma. Do not put spaces in there, or you will accumulate bad security karma. See `www.tldp.org/HOWTO/NFS-HOWTO/security.html` for more information.

Some Other Handy NFS Commands

If you really want to make the best of NFS, you need to know some additional commands. You'll find the following quite useful:

- `/etc/init.d/nfs-kernel-server stop`: Stops NFS

- `/etc/init.d/nfs-kernel-server restart`: Restarts NFS (be careful with this because anyone connected to your NFS server will temporarily find themselves unable to work on any programs accessing NFS-based data)

- `exportfs -ra`: Re-exports the `/etc/exports` file if you've made changes.

To start NFS, you need to run several commands in Konsole, starting with this one:

```
$ sudo portmap
```

`portmap` essentially translates RPC numbers into networking port numbers. When a server (for instance, your Knoppix machine, running NFS server) receives an RPC call, it uses `portmap` to send that call to the right network port. Without `portmap`, NFS doesn't work.

Note Don't know what an RPC is? Head over to Wikipedia and read `http://en.wikipedia.com/wiki/RPC`.

Other commands include stop (`sudo /etc/init.d/portmap stop`) and restart `sudo /etc/init.d/portmap restart`). For more information about portmap, use `man portmap`.

Next, start two services by running the following:

```
$ sudo /etc/init.d/nfs-common start
$ sudo /etc/init.d/nfs-kernel-server start
```

That gets NFS up and running.

With NFS on, anyone running an NFS client on Dante should be able to mount and connect to the shared `/tmp` directory on Homer. To mount the shared directory, run the following commands as root on Dante:

```
# mkdir /mnt/homertmp
# mount -t nfs homer:/tmp /mnt/homertmp
```

The first command creates the mountpoint; the second does the actual mounting. Now you can run `ls /mnt/homertmp` and see the contents of the `/tmp` directory on Homer as though it were part of Dante's local filesystem.

Anyone on Dante can now access that share mounted at `/mnt/homertmp`. Remember that the share was exported `rw`, so anyone using Dante not only has access, but can also read and write documents on that mounted share. That's why many consider NFS to be a little insecure, and why

Samba is so often used, even for sharing between Linux machines. One more word about security: Never connect a machine running `portmap` directly to the Net, or you are opening yourself up to vulnerabilities. NFS is powerful, but it can also leave sensitive files wide open, so be careful!

Tip For a brief overview of NFS, the Wikipedia has a nice article at `http://en.wikipedia.org/wiki/Nfs`. To learn more about NFS, read the "Linux NFS-HOWTO," available at `http://tldp.org/HOWTO/NFS-HOWTO/`, or "NFS: Overview and Gotchas," at `www.troubleshooters.com/linux/nfs.htm`. You can also set up NFS clients to automatically mount NFS shares using `automount`; to find out how to do so, read the "Automount mini-Howto" at `http://tldp.org/HOWTO/Automount.html`, and "Configuring the NFS automounter" at `http://osr5doc.ca.caldera.com:457/NetAdminG/BOOKCHAPTER-15.html`.

Serving Up Web Pages with Apache

Apache is the world's most popular Web server, and with good reason — it's super powerful, stable, and secure. Basically, if you want to serve Web pages and related resources to folks, use Apache. End of story. Recognizing this, Knoppix includes Apache, and it's quite easy to get it going: As root, simply type `apache` on the command line and press Enter.

Apache is now running, and if you want to verify that, open your Web browser and go to `http://127.0.0.1`. You should see something like the page shown in Figure 3-14.

FIGURE 3-14: The default Apache page on your computer

By default, Apache loads files from /var/www, which means that you need to replace the files in that directory with those that you want to serve, or point Apache to a different directory. If you decide on the former, keep in mind that index.html is the default file, although index.htm, index.shtml and index.cgi will also work.

If you want to go with the latter, open /etc/apache/httpd.conf as root with your favorite text editor, find the line that currently says DocumentRoot /var/www and change /var/www to the directory of your choice. Look down about 25 lines or so and find the line that says <Directory /var/www> and change that one to <Directory new-directory> as well. Save your work and close httpd.conf.

You're not finished yet. You need to make sure that the directory you entered has world-readable and executable permissions, like this: chmod o+rx directory. Any directories containing the one you're trying to serve using Apache must also be world readable and executable as well. Once you're sure that your permissions are correct, enter apachectl restart on the command line as root. Reload http://127.0.0.1 in Mozilla, and you should see the contents of your new directory. Even if you don't have index.html or the equivalent set up, you should see a list of folders and files that you—or anyone else able to connect to your box—can view and download.

Tip

If there's a problem and your content doesn't appear, make sure your path is correct next to DocumentRoot in httpd.conf, save it, and restart Apache (make sure you've got content in that directory!).

You'll never use Apache running on Knoppix to power your business or to serve up pages to thousands of users around the world, but in a pinch, it can be perfect to provide Web pages or any other content via the Web.

Summary

In the modern era of computing, it's all about connectivity, and Knoppix helps make things easy. Whether it's controlling other machines or letting other machines control it, using FTP or its vastly more secure brethren SFTP and SCP, logging in and running commands with SSH, sharing files and printers with Samba and NFS, or even serving up Web pages with Apache, Knoppix is ready and able to do the hard work that makes your life easier.

This is important stuff, and it's the base for a lot of later information about data recovery, so make sure you take some time to really familiarize yourself with the various options that Knoppix makes available to you for connecting to other machines and resources. You won't regret it—and it may just save your bacon down the road.

Rescuing and Recovering Systems Using Knoppix

Fixing Linux with Knoppix

Knoppix is a variant of Linux, so it's no surprise that Knoppix can be used to fix problems that crop up in other Linux distros. Machines running Linux are going to face problems: Humans make Linux, after all, and humans also use Linux, so errors, mistakes, and bugs are bound to occur.

Fortunately, there's Knoppix.

This chapter explores some of the fixes that have worked for the authors and will likely work for you, too.

Ensuring That a Machine Will Run Linux

Will a particular machine even work with Linux? Here are a few ways to find out:

> **Ask the manufacturer:** Good luck. Most computer makers still treat Linux like the crazy aunt in the basement, not to be seen and definitely not to be spoken of. This is changing, and some vendors now support Linux, but only on a selected few machines. What if you want to run Linux on a nonsupported machine? Don't ask the manufacturer for advice about that because you won't get any.

> **Ask someone who already has the machine:** If a friend owns the same computer and runs Linux, great! That's not very likely most of the time, however. You can also search the Net, and oftentimes you'll find good info, especially if you're curious about a laptop. Still, it can be a definite exercise in frustration looking for solid info about a particular machine, with hours wasted and no solid data available.

Tip

The best Website, bar none, for Linuxheads interested in laptops is Linux on Laptops at `http://linux-laptop.net`. If you own or are thinking of purchasing a laptop and you want to find out how well it runs various flavors of Linux, you need to visit Linux on Laptops.

- **Test the machine:** If you can get to the machine, test it to see whether it runs Linux. Take a Knoppix disk into your local computer shack and ask if you can try the disk in the machine in which you're interested. If the machine boots and works, it more than likely supports just about any version of Linux; if you find problems with Knoppix, you're probably going to have problems with any other Linux, so that computer should be avoided.

- **Take your chances:** This is always an option. Order the box, and try to install Linux on it. If you have problems, test the machine with Knoppix and note what works and what doesn't. Then begin punching things into Google until you get answers. One of those answers, of course, can be that Linux simply will not work with that computer, and you need to send it back. This drastic step is growing more and more rare, fortunately, but it's still true for a few misbegotten manufacturers who don't yet realize that their lack of support of Linux is going to cost them dearly in the long run.

Knoppix is an excellent tool for verifying the Linux-readiness of a particular computer.

Repairing Boot Issues

There's always a sinking feeling, deep in the pit of your stomach, when a system won't boot. In the past, a failure to boot meant you'd spend hours fiddling with config files in an often fruitless attempt to fix the problem, or worse, a re-install of the OS. Now a boot problem doesn't have to mean a big time loss because Knoppix can often be used to fix issues that arise when you first start up your computer. In fact, you may be surprised just how easy it is to wield Knoppix as a powerful fix-it tool.

 Note We know that we sure could have used Knoppix eight years ago when we tried to install Red Hat on a Windows box to create a dual-boot machine and instead ended up staring in horror at the blinking `LI..` on the computer monitor, certain that we had lost a lot of data on the hard drive. Oh, the humanity!

Restoring a Missing MBR

Quite often, the cause of a boot issue involves a corrupted or missing MBR (Master Boot Record). The MBR is vitally important to your computer. It is a 512-byte area at the beginning of your hard drive that contains two critical items: the information that enables your computer to boot, and your partition tables. If your MBR gets messed up, you're normally up a creek. How does the MBR get messed up? Well, attempting to create a dual-boot system but installing Windows after Linux usually does the trick nicely (always install Windows first, and then install Linux!), and so will running `fdisk /mbr` from within Windows. Sometimes it just gets corrupted for no discernable reason.

Because the MBR is so vitally important, you really should back it up regularly, just in case disaster strikes. You can back up the MBR from within Knoppix by using the following command (which assumes that you're copying the MBR on the machine named Homer onto a USB flash drive):

```
$ sudo dd if=/dev/hda of=/mnt/uba1/mbr_homer_backup bs=512 ⏎
  count=1
```

The dd command creates images of drives, but this command uses the bs (block size) option to tell dd to output only 512 bytes at a time, while the count option means that dd should only do so once. Because the MBR is contained in the first 512 bytes of the hard drive, this command copies it. (For more information on the dd command, see the section "Backing Up Partitions" later in this chapter.) Now the boot sector and the partition table for Homer are backed up on your USB flash drive, which should make you feel safer.

Tip   Yes, you can use Knoppix, but really, you should back up the MBR no matter what OS you're using. Don't wait until you're using Knoppix to perform the backup!

With your MBR backed up, you can restore it if it ever gets nuked. To do so, simply reverse the directories in the preceding dd command:

```
$ sudo dd if=/mnt/uba1/mbr_homer_backup of=/dev/hda bs=512 count=1
```

Keep in mind that this will restore both your boot code and your partition table. Every time you change your partition scheme, you must back up your MBR again (fortunately, most people rarely if ever alter their partitions, so one backup should do the trick). If you have not changed your partitions, this command should be just fine. If, however, you have altered your partition table since the original backup of your MBR (Bad computer user! Bad!), then you want to run the following command:

```
$ sudo dd if=/mnt/uba1/mbr_homer_backup of=/dev/hda bs=446 count=1
```

The MBR's boot code is located in the first 446 bytes of that 512-byte area; the last 66 bytes contain the partition table. Restore the first 446 bytes and you have your boot code back; restore the full 512 bytes and you have your boot code and partition table back. Now that is good stuff to know!

Caution   Be very careful typing those numbers in the dd command! Fat-fingering them and typing 521 instead of 512 can lead to disaster.

Fixing LILO

LILO (LInux LOader) is the old standby when it comes to Linux boot loaders, the code that resides in the first 446 bytes of the MBR. It's possible to break LILO by upgrading the kernel and misconfiguring lilo.conf, the LILO configuration file. It can be broken in other ways as well. Fortunately, you can fix it.

To restore LILO, you need to know which partition on your hard drive was your root partition. To find this out, locate the partition containing /etc/lilo.conf. In many cases, this will be /dev/hda1, but not always, so be very sure about which partition you need to work with. The examples in this section assume it to be /dev/hda1.

By default, Knoppix mounts partitions without the dev option turned on; however, to repair LILO, you must mount the root partition with the dev option turned on (if you're curious, the man page for `mount` explains that the `dev` option tells Linux to "Interpret character or block special devices on the filesystem"), like this:

```
$ sudo mount -o dev /mnt/hda1
```

To repair LILO, you need to fool it into thinking that `/mnt/hda1` (or whatever your root partition may be) under Knoppix is actually `/` if the machine had booted without Knoppix. To do this, use the `chroot` command, which tells processes started with it to treat a given directory as the root directory. Now that the `/mnt/hda1` partition is mounted, restore LILO by running the following:

```
$ sudo chroot /mnt/hda1 lilo
```

This tells the system to treat `/mnt/hda1` like it was actually `/`, and to run `lilo`, which restores LILO just the way you want it. Take Knoppix out, reboot, and LILO should work.

Fixing GRUB

The process for fixing GRUB (the GRand Unified Bootloader), a more modern bootloader than LILO, is pretty much the same as fixing LILO. You first need to find the partition on your hard drive that acts as the root partition and holds the GRUB config file `/boot/grub/menu.1st`. You need to mount the partition that contains GRUB's config file with the `dev` option turned on, like this:

```
$ sudo mount -o dev /mnt/hda1
```

Just as with LILO, you need to use `chroot` with GRUB, but the full command is different because, of course, this is a different bootloader:

```
$ sudo chroot /mnt/hda1 grub-install /dev/hda
```

Now reboot, and GRUB should work. Woohoo!

Note   More and more distros are using GRUB instead of LILO because it's a newer, more flexible, more powerful boot loader. It's really in your best interest to learn it.

Working with Key System Files

You are making good backups of your systems and especially your data, right? Right? Even so, sometimes you need to open the hood and get your hands dirty messing around with the files that help Linux run smoothly. Be careful doing so because one mistake can lead to worse problems. Keep your head about you, double-check everything you type, and success will be yours.

Resetting Forgotten Root Passwords

Sometimes you're given a box to administer, and guess what? The person who knew the root password is nowhere to be found. What can you do? Why, use Knoppix, of course! With Knoppix, you can easily change the root password — or, more accurately, remove the root password so that you can then change it to whatever you want.

As always, make sure you have permission to change passwords on the machine before you do so.

After booting with Knoppix, mount the partition containing the /etc directory in which you're going to muck about. Make sure that it's writable — right-click on the partition icon, choose Properties, open the Device tab, uncheck Read only, click OK, and then click on the partition icon to mount it.

After mounting the partition, run cd /etc and then use your favorite text editor to open the /etc/shadow file (we prefer vi, but you can use any editor you want, as long as you're running it as root). Once /etc/shadow is open, find the line containing root's information, as shown in the following example:

```
root:$1$k2xzdNaz$X.Fq9Xgp9.dhkTszwt4FP1:12893:0:99999:7:::
```

Delete the stuff between the first and second colons, so that the line now looks like this:

```
root::12893:0:99999:7:::
```

Save the text file, and the next time you reboot, root will not have a password. This is obviously a very dangerous situation, so you should assign root a new (good) password as soon as possible.

Now that was pretty easy, wasn't it?

Fixing X

A frequent complaint on listservs is that someone's Knoppix boots just fine, and X works fine, but after installing a distro of choice, X doesn't load, or if it does, things look terrible.

This usually isn't that hard to fix. Boot again with Knoppix, and find the file /etc/X11/ XF86Config-4.

Copy the file to a USB flash drive, or email it to yourself, or store it on another machine on your network. (It's helpful to print the file, too, so that you have a hard copy somewhere.)

Now take Knoppix out and reboot the distro that's giving you problems. If you can, you want to open the XF86Config-4 file on the problematic distro and compare it to the "good" XF86Config-4 file that Knoppix generated. If possible, print out the XF86Config-4 file on the "bad" distro and compare it to the "good" XF86Config-4 file. Hard copy is sometimes easier to use for comparison. Keep in mind that a Knoppix XF86Config-4 file contains options for a million different configurations, so don't just copy blindly from the Knoppix file to your distro's file. You want to focus on these parts of the Knoppix file:

- **Section "Module":** Check whether Knoppix loads some modules and your distro doesn't. Try editing your distro's XF86Config-4 file to load those modules. Of course, that might not work if the modules aren't on your system, but it most likely won't hurt anything either.

- **Section "InputDevice" (there will be several, for your mouse and keyboard):** Wheel mouse not working? Look here.

- **Section "Monitor":** Pay attention to HorizSync and VertRefresh. Be very careful editing those numbers; a mistake can fry your monitor!

- **Section "Device":** Look at the driver. In fact, this is quite often the problem. Change it to vesa, save, and restart your machine to see whether that fixes your problem. Vesa is a generic driver, so you're not going to get the best graphics in the world, but at least you'll be able to use your machine to try to track down something better.

- **Section "Screen":** What you want is DefaultColorDepth, which will lead you to the resolutions your monitor uses. If you know that your video card and monitor support a higher resolution, try adding it to the appropriate Modes line in the Subsection "Display" area.

Whatever you do, back up your original XF86Config-4 file before you begin editing it. You just might make things worse, and it would be nice to revert back to a file that at least kind of works. Then you can begin again. Keep in mind that tinkering with XF86Config-4 is sometimes akin to voodoo, especially for newbies, so don't be afraid to turn to friends, online resources, or your local Linux users group for help.

Note

The XFree86 developers shot themselves in the foot with their unwise licensing changes in 2004 (see http://en.wikipedia.org/wiki/XFree86 for the gory details), resulting in the abandonment of XFree86 by virtually the entire Linux world and a migration to the Xorg project (see www.x.org). Xorg offers several advantages over XFree86, including licensing palatable to the GPL and a more open developer community. Expect Knoppix to switch to Xorg sometime in the future, but don't panic—you won't have lots of new stuff to learn. Xorg's main config file is found at /etc/X11/xorg.conf instead of /etc/X11/XF86Config-4, but other than that, the formats of the two files are remarkably similar.

Performing a Filesystem Check

Occasionally a hard drive begins acting very, well, strangely. Copying files to and from the drive might take forever, even for a few tiny files, and produce scads of worrisome error messages. These signs indicate that it's time to give the drive the once over. Obviously, you can't really check a drive by running programs that reside on that same drive; instead, boot with Knoppix and then run a variety of programs to check your hard drives for errors.

Caution

Make sure that any drives you're checking are not mounted. Once again: You should only check filesystems on unmounted drives!

The command you use to check the filesystem depends on the filesystem the drive is formatted to use. To find out what filesystem was used, take a look at /etc/fstab. The following examples use /dev/hda1, but just substitute the partition or drive that you'd like to check.

Examining and Repairing Ext2 and Ext3 Filesystems

This one is easy. To scan and repair a filesystem formatted with ext2 (nonjournaled) or ext3 (journaled), run this command:

```
$ sudo e2fsck -C /dev/hda1
```

The -C option displays a useful progress bar, which is always handy. If you want to see additional output, including the actual commands that fsck is using, add the -V option to the command.

If you want e2fsck to look for bad blocks on your hard drive, add the -c (lowercase) option (this is a different option than the uppercase -C), which runs the badblocks program. If badblocks finds that any areas on your hard drive are damaged, it adds them to a list that the system keeps, so that they are unused in the future.

When you run e2fsck, you may be asked a lot of questions — hundreds if your hard drive has a lot of problems. If you just want e2fsck to fix your drive automatically, add the -p and -y options. Most of the time, this isn't a big deal, but it may sometimes do things you weren't expecting (to be honest, though, we usually use these options because we're lazy and don't feel like typing the same letter over and over again).

Examining and Repairing ReiserFS Filesystems

Ext3 is a good journaled filesystem, but in recent years ReiserFS has been gaining a lot of converts. To check and repair a ReiserFS-formatted filesystem, use the following:

```
$ sudo reiserfsck --fix-fixable /dev/hda1
```

The --fix-fixable option does just that: It tells reiserfsck to fix the easy problems. If reiserfsck finds additional problems, it lets you know and suggests additional options to use, including some of the following:

- --rebuild-sb: If reiserfsck complains that "read_super_block: can't find a reiserfs filesystem," and you know for certain that the filesystem uses ReiserFS, you probably need to use this option.

- --rebuild-tree: reiserfsck tells you to run this command when it needs to rebuild the entire filesystem tree, and, no, this is not a good sign. Be sure to back up the partition using dd or the equivalent before using this option!

- --yes: This tells reiserfsck to assume "yes" as the answer to all questions, so that it runs without asking you a million things. Be cautious about using this option.

Examining and Repairing FAT32 (VFAT) Filesystems

Yes, FAT32, known as VFAT to Linux users, is a Windows filesystem, but it is widely used in the Linux world as well, especially on partitions shared between Linux and Windows installs, and on USB flash drives, digital camera storage cards, and other portable devices. It's therefore a good idea to know how to check and repair partitions formatted with VFAT using the command:

```
$ fsck.vfat -a /dev/hda1
```

The -a option automates the process, taking the least dangerous method each time there's a problem. If you want to be asked every time there's an issue, use the -r option instead. If you don't use -a or -r, the filesystem is examined, but not actually repaired.

If you want to watch `fsck.vfat` at work, tack on the `-l` option, which lists each file as it's examined, and the `-v` option, which tells the program to be more verbose. To mark bad clusters, use the `-t` option.

Examining and Repairing Other Filesystems

There are more filesystems, of course, but the ones covered here are the most common. Some of the other filesystems you may encounter, and the commands to use, are as follows:

- JFS: `fsck.jfs` (for more info, see `man fsck.jfs`)
- XFS: `xfs_check` (for more info, see `man xfs_check`)
- NTFS: `ntfsfix`, which you should use after writing to an NTFS-formatted partition under Knoppix because, as `man ntfsfix` puts it, "MS `chkdsk` is well known for its stupidity when fixing altered partitions." Keep in mind that `ntfsfix` is not a replacement for the Windows `chkdsk` command but a tool designed to keep that particular software from freaking out.

For more information about any of the filesystem commands, try `man e2fsck`, `man reiserfsck`, and `man fsck.vfat`. For more on filesystems in general, see `man mount` under Linux, or check out `http://en.wikipedia.org/wiki/Filesystem`.

 Note `rm` usually means that a file is gone, and it ain't coming back. However, it is possible to undelete files that you removed on your Linux box. To find out how, check out "Performing Forensics with the Coroner's Toolkit" in Chapter 6.

Working with Linux Partitions

You can check your hard drive, but sometimes you need to specifically work with the partitions on your hard drives. Fortunately, Knoppix provides some excellent tools that enable you to create, manipulate, and restore partitions on your machines.

Partitioning with QTParted

If you've spent any time in the Windows world, you may be familiar with PartitionMagic, a popular — and powerful — program that makes it really easy to work with partitions, even those formatted with NTFS. Think of QTParted as a free, open-source PartitionMagic, and you'll be on the right track with this essential software.

To start QTParted, from the K menu select System ➔ QTParted. You'll see something similar to what is shown in Figure 4-1.

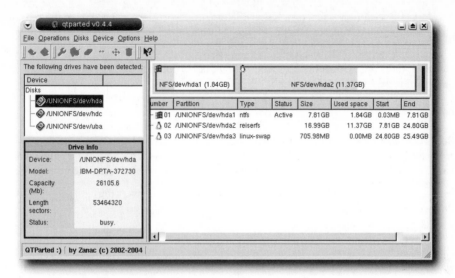

FIGURE 4-1: QTParted enables you to work with partitions from within Linux.

Out of the box, QTParted can do the following:

- Create Ext2 and Ext3 partitions, but not resize them
- Create JFS partitions but not resize them
- Create XFS partitions but not resize them
- Neither create nor resize ReiserFS partitions
- Create and resize NTFS partitions

Using QTParted is pretty easy. Right-click on a partition to get its properties, or to format, resize, move, and delete it; right-click on free space on a disk to create a new partition. If you've ever used PartitionMagic, you should be right at home, and if you haven't, you'll pick this up quickly.

Note two caveats about using QTParted. First, if you right-click on a partition that's already been formatted with ReiserFS, you're only going to have the options Property, Format, Delete, and Set Active. What happened to Resize and Move? To get those capabilities, use APT to install software with the following two commands:

```
$ sudo apt-get update
```

```
$ sudo apt-get install progsreiserfs
```

After running these two commands, you're told that some extra packages will be installed and some others will be removed, and asked whether you want to continue. Type Y and press Enter, and in a few moments the installation completes.

Restart QTParted, right-click on a ReiserFS-formatted partition, and you'll see the full complement of options: Property, Format, Resize, Move, Delete, and Set Active.

The second caution concerns ext3: You cannot resize a partition formatted with that filesystem. However, there is a workaround. It's a bit tedious, but it does the job. First, convert your ext3 filesystem to ext2 with this command:

```
$ sudo tune2fs -O ^has_journal /dev/hda1
$ sudo e2fsck /dev/hda1
```

Remember that ext3 is really just ext2 with journaling. You just removed the journaling, so now you're back to ext2. Don't forget to change /etc/fstab as well, running as root and using your favorite text editor, so that the partition listed there as ext3 is now correctly identified as ext2.

Now use QTParted to resize the partition. When you finish, convert the ext2 partition back to ext3 with this command:

```
$ sudo tune2fs -j /dev/hda1
```

Change /etc/fstab so that the partition once again is identified as ext3, and you're in business. Tedious, yes, but it works!

Note For more on QTParted, check out its home page at `http://qtparted.sourceforge.net`. Because QTParted is really a GUI for the GNU Parted program, you also may want to check that command-line-based app out at `www.gnu.org/software/parted/parted.html`.

Backing Up Partitions

Recently one of us had a problem with one of our hard drives and needed to back up all the data on one of the partitions before the drive failed entirely. Some of you are already thinking, I know what to do: use dd! Normally, dd is just fine if you want to copy all the data from one block device to another device or file, but it does have its limitations, especially if the disk has errors on it. Sure, you can use the `noerror` option, but it's still going to go verrrrrrrry slooooooooowly. Knoppix includes something better than dd for cases in which the hard drive has bad blocks on it: dd_rescue.

Those of you who have used dd know that you typically use it like this:

```
$ dd if=/dev/hda of=/dev/hda.img
```

Basically, you give the command (dd) and then specify the input file (if) and the output file (of). The dd_rescue command is very similar, but without the if= and of=.

Note For more details about how to use dd_rescue, type man dd_rescue. The dd_rescue Web page also explains several key features of the program; it can be found at `www.garloff.de/kurt/linux/ddrescue/`.

Here's a simple example that uses dd_rescue to create an image of a partition:

```
$ sudo dd_rescue /dev/hda1 /mnt/hdb1/hda1.img
```

This copies an image of /dev/hda1 to hdb1. It assumes, of course, that there's room on hdb1 for all of hda1. If there's not, you'll have to use another partition.

The following command restores the disk image of hda1:

```
$ sudo dd_rescue /mnt/hdb1/hda1.img /dev/hda1
```

That was easy — it's just the reverse of the initial command.

Next is something that would be useful if you have only limited partitions on a machine or, for example, if hdb1 couldn't contain hda1: Use dd and ssh to create an image on another machine:

```
$ sudo dd_rescue /dev/hda1 - | ssh username@machine 'cat ⊃
  > /home/username/hda1.img'
```

You'll be prompted for a password; enter it, and then wait for dd_rescue to do its job. Needless to say, this can take a while if you're dealing with a large partition. If you get an error message such as

```
dd_rescue: (warning): output file is not seekable!
dd_rescue: (warning): Illegal seek
```

while you're running this command, it's safe to ignore it. It's just dd_rescue being overly cautious.

To restore the image from another machine using ssh, use this command, entering a password when prompted:

```
$ ssh username@machine 'cat /home/username/hda1.img' ⊃
  | sudo dd_rescue - /dev/hda1
```

Once again, you may have to wait a while. Watch TV. Go for a walk. Read a book. Better yet — read this book!

Tip   It's a good idea to fsck any images you create by running sudo fsck -y /mnt/hdb1/ hda1.img after you create the image, especially if the partition you were backing up had problems to begin with.

Finally, you can use tar and ssh to compress the partition and copy it to another machine:

```
$ tar zcvf - /mnt/hda1 | ssh username@machine 'cat→/tmp ⊃
  /hda1_bak.tar.gz'
```

Of course, you have to enter a password once more. Again, this process could take a long time, but you end up with a compressed copy of your partition.

To restore the partition, use the following command:

```
$ ssh username@machine 'cat /tmp/hda1_bak.tar.gz' | tar zxvf -
```

Don't forget the dash on the end! This process can take a while, but your partition will make it back onto your hard drive, which is the goal.

Caution

Keep in mind that when you untar `hda1_bak.tar.gz`, everything is going to be recreated in a `mnt/hda1` directory subdirectory from which you run the command, so you'll have to manually move your files and folders to the root of your hard drive.

What if you don't want to leave the copied images on another hard drive? If the images you've created are small enough, you can burn them to CD; if they're larger, burn them to DVD. If an image is too big for that, use the `split` command to break the file into sections and burn each section to disk. If you ever need to join the sections again, copy each section from your disk(s) and use the `cat` command to rejoin them (you can avoid this scenario by backing up to external hard drives).

To break up a 10GB gzipped tar file (named `hda1_bak.tar.gz` in this example) into two smaller files suitable for burning onto two DVDs, you'd use the following:

```
$ split --bytes=4000m --verbose hda1_bak.tar.gz hda1_bak
```

This command produces three files: `hda1_bakaa`, `hda1_bakab`, and `hda1_bakac`. The first two are 4GB each, and the last one is 2GB (all that's left of the 10 GB original). Burn them onto DVDs and you're good to go.

When it's time to rejoin what you've burned onto DVD, copy the three files from the DVDs and onto a hard drive, and then run the following:

```
$ cat hda1_bak* > hda1_bak.tar.gz
```

After some time, you have your single file back. Use `ssh` and `tar` to restore it to your hard drive on another machine, and you're as good as new!

Restoring Lost Partitions

OK, you've done it: you deleted your MBR, or at least the partition table, and you don't have a backup. Time to erase the hard drive and start over, right? Wrong! Before you take that drastic route, boot with Knoppix and see whether Gpart (which stands for Guess partitions) can save your bacon.

Gpart looks for areas of your hard drive it can identify as partitions, and then creates a partition table for them. Yes, it seems like magic, and it doesn't always work, but it's better than just throwing in the towel. What can it hurt?

Better still, Gpart supports a wide variety of filesystems, including but not limited to the following:

- FAT and VFAT
- ext2 and ext3
- Linux swap
- NTFS
- ReiserFS

Before you actually turn Gpart loose on your hard drive, run the program in demo mode, so that it shows you what it would do. Here's how:

```
$ sudo gpart /dev/hda
```

You point Gpart at your hard drive, not at a partition—which makes sense because you don't have any partitions at this point!

Eventually—Gpart can take a long time to work, so be patient—you should get some output. Look over it carefully, and if Gpart seems like it will work for you, then it's time to run the program in write mode:

```
$ gpart -W /dev/hda /mnt/hda
```

If all goes well, you should now be able to boot, with your partitions newly raised from the dead! Thank Knoppix and Gpart next time you get a chance. They made your life easier, that's for sure.

 Note For further info on Gpart, including what to do when `gpart` doesn't work right away, check out `www.stud.uni-hannover.de/user/76201/gpart/`, the project's home page.

Summary

Even the best of us can occasionally make mistakes or have things spin wildly out of control. When times get tough, the tough pull out Knoppix, boot with it, and fix their issues. From just making sure that a machine will run Linux to patching up problems with booting, to repairing important files used by Linux, to retrieving busted partitions, Knoppix is there to solve your problems and keep you looking as cool as you really are.

Fixing Windows with Knoppix

Y ou or someone you know will encounter a seemingly unfixable problem with a Microsoft Windows operating system environment at one time or another. When this occurred in the past, most users would reinstall their operating systems, sometimes wiping out significant amounts of data that was needed on the system. Now you can use Knoppix to (often) correct your Windows system problems without losing any data and save the time associated with reinstalling all of the operating system files and applications.

Resizing Windows Partitions

Partitioning is a simple scheme for segmenting your physical hard drive into different sections. Power Windows users typically partition their hard drive for performance and backup reasons or to allow for different operating systems to be installed on it. When the system is first partitioned, the drive sizes are determined by the installer's experience and the projected needs for each partition. As time goes on, the partitions' size requirements may change, necessitating resizing.

Many commercial applications, such as PartitionMagic, enable you to repartition your hard drive. They can cost $60 or more, however, and you can get the same base functionality using tools included natively with Knoppix for no cost. This section explains how to resize your Windows partition or other types of partitions using Knoppix and QTParted, which is a user-friendly graphical front end for the command-line partition resizing tool *parted*.

QTParted works on the following Windows partition types (as well as non-Windows file system types):

> ➤ **FAT16:** Used primarily with Windows 3.1 and earlier versions of MS-DOS

> ➤ **FAT32:** Used by Windows 95, 98, and ME primarily

> ➤ **NTFS:** Used by the NT based versions of Windows, including NT, 2000, XP, and 2003

Preparing to Partition

Before you resize your partitions, defragment your hard drive if you can. This process, put very simply, rearranges the hard drive, putting your files together in as logical a manner as possible, usually in a group, and checking for errors.

Although partitioning with the tools described in this chapter are time tested and have been used by many, many people, there is always the chance of an inadvertent input error on your part or the possibility of some other unforeseen circumstance, so back up your important data.

Determine what you want the filesystem layout to be after you have resized your partitions, including the sizes of the partitions. You will need this information to use the tool in the most effective manner. For example, if you have a single partition on the entire hard drive consisting of 100GB and you want to make room for a secondary Windows or Linux partition of 10GB, you would resize the primary partition to 90GB, leaving 10GB for the new partition to be created.

The QTParted tool cannot create space where none exists, so ensure that you have the requisite amount of space available before you attempt to resize. If your primary 100GB partition is filled with 98GB of data, for example, you'd only be able to create a new 2GB partition because that's how much space is available.

QTParted Partitioning

Ready to partition? Boot your Windows machine with Knoppix and choose Knoppix→ System→ QTParted. A screen similar to the one shown in Figure 5-1 opens.

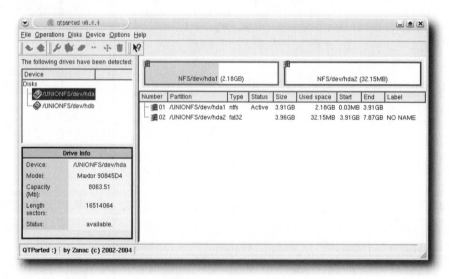

FIGURE 5-1: QTParted's startup screen

A list of detected disks appears on the left. Information about the selected disk appears below it, and the right window lists its current partitions. In Figure 5-1, QTParted shows that the first disk (/UNIONFS/dev/hda) has two partitions, both of which are Windows filesystem types, indicated by a tiny Microsoft Windows icon in the Number column. The Type column identifies the filesystem (NTFS, FAT32, or FAT16).

The partition graphics above the list also show how much used space each has. In the example, the NTFS partition uses 2.18GB of its 3.91GB space, and the FAT32 partition uses 32.15MB of its 3.98GB.

To begin the resizing operation, right-click the graphical box of the partition you want to resize (alternatively, highlight the partition in the list and right-click), and select Operations➔ &resize. The QTParted Resize Partition dialog opens (see Figure 5-2).

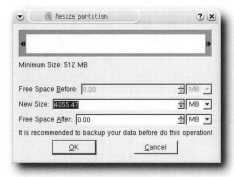

FIGURE 5-2: QTParted's Resize Partition dialog.

You can use the graphical window at the top by left-clicking the arrows at the sides to make the partition larger or smaller, or you can enter the partition size value you want in the New Size text box. Figure 5-3 shows a partition being resized to 1GB.

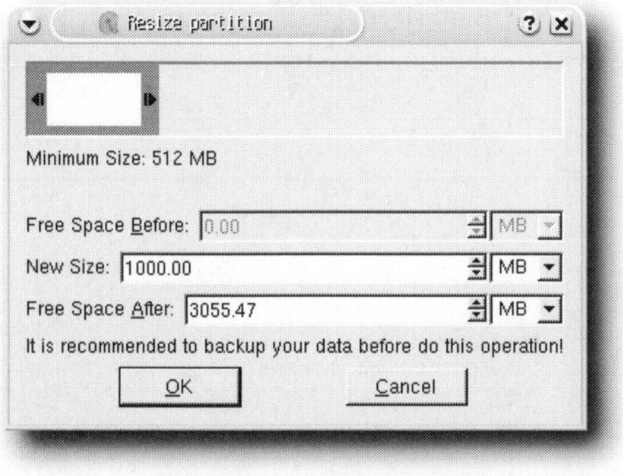

FIGURE 5-3: Sizing a partition to 1GB

When you have the information entered correctly, click OK (you are not making anything permanent yet.)

The main screen shows your modifications (see Figure 5-4): two partitions and a gray box indicating how much free space you'll gain after resizing. The new FAT32 partition is now 996.22GB and there's 2.99GB of free space. The resized partition is a solid color, indicating it has not been committed yet; you can't format the drive until it has been committed.

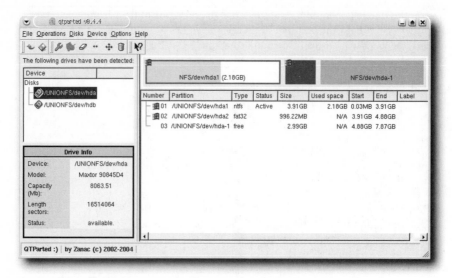

FIGURE 5-4: QTParted displays the changes you want to make.

If you make a mistake, you can undo everything until you do commit a little later in the process. To undo any changes, select File → &Undo and the system will return to its previous state.

Now you can create another partition in the free space by right-clicking on the gray box and selecting &Create (or by selecting Operations → &Create). The Create Partition dialog opens, as shown in Figure 5-5.

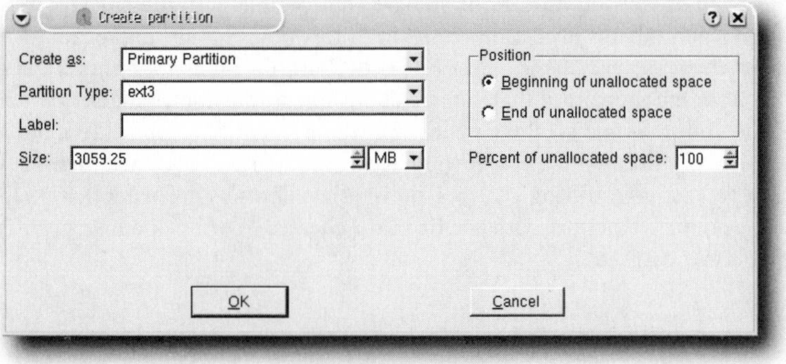

FIGURE 5-5: QTParted's Create Partition dialog box

Click the arrow at the right of the Create As text box and select the kind of partition you want (Primary Partition or Extended Partition). There is a limitation of four primary partitions imposed on a system by the master boot record, which was a restriction from the early days of PCs. To get around this constraint, the extended partition was created to allow for more partitions on a drive. An extended partition is created by separating one of the four primary partitions into more divisions, called *logical partitions*. Most operating systems are loaded on a primary partition and boot from there. (Linux is an exception because it can be booted from a logical partition.). If you create an NTFS partition of 2.99GB (all of the free space) as a secondary partition for backups within Windows, the result would be as shown in Figure 5-6.

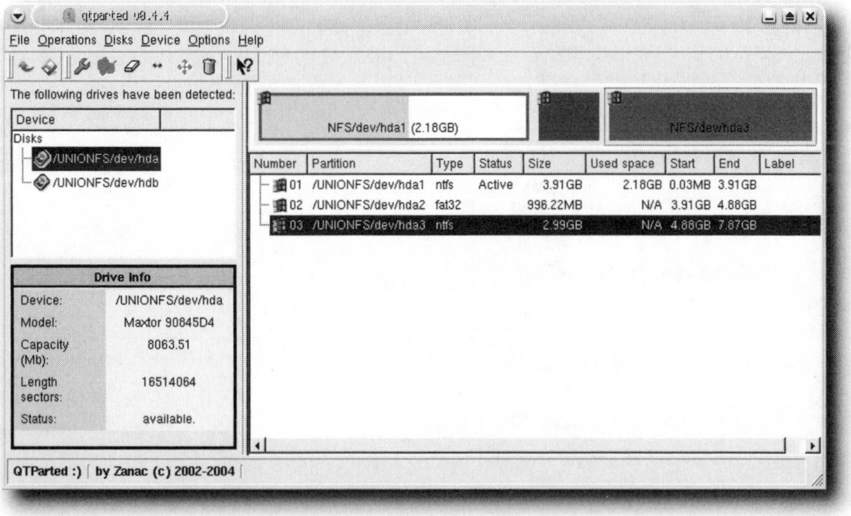

FIGURE 5-6: Creating a partition in QTParted

After you have made all of your modifications and are comfortable with the changes, you need to make your changes permanent (everything done until this point is "virtual," or for show only). To make your changes permanent, select File → &Commit. Figure 5-7 shows the warning dialog box that appears, indicating that you are about to commit the changes to the hard drive for good. (The grammar and spelling are awkward in parts of this application, but will most likely be corrected in future releases.) If you have a swap partition (virtual memory) on the drive for which you are committing changes, prevent problems by ensuring that swap is turned off, either by booting Knoppix with the noswap cheatcode or by opening a terminal window and typing swapoff -a.

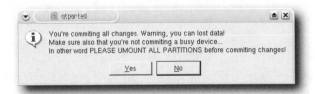

FIGURE 5-7: QTParted's commit warning

Select Yes. A window displays the progress of your modifications and the estimated time until completion. If everything is successful, your changes are made on the hard drive and you'll see a dialog box similar to one shown in Figure 5-8.

FIGURE 5-8: Partitioning was successful.

After you have completed the resizing, you can format your new partitions using QTParted — just select Operations → Format.

Taking Charge When Key System Files Have Problems

Sometimes Windows has files that are corrupted or missing, which seriously impairs, or even prevents, the operation of the system. If you've encountered this before, you know that one of your options is to start from scratch or try to recover the system using the draconian Windows Startup and Recovery system. The toolset included in that tool is sparse at best and difficult to use. Knoppix, conversely, provides a friendly and very powerful environment in which to fix certain issues you may encounter when problems pop up.

By default, Knoppix can read a large set of filesystems right out of the box, but it doesn't support writing to certain filesystems. There are some known issues with Knoppix 3.8 and later regarding writing to NTFS filesystems (the default for Windows XP and later). Those filesystems require the use of a program called `captive-ntfs` (`http://jankratochvil.net/project/captive/`) to allow write access, which is crucial for editing files on the systems. Knoppix 3.8 and later does not include `captive-ntfs` by default because of lack of active project development and other concerns regarding corruption of data. (There is another system in place — UnionFS — that promises to provide this support in the future. It isn't fully developed yet, so it currently only gives the appearance of writing to the NTFS partition.)

Earlier versions of Knoppix (3.7 and earlier) include `captive-ntfs`, but if you are using Windows XP Service Pack 2 (SP2), take the steps identified in `http://kb.bitdefender.com/site/KnowledgeBase/viewArticle/en/100/Problem_with_LinuxDefender_and_Windows_XP_SP2_.html` to enable read/write capabilities.

Accessing boot.ini to Resolve Start Issues

The `boot.ini` file is used by Windows NT-based systems (NT, 2000, XP, 2003) to boot the system into the correct operating environment by displaying a list of Windows-recognized operating systems and directing the system toward the selected environment. If the file is corrupted, damaged, or missing, you cannot boot your Windows system properly. The `boot.ini` file can become corrupted if you reboot your system improperly, or may be missing if someone deletes it accidentally, or, well, there are many other causes for that error.

If you boot your system and get an `invalid boot.ini` or `Windows could not start` error message, the most likely culprit is an invalid or corrupted `boot.ini` file. To correct this problem, you need to either edit your existing `boot.ini` file or create a new, generic one. First, you must make the Windows partition that your core system resides on writable (Knoppix makes all existing partitions read only) by right-clicking the drive on the desktop and selecting Properties. In the Device tab, make sure that Read Only is unchecked to make the drive writable. Don't do this if you're working on an NTFS partition.

Modifying NTFS partitions (the Windows XP default) can cause significant problems, so perform the write function on FAT partitions only.

Once you have the capability to write to the filesystem, locate the Windows top-level directory on what is usually the Windows C: drive (typically on the drive labeled HDA1). Click on the drive on your desktop labeled Hard Disk Partition HDA1 In the top level is a file called `boot.ini`. Create a copy of the file by right-clicking it and selecting Copy. Then paste the copy in your Windows directory in case you need to refer to it later.

When you open your drive in Konqueror, the `boot.ini` folder is in the directory (see Figure 5-9) if you did a default install of Windows and have selected the correct hard drive (HDA1). If you have set up Windows differently, look in your Windows boot directory for the `boot.ini` folder).

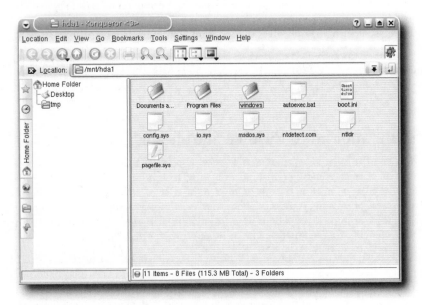

FIGURE 5-9: Open your Windows hard drive in Konqueror.

Open the file with your favorite editor. Figure 5-10 shows a `boot.ini` open in KWrite.

FIGURE 5-10: A boot.ini file open in KWrite

The following, from a Windows XP Home Edition, is a typical generic boot.ini file:

```
[boot loader]
timeout=30
default=multi(0)disk(0)rdisk(0)partition(1)\WINDOWS
[operating systems]
multi(0)disk(0)rdisk(0)partition(1)\WINDOWS="Microsoft Windows XP
Home Edition" /fastdetect
```

timeout specifies how long the system should wait for user input while the boot menu is being displayed.

default identifies which selection from the Windows recognizable operating systems (identified in the [operating systems] section) will be booted if the user makes no selection in the boot menu. The [operating systems] section identifies all Windows recognizable operating systems that can be booted by the boot menu.

multi denotes that this system has an IDE or ESDI drive, and is almost always 0. If you are using a SCSI drive with no BIOS support, this is scsi(0) instead of multi(0). (Note that Windows NT systems using SCSI drives have multi.) The disk designator is 0 if multi is listed as the adapter. If scsi is the adapter in use, you would indicate the scsi bus number. rdisk identifies what controller the disk is on, such as rdisk(1) for the secondary disk, rdisk(0) for the primary. If you are using scsi, this option is always 0.

partition indicates the partition on which the file to boot resides. If you are on the second primary partition, you would write partition(2). This should never be 0 because there is no partition 0. The last portion identifies the directory in which Windows resides (in this case, \WINDOWS (this could be anything depending on the version of Windows and how the system was installed). Everything after the equals sign and in quotes shows what is displayed in the boot menu to the user regarding booting.

Most boot.ini problems you encounter will be file corruption (or misconfiguration if you are hand-editing the file). You can use the preceding information to recover by simply replacing or adding the default lines.

For specifics on configuring the boot.ini file, go to http://support.microsoft.com/?kbid=289022.

When you have completed editing the file, save it. Remove your Knoppix CD and reboot the system into Windows.

Editing the System Registry When It Goes Bump in the Night

The registry is the central Windows location for all system-specific information, including configurations and settings, for Windows 95 and all later versions. The registry can be edited very easily by using the Windows native program regedit within Knoppix. Just type the following command in a console window:

```
regedit
```

This command invokes *Wine* and pulls up the Windows Registry Editor, as shown in Figure 5-11. (Wine is an open-source implementation of Windows APIs that runs on top of Linux. Some folks think of it as a Windows emulator, but Wine's developers call it a Windows *compatibility layer* for UNIX.)

All of the functionality you find running the Registry Editor in Windows is available under Wine, including importing a backed-up registry and saving a modified registry.

Some of the variant versions of Knoppix include an excellent Linux-native Windows Registry Editor called Offline NT Password and Registry Editor (chntpw), a program that enables you to modify the Windows registry as well as Windows passwords. You can get more information on chntpw at http://home.eunet.no/~pnordahl/ntpasswd/. The standard Knoppix versions 3.8 and later do not include chntpw by default, but the software is available through APT (sudo apt-get install chntpw), described in Chapter 1, as well as through the Klik program.

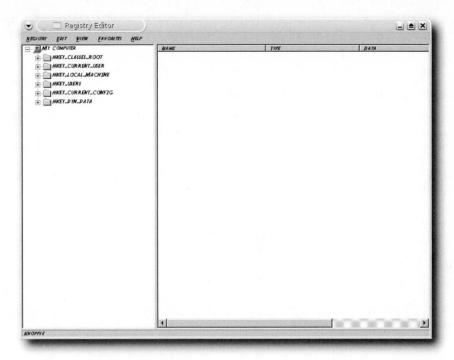

FIGURE 5-11: Using the Registry Editor in Linux

Recovering Data

If your Windows system crashes completely and cannot be recovered using the Registry Editor or the boot.ini, you may face some serious problems if important data on the system wasn't backed up. Knoppix can come to your rescue by enabling you to access your Windows partition and save your important data to multiple devices for restoration later. These methods include using USB jump drives (also called *flash drives* or *key drives*), using CD-Rs and DVD-Rs, and copying data over the network. This section explains how to recover and save the data that you'll restore after you have reinstalled Windows following a crash.

Preparing for Data Recovery

The most common mistake when recovering data from a system is failing to retrieve all of it because of haste. What you leave behind is typically the data you end up needing the most, so take your time and ensure that you are capturing everything valuable. The most common area for data storage is in the Documents and Settings folder (usually /mnt/hda1/Documents and Settings), which is Windows' default for saving most user documents, music, pictures, and so on. If there are any nonstandard directories into which you or your users save data, consider those as well.

Tip

After you have saved all the files you think you need, it is always a good idea to verify that the data you saved is correctly archived. Navigate the backup medium and open random files (those that can be opened) to ensure that the data is valid.

Saving Data to a USB Jump Drive

Knoppix recognizes your USB jump drive almost immediately after the drive is plugged in. From that point, it is a trivial matter to save data from your Windows partition to the key drive, which is represented by the USB icon on the desktop. To save to the jump drive, you only need to make it writable by right-clicking the jump drive icon, and selecting Properties. Select the Device tab, which looks much like the dialog shown in Figure 5-12, and then uncheck the Read Only box to enable writing to the drive. Click OK to close the window, and you're good to go.

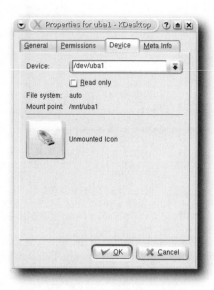

FIGURE 5-12: The USB jump drive is set to read-write once you uncheck the Read Only box.

Mount the drive by right-clicking on the drive icon and selecting Mount. You can use the command line in conjunction with the cp command to move files between the hard drive and the jump drive (typically /dev/uba1). Alternatively, you can open two Konqueror windows (see Figure 5-13) and drag and drop.

Your only limitation to saving files this way is the speed of the file transfer and the capacity of your jump drive, although 1GB and 2GB jump drives are available for very reasonable prices, and you can use more than one if necessary.

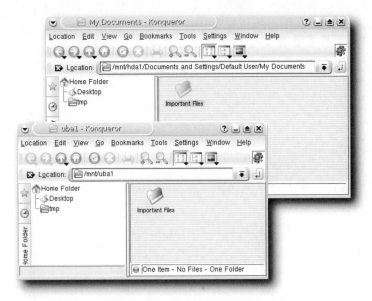

FIGURE 5-13: Saving files to the jump drive from Windows

Burning Data to a CD or DVD

Burning the files you need to a writable CD or DVD is made very simple in Knoppix, which includes K3b (discussed in depth in Chapter 1), a user-friendly CD recorder that's on a par with the most expensive commercial software. Select Knoppix → Multimedia → K3b Program to open it. The application's screen is similar to that shown in Figure 5-14.

Note There's a glitch in K3b's capability to burn DVDs or CDs in Knoppix 3.8.2, but that should be resolved by Knoppix 4.0.

Select New Data CD Project or New Data DVD Project from the window. Navigate to the files you want to save and drag and drop them to the Current Projects section of the screen. Figure 5-14 shows the /mnt/hda1/Documents and Settings file already being saved to a DVD. The graph near the bottom of the screen shows the size of the file (more than 890MB). After you have put all the files you want to save into the Current Projects section, click the Burn icon at the top left corner of the application window. A dialog box similar to the one shown in Figure 5-15 appears.

After you have set any user-specific settings you need (see Chapter 1 for all the gory details), click the Burn button to begin the writing process. When K3b finishes, navigate the finished CD/DVD to ensure that the data is properly encoded.

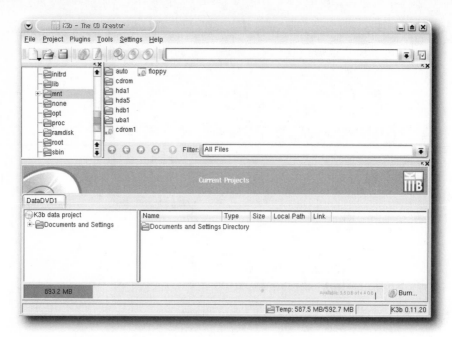

FIGURE 5-14: Burning files to a CD/DVD using K3b

Emailing Data to Yourself

Another option that many people don't think of is to email the data to yourself. With today's large-capacity sizes of both Web-based email services (thank you, Gmail!) and personal email services, you can generally send any data you need backed up via email with no worries about the capacity of the mail account. You do, however, still need to take into account that your email service probably has some limit on the size of attachments. For example, Gmail limits attachments to a maximum of 10MB.

To save data by email, simply use KMail (covered in Chapter 2) or Thunderbird, available via Knoppix → Internet. Set these up to use your POP or IMAP account, and then attach your recovered files and send the mail. If you use a Web-based email account such as Yahoo! or Gmail, you can simply use Firefox or another Web browser and attach the files as you would normally.

Be aware that email is not typically an encrypted method of transmission, meaning that someone intercepting your files will be able to read the data.

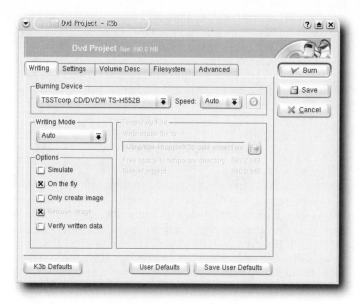

FIGURE 5-15: Starting the backup process

Copying Data over the Network

Knoppix includes the capability to transfer your important files over a network if that is the method you prefer. By far the easiest way to accomplish this is to have your Knoppix system run an SSH server for you. SSH provides the capability to interactively log into your Knoppix system as well as transfer files, all over an encrypted transmission, meaning that should anyone intercept your communication, he or she would have a very difficult time deciphering the actual data. If the system to which you are transferring the files resides on a Linux or Knoppix system, the capability to SFTP files is already built into the system. If you are transferring your files to a Windows system, you need to download an SFTP client (one recommend free version is WinSCP, available at http://winscp.net.)

Note   For more about SFTP, see Chapter 3.

To enable a remote Linux or Windows system to connect to the Knoppix system you want to back up, start the SSH server on the Knoppix system by selecting Knoppix → Services → Start SSH Server. A key used for encryption is generated in the window that opens. Enter a strong password, and then enter it the second time the same way. The password you enter here is used when logging into the system via SFTP, and it is case sensitive, so make sure that you remember your exact password.

You need to know your system's IP address (use the command `ipconfig eth0` to determine your IP address; it is four sets of numbers separated by dots, such as 192.168.1.1). Using WinSCP or another SFTP/SCP client, connect to your Knoppix machine with the IP address. Enter **knoppix** as the username, and then enter the password you created earlier. Now you can navigate the filesystem to find the files you want to copy to the remote system using SFTP commands if you are connecting via the command line or by dragging and dropping if you are using a graphical application such as WinSCP.

Summary

Knoppix provides a wealth of tools for Windows recovery and maintenance that enable you to recover the system without even logging into Windows. This chapter has shown you how to resize a Windows partition using QTParted and how to back up and modify your Windows files in the case of disaster. With the information provided in this chapter, you're well on your way to saving your sanity the next time Windows flakes out. Just be sure not to gloat to other Windows users the next time they face problems. Instead, smile knowingly and give them a copy of Knoppix . . . and this book!

Assessing Security with Knoppix

chapter

6

Security is vitally important to everything we do. Think about it: We drive well-built cars and wear seat belts, avoid unsafe areas of town, and safeguard our computer systems and networks as best we can against criminals, spammers, and miscreants. You can use Knoppix to help protect your computers, but you can also use it to learn more about security. You may even find that it's fun along the way.

Encrypting Data with GnuPG

Encryption is one of those things that can really raise the hackles of some folks, primarily those in government who want to limit the use of it by ordinary Joes like you and me. However, there is no good reason not to use encryption. We all have information that we'd like to keep secret, whether it's related to business or our personal lives, and encryption is the way to do it.

One of the best tools for encryption is *GnuPG*, the *Gnu Privacy Guard*. GnuPG uses public key cryptography, which means that you possess two keys: a private key that you use to decrypt messages sent to you, and a public key that others use to encrypt messages meant for you. This setup necessitates public keys being exchanged between people who want to send each other encrypted files, as you'll see.

Note Don't know what encryption is? Read `http://en.wikipedia.org/wiki/Encryption`, or, if you're feeling more hardcore, check out Niels Ferguson and Bruce Schneier's *Practical Cryptography*. Want to learn more about public key cryptography? Head over to `http://en.wikipedia.org/wiki/Asymmetric_key_algorithm`.

You can actually use GnuPG for a variety of tasks:

➤ Encrypting and decrypting email

➤ Encrypting and decrypting files on your computer

➤ Signing a file with an electronic signature, or verifying the authenticity of a file by checking its digital signature

➤ Verifying, or signing, other folks' public keys

in this chapter

☑ Encrypting data with GnuPG

☑ Testing for vulnerabilities

☑ Sniffing packets on a Network

☑ Performing forensics after a crack

☑ Wiping a hard drive

To use GnuPG, you need a *key pair*. You can generate the keys from scratch or import an existing set of keys. The following sections show you how to do both.

Generating GnuPG Keys

To start the process of creating your own set of GnuPG keys, run this command:

```
$ gpg --gen-key
```

Then choose what kind of key you want to use. The options are as follows (that's right — there is no 3 in the list; I don't know why):

1. DSA and ElGamal (default)

2. DSA (sign only)

4. RSA (sign only)

The default of 1 is just fine, so either type 1 and press Enter, or just press Enter to accept the default. Choose the size of your key. Once again, the default, 1024, is okay, so press Enter. Next, decide the length of time the key is going to be valid. 0, the default, means that the key will never expire. This is acceptable, if you intend to keep the key and re-use it in the future, or as long as you don't publish the public key to a keyserver and then neglect to either use the key ever again or delete it, thereby cluttering up public keyservers.

If you know for certain that you're only going to use the key for a brief period of time, select a key life span corresponding to that time. For example, if you need it for one week, type 1w and press Enter. GnuPG asks you to verify the life span of the key, so make sure it's what you want, type y, and press Enter.

Create what GnuPG calls a *User-ID*, which is actually composed of three questions. Answer them all, pressing Enter after each one. First, you need to enter a real name, like Scott Granneman; then an email address, like scott@granneman.com; and finally, a comment, which can be anything from an organization name, to a city and state (such as St. Louis, MO), to a URL, to anything at all. If the User-ID is okay, type the letter O; if it's not, make your changes and then type O. Press Enter.

Next, and perhaps most important of all, you must type the passphrase that will be used to protect your secret key. If you lose this, or if someone else can guess your passphrase, your security is compromised, so it's imperative that you pick something strong and secure. Keep in mind that you can use a passphrase, not just a password, which should help strengthen your security. Passphrases can include spaces and other special characters.

Tip   You may want to read the SecurityFocus article titled "Pass the Chocolate" (http://security focus.com/columnists/245), which has many tips for generating strong passwords. It's easy to apply its advice to passphrases.

Type in your passphrase (please make sure it's a good one!) and press Enter, and then do it again so GnuPG can make sure your passphrases match. Immediately you're going to see a lot of gibberish go by on the screen because GnuPG uses random data to generate your keys. Help GnuPG out a bit by moving your mouse, typing on the keyboard, or running a program in the background so that the disk is active. After a short time, GnuPG quits, and your new keys will have been created.

To verify that things worked, enter the following on the command line:

```
$ gpg --list-keys
```

You should see something like this:

```
/home/knoppix/.gnupg/pubring.gpg
-------------------------------
pub   1024D/65D0FD58 2003-07-11 CA Cert Signing Authority (Root CA)
<gpg@cacert.org>
sub   2048g/113ED0F2 2003-07-11 [expires: 2033-07-03]

pub   1024D/9E2BD1F2 2003-08-05 CA Cert Signing Authority (Low Security Key)
<lowgpg@cacert.org>
sub   2048g/456D7D4B 2003-08-05 [expires: 2033-07-28]

pub   1024D/A2DE1C11 2005-04-10 Scott Granneman (St. Louis, MO)
<scott@granneman.com>
sub   1024g/9D7F447C 2005-04-10
```

The first two keys come along with GnuPG, so they're expected. After that, you should see your new key listed. Success! Now you need to actually encrypt and decrypt something. If you don't need to import any GnuPG keys that you already use, you can skip the next section and jump ahead to "Using GnuPG Keys."

Importing GnuPG Keys

If you already have a collection of GnuPG keys, which GnuPG calls a *GPG keyring,* you can import it easily enough. If you've booted Knoppix on a machine that contains your keyring, it's really easy. Mount the drive that holds the keyring (hda2, for example), make sure you know where the keys are stored (they should be in the ~/.gnupg directory), and then run the following command:

```
$ gpg --import /mnt/hda2/rsgranne/.gnupg/pubring.gpg
```

Make sure you import the pubring.gpg file, not the secring.gpg file.

You should see something like the following on your console (email addresses have been changed to preserve privacy):

```
gpg: key 6503F88C: public key "Scott Granneman (www.granneman.com)
<scott@granneman.com>" imported
gpg: key E4A3CAF1: public key "eric mckinley <erickmckinley@localhost.com>"
imported
gpg: key 35745FEB: public key "Jans Carton <JansCarton@localhost.com>" imported
gpg: key 1768928B: public key "intake <intake@locahost.org>" imported
```

```
gpg: key 59B1ABA8: public key "Bryan_Consulting (www.bryanconsulting.com)
<bryanconsulting@localhost.com>" imported
gpg: key 4D95C51B: public key "Alan German <alangerman@locahost.com>" imported
gpg: Total number processed: 6
gpg:                  imported: 6
```

That was easy! What if you don't have a keyring on your machine? You can always import keys from a keyserver on the Net into your keyring. For instance, to import Klaus Knopper's GnuPG key (used to verify that you downloaded the correct ISO images, signed by Klaus Knopper himself), use the following command:

```
$ gpg --keyserver keyserver.veridis.com --recv-keys 0x57E37087
```

How did I know that 0x57E37087 is Klaus' key? I went to http://keyserver.veridis.com, a Website that indexes public keys, clicked on the PGP KeyServer link, searched for "Klaus Knopper," and then copied the Key ID on the results page. Go ahead and search for "Scott Granneman" if you'd like. I'm there, although only the most recent key is good.

To verify that you have Klaus in your keychain, enter gpg --list-keys and see if he shows up. He's there? Good. If he's not, search http://keyserver.veridis.com (click PGP KeyServer link) yourself to see whether you can find his key, and then import it.

You can also import keys if they're made available to you as an ASCII file, usually ending with the .asc extension. For instance, head over to http://keyserver.veridis.com and search for "Linus Torvalds," which currently brings up four results. Click on the Key ID next to torvalds@transmeta.com, and you'll be prompted to download a file named pubkey.asc, which is the key for that particular ID. Save the file on your hard drive (the Desktop is always a good place to put such things), and then enter the following:

```
$ gpg --import ~/Desktop/pubkey.asc
```

GnuPG will report that it has imported the public key for Linus Torvalds into your keyring. Success! Go ahead and delete pubkey.asc from your Desktop because you no longer need it.

Now it's time to start using your keys.

Using GnuPG Keys

Before you can use GnuPG, you have to sign the keys in your keyring. In other words, you need to assert that the keys you possess belong to the folks to whom they're supposed to belong. Ideally, you'd know this because you received the key directly from the individual. If you don't get the key personally, you'll have to verify the key's ownership in some way that satisfies you. If you're sure that a key from Klaus Knopper actually belongs to Klaus, you need to run the following command:

```
$ gpg --sign-key "Klaus Knopper"
```

Note   How did I know to use "Klaus Knopper" in the command? Because I ran gpg --list-keys first and verified the name associated with the key. In actuality, you can use anything unique for the key, including "Klaus," "Knopper," "knoppix@knopper.net," or "57E37087" (the User-ID).

When you run the `--sign-key` command, you're asked several questions:

- Do you want to sign all the user IDs associated with the key? Answer y and press Enter.

- How carefully have you performed the verification? It really doesn't matter what your answer is because the process continues regardless, but it does force you to think about what you're doing, and that's never a bad thing when it comes to security. Do your best to at least be able to truthfully answer that you have done casual checking. Make your choice, and press Enter.

- Do you really want to sign the key? Yes, you really want to sign the key, so type y and press Enter.

Type your secret passphrase, to prove that it's really you who's trying to sign the key in your keyring, and press Enter. You're back at the command prompt. (In the best UNIX tradition, success is quiet; in other words, if things work, UNIX just continues trucking along. Only problems merit feedback.)

You need to repeat this process for every key in your keyring. If you sign a new key immediately whenever you add it to your keyring, you get it over with and can start using the key right away.

With Klaus' key signed, create and encrypt a file as if you were going to send it to him. From the K menu select Editors → KWrite, and type `This is a file I'm going to encrypt ... bwahahahahaha!` Save the file on your Desktop as `secret.txt`, minimize KWrite, and go to your shell (Konsole on the panel, if it's not already open). `cd` to your Desktop, and run the following command:

```
$ gpg -r "Klaus Knopper" --encrypt secret.txt
```

Note Please don't inundate Klaus with encrypted files. He's too busy working on Knoppix to mess around with a bunch of test encryptions sent to him by every yahoo reading this book.

After a few seconds, you're back on the command line (again, silence means success). Enter `ls`, and you'll see that in addition to the original `secret.txt` file, there's now a `secret.txt.gpg` file next to it. The file is encrypted, but it's in a binary format. If you wanted to email it to Klaus (and, again, please do not!), you'd need to actually attach `secret.txt.gpg` to your email message.

To generate ASCII text output, do this instead:

```
$ gpg -r "Klaus Knopper" --armor --encrypt secret.txt
```

Again, `ls` informs you that there's a new file in this directory: `secret.txt.asc`. It can be viewed by using the command `cat secret.txt.asc` and looks something like this:

```
-----BEGIN PGP MESSAGE-----
Version: GnuPG v1.2.5 (GNU/Linux)

hQEOA4SWCtGmm0R2EAP+MRP7e4SJW8vddpbCv+RTw8kMrqp8MdJ1KTirWVQJ6+2b
qg9ktjkXIurX9Ce33FRMtiKX1SUgBYfE8M08JXAMgS6bDPLWfIatHFLTyEGYp2Dx
```

```
s23EQ7c8XK16yjOcLKgJihq11KrBcCru8QsapcOLVlhdqFcXt9K8eRoXehb+kXcE
AMVwFkL+MaLjJX+r4BC1oXerfF1jE+SjgheUHY82weEgLppUvKezcWAdfyNCZQMV
7HkLBrGnISqaxMTtkafk/cNT6/kYfzoNjpxXjrbTap3D3qSnffD4Wo7/czeSyLko
+VHOhe86ZK0eyxYuE7cg1okvVZdAVgo6dYH0/rDcQwDG0nIBvcZ5LfP4xGS1oG/M
N88O7xl2qxoTST4TcFHLlUS7O6KXHoifxAt/nRcRctkrkkJyorUnWL2RXVrE21f
5LeFVrM+Y8R89rhcShlG44NsAn2m0GkzjXNV1QBcbzhfFq95D/cq7TriP5tHlBFV
Djs5Cv0=
=fm66
-----END PGP MESSAGE-----
```

You can attach the ASCII file to an email, or you can copy and paste the text — all of it, even the BEGIN and END lines! — into an email message directly.

You can go even further. Beyond simply encrypting the file, you may want to digitally sign it, so that the recipient can ensure that the file really came from you. To encrypt and sign the file, use this command (leave off --armor if you want to generate a binary file instead of an ASCII file):

```
$ gpg -r "Klaus Knopper" --armor --sign --encrypt secret.txt
```

When you run that command, you're asked for your passphrase, which makes sense because you have to verify your signature. When the process is complete, you once again end up with a file named secret.txt.asc, but this time cat secret.txt.asc shows it to be a bit longer because it contains your digital signature as well:

```
-----BEGIN PGP MESSAGE-----
Version: GnuPG v1.2.5 (GNU/Linux)

hQEOA4SWCtGmm0R2EAP/XDgpwXRT7O2LEcbKvGb3ufIhWz52b8TpXkurSN1C25IR
zWX60G437Q+piTnU13Px1kiFsPqsOJgxfRC4UwzAr7M5+78HSQ7C0Udhljm0dASn
OgSqsl5ApdiRVNgEPlYfpsy/Te+cV8QBfGnkFrbw27SkpfO9M8+MryzbSRnDZ4wD
/1zy2zUSxtSd/wymaXKhhnH/J4zAAI9k5QP3N/AH3R4UbEOpohmcoz1/Zmdr5FUT
z+M6R9jixndRyAS65SEIDRa5/hq+HBslRvgcbKY2sbE6G+4wYLJgLKTB/dLhtaUd
F134PEQLPt7fYl/7KaKpyPFb+L3JOaElGwr0cbUX93z50r0BbHDhr8BaUh3AclUb
cCmb9adys14Kz+pQbzu0XsRityzAE6dm83RZXX0GtAb/MWLjbJ3D/kUAz6BL2hbd
iIXW+t09G+YJcK4gTyib9MtujQTmZRiRTaQSpL7bJuGLVZyNvNjXnOMdtufNIQy9
IaW55RQqyZw4p1Ey31IXp2P+mQNTtCskyuIoV4dT/kugF8q1Fn4KVZylu9iwTA/P
GJqcCeqeQ2s97YsCs7ppE9o5MTwpwY2sDjqW3uL0ZQU=
=UBSD
-----END PGP MESSAGE-----
```

Of course, you may not want to include both your original document and your signature in one file, so instead you might want to use this command:

```
$ gpg --detach-sign secret.txt
```

The output is a file named secret.txt.sig, which is a binary file containing your digital signature. If you want to create an ASCII equivalent, suitable for pasting into email messages or posting on a Website, do the following:

```
$ gpg --output digitalsig.sig --armor --detach-sign secret.txt
```

This uses the --output option, which enables you to specify the name of the ASCII file you're creating. You don't need to use it per se, but if you left it out, the resulting digital signature file would be named secret.txt.asc, the same as the output of the gpg -r "Klaus Knopper" --armor --sign --encrypt secret.txt command you used previously. In other words, you would overwrite your encryption with your signature (or vice versa, depending on the order in which you ran the commands)!

You can combine the commands and do everything at once:

```
$ gpg -r "Klaus Knopper" --armor --encrypt secret.txt ; ⤶
    gpg --output digitalsig.sig --armor --detach-sign secret.txt
```

The result? Two files (in addition to the original secret.txt file, which remains untouched): digitalsig.sig and secret.txt.asc, suitable for pasting into email messages or attaching.

Tip You can always specify yourself as the recipient, thus protecting your important files from prying eyes.

So you send Klaus your encrypted file and your digital signature. What does he do with them? First he verifies your signature — and this assumes, of course, that he's already imported your public key into his keyring. To verify your signature file, he runs the following:

```
$ gpg --verify digitalsig.sig secret.txt.asc
```

Klaus can either decrypt the attachment, once it has been saved, or copy and paste the text into a new file and then decrypt that. To perform the decryption, he simply enters one of the following on the command line:

```
$ gpg --output secret.txt --decrypt secret.txt.gpg
$ gpg --output secret.txt --decrypt secret.txt.asc
```

When Klaus presses Enter, he's prompted to enter the password for his secret key; after he does so, GnuPG does its work and the file is decrypted, so that secret.txt appears and Klaus can now read your message. If Klaus didn't use the --output option, GnuPG would simply place the output of the decrypted file on the console. Another way around that would be to use this command:

```
$ gpg --decrypt secret.txt.gpg > secret.txt
```

With GnuPG in your arsenal, you have industrial-strength encryption available to protect your secrets. It's a shame that more people don't know about GnuPG and encryption, but you can help spread the word and educate folks with Knoppix. Go forth and proselytize!

Note man gpg has a lot of great information if you want to learn more. The GnuPG Website is an excellent resource, at http://gnupg.org, containing HOWTOs, FAQs, guides, and more.

Testing for Vulnerabilities

It's not enough to want to batten down the hatches if you don't know which hatches need battening. On a computer system, you need to know where the possible holes are, and Knoppix can help you test for and then mitigate vulnerabilities.

Verifying the Absence of Rootkits with Chkrootkit

If your computer gets cracked, *rootkits* (also called *root kits*) are definitely a concern. Basically, a cracker can leave a rootkit behind that lets him easily access and control the machine in the future, while making it hard to detect his comings and goings. There are two kinds of rootkits: kernel level, which replace pieces of the Linux kernel with malicious code, and application level, which replace regular programs (such as ls, cd, less, and so on) with seemingly similar programs that are actually Trojan horses up to no good. With Knoppix, you can root out the rootkits and keep your computer safe.

Note   For more information on rootkits, see the Wikipedia article at http://en.wikipedia. org/wiki/Rootkit, or view search results at SecurityFocus with http://search. securityfocus.com/swsearch?query=rootkit&sbm=infocus&metaname=all doc.

Knoppix uses a command-line program called chkrootkit to do its work. It tests for (at this time) 59 different rootkits, worms, and LKMs (Linux Kernel Modules, the kernel-level rootkits discussed previously). Check out the complete list at the chkrootkit Website, www. chkrootkit.org.

To run chkrootkit, open your terminal and enter the following command:

```
$ sudo chkrootkit
```

Immediately chkrootkit kicks into action, scanning your machine for known rootkits and poking about, looking to see if anything has been tampered with. As it works, the program spits out its progress on your command line, leading to about a hundred lines or so that look like this:

```
Checking 'timed'... not found
Checking 'traceroute'... not infected
Checking 'vdir'... not infected
Checking 'w'... not infected
Checking 'write'... not infected
Checking 'aliens'... no suspect files
Searching for sniffer's logs, it may take a while... nothing found
Searching for HiDrootkit's default dir... nothing found
Searching for t0rn's default files and dirs... nothing found
```

If a nasty were on your computer, you'd see the name, following by INFECTED. Clearly it's a bit overwhelming to see a list of everything that's not infected because it would be easy to miss the one line informing you that you are infected, so it's better to run chkrootkit with the -q (for "quiet") option, like this:

```
$ sudo chkrootkit -q
```

The -q option will only show you warnings or lines indicating an infection, which should make things crystal clear. Much better!

Tip

When you run chkrootkit on Knoppix, you're going to see these warnings:

```
/usr/bin/strings: Warning: '/' is not an ordinary file
```

```
You have    8 process hidden for readdir command
```

```
You have    8 process hidden for ps command
```

```
Warning: Possible LKM Trojan installed
```

Don't freak out—because of the way Knoppix works, these lines show up. Your readdir and ps commands are not infected.

If you think that some particular programs are fishy, check them by specifying the programs on the command line, like this:

```
$ sudo chkrootkit ps tar ls
```

The results are reassuring, to say the least:

```
ROOTDIR is '/'
Checking 'ps'... not infected
Checking 'tar'... not infected
Checking 'ls'... not infected
```

Of course, if you use the -q option, chkrootkit only lets you know if one of those programs is infected.

Because you're using Knoppix, any examinations performed by chkrootkit operate, by default, on the Knoppix CD itself. While this is interesting, it isn't particularly helpful. More likely, you'll want to use Knoppix to examine a system that you suspect is compromised. In such a situation, use the -r option, which tells chkrootkit to scan a different drive as though it were the root drive. For example, your machine's hard drive is probably located at /mnt/hda1 once you've booted Knoppix, so you'd run the following to check it:

```
$ sudo chkrootkit -q -r /mnt/hda1
```

Adjust, of course, to suit your partitions.

Tip

Don't forget that because chkrootkit runs on the command line, it's easy to set up a cron job that does an automatic scan every night at a specified time and then sends a report to you letting you know if anything amiss was detected. This isn't as applicable when you're using Knoppix because you'd typically run just a single scan on a system and be done with it, but it's still useful to know. In /etc/crontab, add a line like the following (adjust the path to chkrootkit as appropriate for your system):

```
0 3 0 0 0 (chkrootkit -q 2>&1 | mail -s "chkrootkit scan report"
email@youraddress.com)
```

Unfortunately, if you find that the system you're examining has in fact been rooted, your best option is just to reinstall your OS and make sure that all updates have been applied and that the system is hardened before turning it loose back on a network. It's no fun, but that's the only way to ensure that you don't miss something and continue to allow some miscreant access to your box.

Scanning for Open Ports with Nmap

To find out what ports are open on a machine, the gold standard is Nmap. Nmap actually does its job in three steps: pinging the computer in question (or several, if you want) to determine whether it's on the network, scanning ports to ascertain what services are running on the machine, and figuring out the operating system of the box. Each of these steps is almost endlessly configurable within Nmap, enough so that a short book could be written on the software. This section focuses on common tasks for which you would use Nmap.

Note If you don't know what ports are, check out `http://en.wikipedia.org/wiki/Port_(computing)`, `http://en.wikipedia.org/wiki/Socket`, and `http://en.wikipedia.org/wiki/List_of_well-known_ports_(computing)` for a quick overview.

First, choose the computers you want to scan. If you have only one machine you're interested in, that's easy: just specify its IP address or domain name. If you're interested in several machines, you can give a range of IP addresses — 192.168.0.1-5, for instance — or you can use a mask. It's not easy to remember what the various masks mean, so here's a handy table that may help you keep things straight:

IP Address/Mask	What It Means
192.168.0.1/32	Just that computer: 192.168.0.1
192.168.0.1/24	The entire Class C range of addresses for that network: 253 addresses total First octet is always between 192–223 192.168.0.0–255
172.16.0.1/16	The entire Class B range of addresses for that network: 65,532 addresses total First octet is always between 128–191 172.16.0–255.0–255
10.0.0.1/8	The entire Class A range of addresses for that network: 16,777,214 addresses total First octet is always between 0–127 10.0–255.0–255.0–255

Note For more on IP addresses and classes, read through the excellent "Connected: An Internet Encyclopedia," available at `http://freesoft.org/CIE/Course/index.htm`. Head over to `http://en.wikipedia.org/wiki/Classful_network` for a quick overview, and then play with the IP Subnet Mask Calculator at `http://subnet-calculator.com/subnet.php`.

Now that you know which machines you're going to query, perform the simplest Nmap scan possible — a look at your own Knoppix box — by running the following:

```
$ nmap 127.0.0.1
```

In just a second or two, you should get this response:

```
Starting nmap 3.75 ( http://www.insecure.org/nmap/ ) at 2005-03-24 23:09 EST
Interesting ports on Knoppix (127.0.0.1):
(The 1661 ports scanned but not shown below are in state: closed)
PORT      STATE SERVICE
68/tcp    open  dhcpclient
6000/tcp  open  X11
Nmap run completed -- 1 IP address (1 host up) scanned in 0.199 seconds
```

Note a couple of interesting things here. The Knoppix box has only two ports open — the DHCP client and X11 — which is pretty good. But notice that Nmap only scans 1661 ports by default, and there are plenty more (ports can go up to 65535) that might hold something interesting.

If you don't care about hiding your scan and you just want to find out what machines are running on your network, try a quick Nmap ping scan, like this:

```
$ nmap -sP 192.168.0.1/24
```

The results for my network are as follows:

```
Starting nmap 3.75 ( http://www.insecure.org/nmap/ ) at 2005-03-24 23:58 EST
Host 192.168.0.1 appears to be up.
Host 192.168.0.6 appears to be up.
Host 192.168.0.10 appears to be up.
Host 192.168.0.13 appears to be up.
Host 192.168.0.100 appears to be up.
Host 192.168.0.103 appears to be up.
Host 192.168.0.104 appears to be up.
Nmap run completed -- 256 IP addresses (7 hosts up) scanned in 3.020 seconds
```

Yup, that's correct: seven machines on my network. It gets more interesting when that same scan is run with root privileges:

```
$ sudo nmap -sP 192.168.0.1/24
```

Here are my results:

```
Starting nmap 3.75 ( http://www.insecure.org/nmap/ ) at 2005-03-25 00:01 EST
Host 192.168.0.0 seems to be a subnet broadcast address (returned 4 extra
pings).
Host 192.168.0.1 appears to be up.
```

```
MAC Address: 00:12:17:31:4F:C4 (Cisco-Linksys)
Host 192.168.0.6 appears to be up.
MAC Address: 00:C0:4F:A1:25:4A (Dell Computer)
Host 192.168.0.10 appears to be up.
MAC Address: 00:B0:D0:FE:87:68 (Dell Computer)
Host 192.168.0.13 appears to be up.
MAC Address: 00:C0:4F:A1:25:89 (Dell Computer)
Host 192.168.0.100 appears to be up.
MAC Address: 00:C0:4F:A1:27:BF (Dell Computer)
Host 192.168.0.103 appears to be up.
MAC Address: 00:0D:88:66:FB:87 (D-Link)
Host 192.168.0.104 appears to be up.
Host 192.168.0.108 appears to be up.
MAC Address: 00:11:D8:90:D6:7F (Asustek Computer)
Host 192.168.0.255 seems to be a subnet broadcast address (returned 4 extra
pings).
Nmap run completed -- 256 IP addresses (8 hosts up) scanned in 4.390 seconds
```

When run by root, Nmap gives you the MAC address of each machine's NIC, and the manufacturer of that NIC (of course, now that you know the NICs, you can try to spoof them, but that's a different book).

Realize that the last two scans were in no way hidden. Any admin reviewing logs on the machines just scanned would have to notice something fishy going on. Nmap, however, can do much more to hide itself.

Caution

Now that you've done your machine, try your local network—as long as it's your network. Do not try this at work without permission, and do not use Nmap against random IP blocks or machines on the Internet. You may get visits from the authorities that will not be any fun. With that warning out of the way, if your LAN uses 192.168.0.x as its base, try `nmap 192.168.0.1/24`; if you use a different scheme, fill those numbers in and go to town.

For a stealthier scan, use SYN scanning. Here's an example of running SYN scanning against one machine on a LAN:

```
$ sudo nmap -sS 192.168.0.6
```

You have to use `sudo` because a stealth scan requires root privileges. Try it without `sudo`— Nmap immediately shuts you down. When the scan finishes, Nmap gives you some new information (in this example, some lines have been redacted for the sake of brevity):

```
Interesting ports on 192.168.0.6:
(The 1653 ports scanned but not shown below are in state: closed)
PORT     STATE SERVICE
22/tcp   open  ssh
139/tcp  open  netbios-ssn
445/tcp  open  microsoft-ds
631/tcp  open  ipp
901/tcp  open  samba-swat
2049/tcp open  nfs
MAC Address: 00:C0:4F:A1:25:4A (Dell Computer)
```

A lot more ports are open—not really surprising because this machine shares data back and forth all over the LAN. More important, this scan would be far more difficult to detect.

 Note Why is a SYN scan harder to detect? The inventor of Nmap tells you himself, at http://www.insecure.org/nmap/nmap_doc.html#syn.

For even more information about the target, use the -O option, which tells Nmap to try to figure out the operating system of the machine it's scanning, in tandem with the -v option, which tells Nmap to be verbose (use -vv for even more verbosity). Combining those with the stealth scan on an example Linux box gives you this command:

```
$ sudo nmap -v -O -sS 192.168.0.6
```

This produces a lengthy result, which has been condensed into the following:

```
Starting nmap 3.75 ( http://www.insecure.org/nmap/ ) at 2005-03-25 00:48 EST
Initiating SYN Stealth Scan against 192.168.0.6 [1663 ports] at 00:48
...
The SYN Stealth Scan took 0.21s to scan 1663 total ports.
...
Host 192.168.0.6 appears to be up ... good.
Interesting ports on 192.168.0.6:
(The 1653 ports scanned but not shown below are in state: closed)
PORT      STATE SERVICE
22/tcp    open  ssh
139/tcp   open  netbios-ssn
445/tcp   open  microsoft-ds
631/tcp   open  ipp
901/tcp   open  samba-swat
2049/tcp open  nfs
MAC Address: 00:C0:4F:A1:25:4A (Dell Computer)
Device type: general purpose
Running: Linux 2.4.X|2.5.X
OS details: Linux 2.4.0 - 2.5.20
Uptime 32.150 days (since Sun Feb 20 21:12:15 2005)
TCP Sequence Prediction: Class=random positive increments
                         Difficulty=5555644 (Good luck!)
...
Nmap run completed -- 1 IP address (1 host up) scanned in 2.583 seconds
```

Wow! Lots of stuff here, including open ports and services, the MAC address and manufacturer, OS details, machine uptime (32 days—not bad!), and the difficulty level for getting in to the computer.

You can also adjust the timing that Nmap uses when it scans. Include the -T5 option, and Nmap scans at an "insane" speed (that's Nmap's word, not mine) that will definitely get picked up by anyone looking for something suspicious. On the other hand, -T0, the "paranoid" speed, sends a packet every five minutes or so. Your scan will take a looooong time, but it also will probably go undetected by both machines and humans. Try the numbers between 0 and 5; when I used -T2 against one machine, the scan took 674 seconds—that's more than 11 minutes!

This overview should be enough to get you started with Nmap. It's a powerful tool that anyone involved in security ends up using constantly; in that respect, it's kind of like a hammer to a construction worker. The best thing for you to do now is start reading about Nmap and, more important, play with it.

Note   There's a vast amount of really useful information about Nmap on the Web. The Nmap man page is long and very detailed, but also make sure you visit the Nmap Website, at `http://insecure.org/nmap`, especially Fyodor's "The Art of Port Scanning," located at `http://insecure.org/nmap/nmap_doc.html`. It's a bit out of date now, but still contains an excellent overview you should read.

For tutorials, check out Andrew J. Bennieston's "NMAP—A Stealth Port Scanner" (`http://security-forums.com/forum/viewtopic.php?t=7872`) and Lamont Granquist's short but sweet email guide from 1999 (`http://seclists.org/lists/nmap-hackers/1999/Apr-Jun/0004.html`).

By the way, here's how cool Nmap really is: It was actually used (correctly!) by Trinity in *The Matrix Reloaded*. See for yourself at `http://images.insecure.org/nmap/images/matrix/`.

Checking for Dangerous Weaknesses with Nessus

Nmap tells you about a machine's OS and its open ports, but once you have that information, what can you do with it? Well, if you're a black hat hacker, it's time to pull out Nessus, the open-source vulnerability scanner, and determine whether there are any holes you can exploit. If you're trying to protect a network against black hats, then it's time to pull out Nessus, the open-source vulnerability scanner, and determine whether there are any holes that someone can exploit that you need to repair now.

There are commercial tools costing thousands of dollars that do the same thing that Nessus does for free, which is essentially look at the ports on a computer (usually by making use of Nmap), figuring out what services are running on those ports, and performing a variety of appropriate tests to determine whether any known security vulnerabilities exist on that machine. In addition, Nessus has some compelling features that make it attractive, especially to the Knoppix user thinking of combining Knoppix and Nessus to test a computer or even an entire LAN.

Before configuring Nessus, you need to understand that Nessus is really two interlocking pieces of software: a server and a client. The idea is that you can install the Nessus server on one computer (or more, if you'd like) on a network, and then connect to the server using the Nessus clients installed on any computer. If you're running Nessus on Knoppix, however, you probably don't need such a complicated arrangement. Instead, you'll want to run both the client and the server on the same machine, which is extremely workable.

Nessus uses plug-ins to work. Basically, a Nessus plug-in is a test for a particular weakness. As new security issues are published, volunteers write plug-ins for Nessus to probe the problem. There are thousands of plug-ins for Nessus, testing an amazing variety of exploitable holes. It's important that you update your Nessus plug-ins before you run the program by entering `sudo nessus-update-plugins` on the command line; that downloads any new additions to the Nessus arsenal. New plug-ins are published almost every day, so it's a good idea to run that command whenever you're going to use Nessus.

Note   The Knoppix developers have made it really easy to use Nessus by performing a lot of actions behind the scenes so you don't have to do them. If you want to know the whole process— because you want to run Nessus on a non-Knoppix machine, for instance—you really should read Harry Anderson's excellent three-part series on Nessus at SecurityFocus: `http://securityfocus.com/infocus/1741`, `http://securityfocus.com/infocus/1753`, and `http://securityfocus.com/infocus/1759`.

From the K menu, select System → Security → NESSUS Security Tool — Network Scanner. That starts the server portion of Nessus in the background, and then opens up the Nessus client, which looks like what is shown in Figure 6-1.

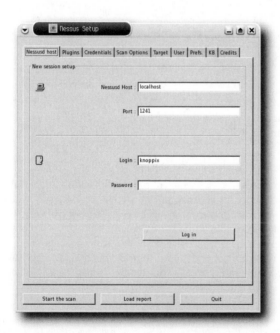

FIGURE 6-1: Nessus is now open and ready to configure.

Knoppix has already set up a user for you, so simply enter `knoppix` in the Login textbox and the Password textbox and click Log in. Nessus asks you about accepting the security certificate it wants to use to encrypt traffic between the client and the server, as shown in Figure 6-2.

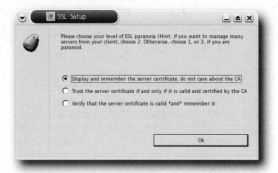

FIGURE 6-2: Nessus sets up an SSL certificate to
encrypt traffic.

Because both client and server are on the same machine, and because you have to trust the
Knoppix developers here, leave the first option chosen, and click OK. Another window opens,
asking if you want to accept the certificate; click Yes.

The next window warns you that dangerous plug-ins have been disabled. Click OK, and you
find yourself logged in to Nessus, with the Plugins tab visible and ready to go, as shown in
Figure 6-3.

Keep in mind that some Nessus plug-ins can cause the machine being probed to lock up or
crash, so Nessus disables those by default. It's easy, however, to enable those plug-ins. The
question is, should you?

If you're testing computers under your control, I recommend enabling the dangerous plug-ins.
After all, the bad guys might very well do so, so shouldn't you? However, you should weigh the
possibility of crashing your machine against any security gains. In other words, yes, it would be
good to make sure that your company's email server is safe against all forms of cracking, but
don't run Nessus to test things during the middle of the work day.

Do *not* run Nessus against computers that are not under your control. Your scan may very well
look like an attack, and you could get into serious trouble with the authorities. Be careful with
Nessus!

If you decide to enable every plug-in, even the dangerous ones, you first have to go to the Scan
Options tab and uncheck Safe Checks. You're now ready to live on the edge.

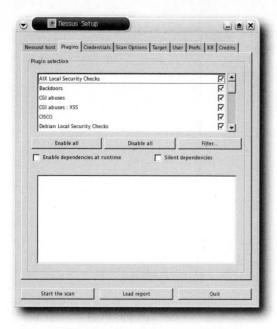

FIGURE 6-3: Choose the plug-ins you want to use
when scanning with Nessus.

Of course, if you don't need to test everything, or you simply can't afford the possibility that
you might crash the computer you're examining, use the defaults. You'll still get a lot of useful
information from Nessus.

You'll recall from the Nmap discussion that there are different kinds of scanning methods you
can use. In fact, Nessus uses Nmap to perform its scans, as you can see on the Prefs tab. The
first option on that tab is TCP scanning technique; I'd use the SYN scan because it's quick and
sneaky.

Note   Because of limited space, this section doesn't cover the entire Prefs tab, but if you're going to
use Nessus effectively, you really should familiarize yourself with all of your options here. The
best place to go for this information is the Nessus Knowledge Base, which goes through every
single option in the program. It's awesome, and you can find it at `http://edgeos.com/
nessuskb/`.

There's one last thing to set, and in some ways it's the most important option of all: the com-
puter(s) you want to scan. Go to the Target tab, shown in Figure 6-4.

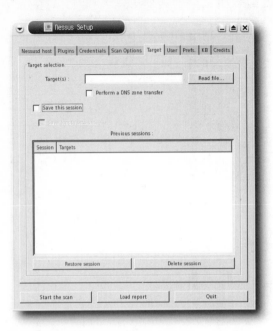

FIGURE 6-4: Choose which computer(s) you want to examine with Nessus.

You can specify targets the same way you can using Nmap, with any of the following:

- IP address
- Domain name
- Range of IP addresses
- Subnet

For example, 192.168.0.6 is a Linux box on my LAN used for file sharing, among other tasks. I enter that IP address in the Target(s) field, click Start the Scan, and Nessus takes off. The window changes to one labeled Scanning Network from Localhost, and a few seconds later the progress of Nessus at work is displayed. A scan can take quite a while, so you may want to move on to other things and let Nessus do its job. Eventually Nessus finishes, and you get a report window, shown in Figure 6-5.

To get to the meat of the report, click on the subnet in the Subnet box to populate the Host box. Then click on the IP listed in the Host box to populate the Port box. The items listed in the Port box are what you need to read. An orange triangle icon next to a list item indicates a Security Warning, and a lightbulb icon tells you that there's a Security Note on that item. Lack of an icon means that Nessus (and Nmap) detected a service running on that port but found no potential problems with it.

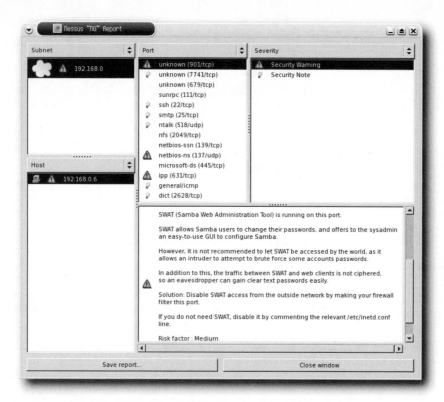

FIGURE 6-5: Nessus presents you with a report after its scan and analysis.

You should look at every Security Note because you might find something interesting, and certainly review every Security Warning. Every time Nessus warns you of a potential problem, it also gives you advice about mitigating the issue, and often includes a link to follow for further information or even a patch.

If you decide to save the report, whether to establish a baseline for that particular system or to show your boss ("Look at all the pretty graphs and numbers!"), click Save Report and then pick the format you'd like to use. You have a variety to pick from, including the following:

- **NBE:** Enables you to open it again using Nessus
- **XML:** Suitable if you want to manipulate the data yourself
- **LaTeX:** Also good for manipulating and creating your own report formats
- **HTML:** An attractive, clickable report, with links to the Nessus Web site for further info
- **ASCII:** Plain text
- **HTML with pies and graphs:** A pretty, graphical clickable report, perfect for your PHB (pointy-haired boss)

The first couple of times you use Nessus, save a report using each of the formats so that you can get a handle on the pros and cons of each one. Either of the HTML formats can be tremendously helpful because they include links to resources that the normal report doesn't provide.

Nessus is an amazingly powerful tool, one that you'll find yourself using often on your own systems. Remember that it's better for you to find out the weaknesses on your own computers and network before the bad guys do, and Nessus is an awesome way to do so. Use it!

Sniffing Packets on a Network

Traffic sent from your computer to another is broken up into small chunks (typically around 1,500 bytes each) called *packets;* when the packets reach their destination, they are reassembled back into a whole. Each packet consists of headers and data. The data is the information being sent, while the headers help get the packet from its source to its destination.

To understand packets sent over the Internet, think of an onion. Start with the data at the center. Wrapped around the data is the Ethernet header, which contains the MAC addresses of the source and destination. Wrapped around that is the Internet Protocol (IP) information, which consists of a lot of data, but most importantly the IP addresses of the source and destination.

Wrapped around the IP layer is the Transmission Control Protocol (TCP) information, which possesses the source and destination ports and the sequence numbers of the packets. That may be the outside of the onion, unless an application of some sort, such as a Web browser or an email program or an IM app, is involved. In those instances, the TCP layer is wrapped in an application layer — such as HTTP, POP3, or AIM — which performs services needed by those applications. And that, usually, is the final layer of the onion.

What do sniffing programs do? Basically, they enable you to see all the traffic on your network, whether it is intended for your machine or not (there is a caveat to that statement, coming up soon). All the packets rushing by and all the various layers that make up those packets — network protocol analyzers such as Ethereal show it all.

Why would you want to do that? Why in the world would you want to know the details of all the traffic going across the network to which you're currently attached? Well, there's the bad guy reason — to grab non-encrypted passwords and data — and the good guy reasons:

- To learn more about network protocols

- To figure out just what the heck is wrong with that %#$&! Samba connection (or NFS, or email, or what have you)

- To audit an organization's network to expose security holes (such as really bad, unencrypted passwords, or folks who aren't using encryption when they're supposed to)

No matter what the reason, you'll find a lot of reasons to use Ethereal, not least of which is that it's really fun.

Note For more on packet sniffing, start with Robert Graham's extensive Sniffing FAQ, available at `http://linuxsecurity.net/resource_files/intrusion_detection/sniffing-faq.html`.

Analyzing Network Traffic with Ethereal

Ethereal has been available for general use since 1998, and in the few years it's been out, it has become one of the premier open-source security tools. It is both powerful and easy to use for basic needs, so including it on Knoppix was a no-brainer. It's also a program that rewards careful study: The more you learn, the more you can do, and the more you will learn — about your network, about networking, and about security.

To get the most from Ethereal, you need to run it as root. Unfortunately, if you try to open Ethereal as root in Knoppix, you are prompted for a root password that doesn't exist. There are two ways around this issue (actually, there are a lot more than that, but these two should do it for you):

- Set the root password. Just open your command line by going to the K menu and selecting System ➔ Konsole. When it opens, enter `sudo passwd`, type in the new root password twice, and press Enter. That's it. The password for root is now changed. When you run Ethereal, you are prompted to enter root's password, which you just created.

- Right-click the K menu and select Menu Editor to open the KDE Menu Editor. Click the + next to Internet to expand it, and then select Ethereal (as root) with a single click. You should now be able to edit the data about this item on the right side of the KDE Menu Editor. Next to the Command field, edit the command to read like the following:

    ```
    sudo gksu -u root /usr/bin/ethereal
    ```

    Further down, uncheck Run as a Different User. Close the KDE Menu Editor. Save your changes and wait while they are made permanent. Now you can run Ethereal as root without having to create a root password.

Open Ethereal by going to the K menu and selecting Internet ➔ Ethereal (as root). The program opens with a screen similar to the one shown in Figure 6-6.

Setting Caption Options

When you first open Ethereal, it seems like you have a lot of options — and you do! — yet getting started isn't that difficult. To begin the process of capturing packets, choose Capture ➔ Start, which opens Ethereal's Capture Options window (see Figure 6-7).

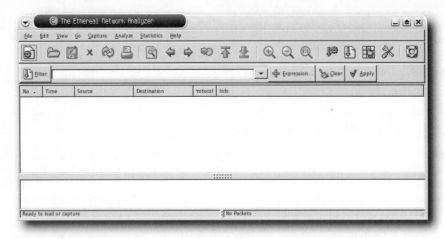

FIGURE 6-6: Ethereal doesn't do much when it first opens . . . but just wait.

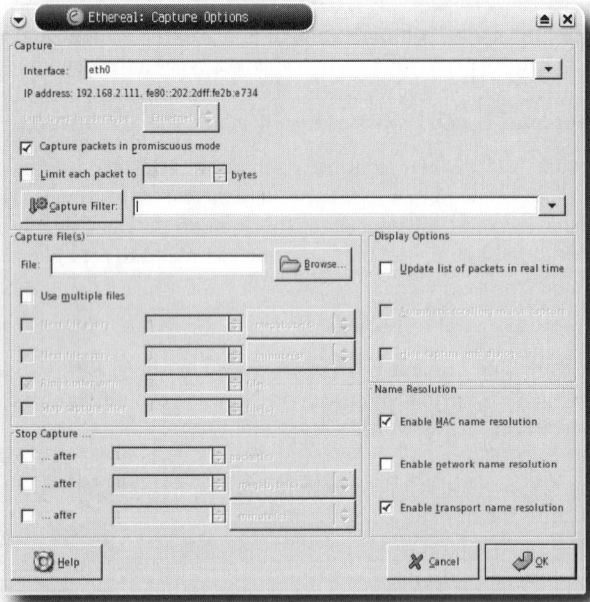

FIGURE 6-7: Choose what you want to capture with Ethereal.

This is a very important window because it determines which packets Ethereal is going to gather. The Interface box should contain the NIC that is connected to the network. If you have only one, it's chosen; if you're using two NICs, select the one you want Ethereal to use.

To grab every packet on the network, even those not bound for your machine, leave Capture Packets in Promiscuous Mode checked. To see only information entering and leaving your specific machine, uncheck this box.

Note If you're on a switched network, you will only capture packets meant for your machine, in addition to the occasional broadcast packet. (Yes, there are ways around that, but that's another book. If you really want to know how to grab other machines' packets on a switched network, use your favorite search engine.)

Because this is your first time using Ethereal and because this isn't a life-or-death situation, check Update List of Packets in Real Time, and, once that's enabled, check Automatic Scrolling in Live Capture. With those two options on, Ethereal shows you the packets it is snarfing as it snarfs them. It's too much information to be useful while it's going on, but it sure looks cool, and it gives you an idea about just how busy your network really is.

Note There are plenty of other options on the Capture Options screen, but they're not applicable to you right now. Nonetheless, you may want to use one of them sometime, so check out the Ethereal User's Guide for the Capture Options dialog box, at `http://ethereal.com/docs/ user-guide-sp/#ChCapCaptureOptions`.

Understanding the Capture

Now that you've told Ethereal what to capture, click OK. The main Ethereal window fills up with data, and a smaller window titled something like "Capture from eth0" (see Figure 6-8) shows you the aggregate of Ethereal's progress, broken down by protocol.

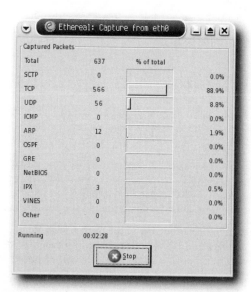

FIGURE 6-8: Ethereal at work

Not surprising, TCP is responsible for the lion's share of traffic because most folks cruise around to Web pages and open their email programs. After a couple of minutes, click Stop so that you can examine what's been traveling about the network. The capture window closes, leaving you with the main Ethereal window, now chock-a-block with data, as Figure 6-9 shows.

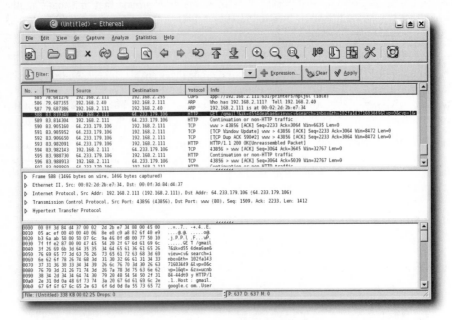

FIGURE 6-9: Ethereal has captured plenty of data for analysis.

The three panes of data, from the top down, are as follows:

- **Packet List pane:** Contains a list of every packet captured and key data about it. When you select a packet in this pane, information about it is displayed in the middle and bottom panes.

- **Packet Details pane:** Breaks the packet you selected in the Packet List pane into its component parts, including headers and data. Each item can be expanded to show further detail by clicking the small triangle to the left of each field. When you select a component in this pane, the corresponding information is highlighted in the bottom pane.

- **Packet Bytes pane:** Displays the actual information sent in the packet. If an item in the middle pane is chosen, the specific information in the bottom pane is highlighted to make it easy to find and read. Conversely, choosing a snippet of data in the bottom pane highlights the specific protocol in the middle pane.

The packet selected in Figure 6-9 shows what happened when I loaded Gmail. You can see that the browser (at 192.168.2.11 in the Source column) sent an HTTP GET request to Google's server (at 64.233.179.106 in the Destination column) in the Packet List pane.

The Packet Details pane shows that the packet consisted of an Ethernet header, an IP header, a TCP header, and HTTP data.

Finally, the Packet Bytes pane reveals the entire packet in a (mostly) comprehensible format. The first column of the Packet Bytes pane shows the offset in the data, the second column shows the data in hexadecimal format, while the third column shows the data in human-readable ASCII format (just because it's human-readable doesn't mean that you'll understand it, though!).

Filtering the Capture

Things get really interesting when you start filtering the mass of data that Ethereal captures. For instance, suppose you want to determine whether anyone on your network is trying to log in to his email using a username and password sent in the clear (Bad user! Bad!). To find out, you want to create a display filter that limits in some way the packets that Ethereal shows you (these are not the same as capture filters, which control the packets that Ethereal gathers in the first place). Click the Expression button in the filter toolbar near the top of the window; Ethereal's Filter Expression window (see Figure 6-10) opens.

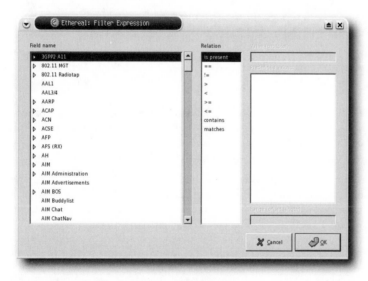

FIGURE 6-10: Create a display filter for Ethereal.

Among the enormous list of possible protocols on the left side of the window, select the one in which you're interested: IMAP. For Relation, choose "contains," and in the Value (protocol) text box (which is active for every Relation except "is present") enter **LOGIN** — that's what IMAP servers expect when a user is trying to authenticate to the server. Now that your filter exists, click OK to go back to the main Ethereal window, where only the filtered results are displayed, as shown in Figure 6-11.

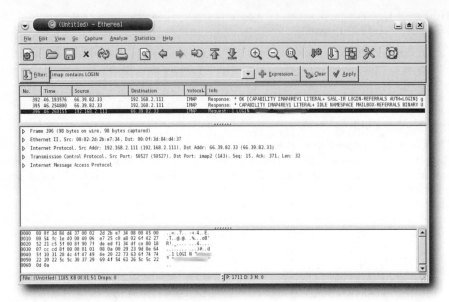

FIGURE 6-11: Clear-text email login and password (blacked out in this figure) are available to nearly everyone. Oops.

Ethereal displays the filter you created in its own syntax: `imap contains LOGIN` (filters are case insensitive). Below that are three packets out of hundreds, and one of those three is dynamite. The third packet — the one that's highlighted — contains the user's name and password, in clear text and easy to read (blacked out here to protect the bad user). Yes, it's that easy.

And it gets easier. When you find a packet that looks interesting, right-click it and select Follow TCP Stream. Ethereal gathers all the packets that are part of that email message, or login sequence, or whatever; joins them together; and then shows you the ASCII text. Try it with one of your own email messages, and prepare to be amazed.

Note When you choose Follow TCP Stream, Ethereal automatically turns that request into a display filter.

Here are some other display filters you can use. Just remove the current filter, enter one of the following, and click Apply:

- `aim && !(aim.channel == 0x5)`: Look for AOL Instant Messenger traffic, but without the annoying Keep Alive packets that appear constantly.

- `(http contains "hotmail") && (http contains "Reply-To")`: Find emails sent using Hotmail.

- (tcp.port eq 110 and tcp.port eq 3457) && (tcp contains PASS) : Find out usernames and passwords sent when folks try to log in to get their POP3 email.

Protecting with Encryption

How do you protect against Ethereal? It's pretty simple, really. Use encryption. That means SSL whenever you have to log in to any Website that needs a username and password, and SSL for any email clients. For the contents of email, use GPG (discussed earlier in this chapter).

Want to scare a friend or family member straight and show her the value of good security? Use Ethereal for a while when she's using the Net to surf and read emails, and then show her what you learned. I have the feeling she'll be a lot more receptive to a simple discussion about the benefits of SSL and encrypted POP3 or IMAP. In that way alone, you can use Ethereal to make everyone safer.

Note Ethereal is an awesome program that offers hundreds of features and tweaks, and I've barely touched on a fraction of its capabilities. To learn more, start with the excellent Ethereal User's Guide, available in HTML or PDF formats at `http://ethereal.com/docs/`.

Performing Forensics with the Coroner's Toolkit

One of the most popular shows on TV right now is *CSI: Crime Scene Investigation*. Every week, an intrepid team of investigators uses forensic evidence and the latest scientific tools to plumb the depths of human crime and malevolence. Using clues such as blood spatters, footprints, teeth impressions, and gunpowder residue, the past can be reconstructed and crimes can be solved.

In the computer world, forensics is a well-known aspect of computer security. When a machine is compromised, it's important for a qualified, knowledgeable person to use tools such as the Coroner's Toolkit (known as TCT) to enable the reconstruction of the computer to learn the following:

- The exact causes of the break-in can be reasonably ascertained
- The extent of the damage can be cataloged
- The evidence can be preserved in a way that can be used in legal proceedings

Caution That last point is especially important. If a court case is to be made, it is imperative that the evidence is gathered and preserved in a way that does not allow for an argument to be made that the gathering and preservation itself changed or manipulated any of the evidence. For that reason, I do not encourage you to intrude yourself if the legal system is going to be involved. Instead, engage the services of a security professional (who may very well run TCT).

The Coroner's Toolkit is actually a collection of software packages, some of which can be run independently, that work together to give you a snapshot of the activities a computer was engaged in at a specific time. It includes the following:

- **Grave-robber:** Runs several other tools that gather together as much information about a computer system as possible.
- **Mactime:** One of the tools used by grave-robber, which you can also run independently, that looks at the last time the following occurred:

- A file was modified (the file's mtime)
- A file was accessed for reading (by ls or cat, for instance) or writing (the file's atime)
- A file's inode was changed, by changing permissions or ownership, for instance (the file's ctime)

■ **Unrm:** Copies all free disk space

■ **Lazarus:** Analyzes data gathered by unrm

Note Don't know what an inode is? Wikipedia tells you at http://en.wikipedia.org/ wiki/Inode. Wondering why creation time isn't listed? Because UNIX-based systems don't keep track of a file or an inode's creation time!

Using Grave-robber

You can run grave-robber against either a live system or a corpse. A live system is just that: one that hasn't been rebooted and is still the site of a suspected break-in. A corpse, on the other hand, is a backup copy of the problematic disk (usually created using the dd command) or a problematic disk that has been mounted on a system.

Insofar as this book is concerned, you're running TCT against a corpse because you would have to reboot anyway to use the software on a Knoppix disk. That mean using the dd command to image the suspected hard drive while it was still alive, booting with Knoppix, mounting the image using the loopback device, and then running TCT against the mounted image, now a corpse (be aware that the last command involving grave-robber is usually run against an entire filesystem, so it can take hours and hours or even days). Here's the quick series of commands:

```
# dd if=/dev/hda1 of=/mnt/hda2/corpse.img
```

Then reboot with Knoppix and continue:

```
$ sudo mkdir /mnt/corpse
$ sudo mount -o loop,ro /mnt/hda2/corpse.img /mnt/corpse
$ sudo grave-robber -c /mnt/corpse -o LINUX2
```

Note For the commands used on a live system, see man grave-robber.

These commands are what you would normally do. While you're learning, though, run grave-robber against the /KNOPPIX/ directory, which should give you more than enough data to play with (this is kind of like using a corpse because /KNOPPIX is on the CD-ROM and is therefore mounted read-only like the corpse in the preceding list of commands). To start TCT, run the following and leave your computer for a while:

```
$ sudo grave-robber /KNOPPIX/
```

Note

For the full list of options that you can use when running grave-robber, check out `man grave-robber`. By not explicitly choosing an option, grave-robber runs with the following options as default: `-i`, `-m`, `-M`, `-P`, `-s`, `-t`, `-l`, `-I`, `-O`, `-F`, `-S`, and `-V`. Use your free time to find out what all of those do!

Eventually, the process finishes (it can take quite a while depending upon the speed of your processor, your CD drive, and other factors), and then you'll see something like this as output on the terminal:

```
Starting preprocessing paths and filenames on Knoppix...
Processing $PATH elements...
/usr/local/sbin
/usr/local/bin
/usr/sbin
/usr/bin
/sbin
/bin
/usr/X11R6/bin
        Processing dir /
        Processing dir /etc
        Processing dir /bin
        Processing dir /sbin
        Processing dir /dev
Finished preprocessing your toolkit... you may now use programs or examine files
in the above directories
```

TCT places two very important log files — `coroner.log` and `error.log` — in your current directory. The first tells you exactly what commands grave-robber ran, and the dates and times those commands ran, as it did its work; the second lets you know — surprise! — about any errors that grave-robber encountered. Both can help you learn exactly what grave-robber does and explain why things don't work as you might have expected them to.

TCT places its output files at `/var/cache/tct/data`, but you need to be root to see them (which makes sense because you run grave-robber as root). The easiest way to view the files is to run Konqueror as root. From the K menu, select System ➔ Root Terminal, logging in as root, and then entering `konqueror` to run that program.

Note

You should have already set a root password to open the Root Terminal. If you haven't, open the Terminal Program on the panel, enter `sudo passwd`, and then assign a new password for root.

Once Konqueror is open, navigate to `/var/cache/tct/data` and start looking at the treasure trove of data that grave-robber has made available to you. Here's an overview of some of the files and folders you should see:

- body: The `mactime` database, used by the `mactime` program
- body.S: File attributes of all `suid` files. The same data is in the body file, but it's called out here.
- command_out/: Output of programs grave-robber executes to find out information about the system, such as `top`, `dmesg`, `arp`, and `netstat`
- conf_vault/: Copies of files that grave-robber found that looked interesting, such as configurations and other critical files

- `proc/`: Images of running processes gathered from the `/proc` filesystem

- `removed_but_running/`: Deleted files that were still running

- `trust/`: Files presenting information about trust relations between computers and users, such as cryptographic keys from GPG and SSH, command histories, and `.forward` files

As an intrepid forensics investigator, your job is to look over these files and try to reconstruct the machine's state when grave-robber was run against it. This is going to take experience and time, so jump right in. Look at everything, try to figure out what it signifies, and glean all that you can from the data you have. No one said it was going to be easy!

Running Mactime

The `mactime` command is a bit easier to get a handle on. Remember that it can be run independently of grave-robber, which means that you could start with it and master that tool before moving on to the full glut of data provided by grave-robber. For a quick look at how to utilize mactime, run it against the `/etc/init.d` directory, which holds a lot of the programs run as services on your Knoppix machine:

```
$ sudo mactime -y -R -d /etc/init.d 1/1/1970
```

The options used in this command mean the following (for the full list of options, use `man mactime`):

- `y`: Display the date as YY MM DD, instead of MM DD YY, which makes for better sorting.

- `R`: Process the current directory, and all subdirectories, recursively.

- `d`: Use the following directory instead of a database (`/etc/init.d` in this example).

- `1/1/1970`: Show all files modified, accessed, or changed after this date (in this example, the UNIX epoch, seen by UNIX systems as the start of time); it's also possible to use a range, such as 4/1/2005–4/8/2005.

Note For more information on the UNIX epoch, see the Jargon File at `http://clueless.com/jargon3.0.0/epoch.html` or Wikipedia's in-depth "Unix time" article at `http://en.wikipedia.org/wiki/Unix_epoch`.

The example command should produce output containing at least some of the following:

```
99 Nov 07 10:35:31      2213 m.. -rwxr-xr-x root      root      /etc/init.d/rc
99 Nov 13 11:24:46      1909 m.. -rwxr-xr-x root      root
/etc/init.d/bootmisc.sh
00 Feb 11 05:52:19      1478 m.. -rwxr-xr-x root      root
/etc/init.d/mountnfs.sh
00 Apr 03 07:57:46      1074 m.. -rwxr-xr-x root      root      /etc/init.d/atd
00 Jun 05 12:36:19       853 m.. -rw-r--r-- root      root      /etc/init.d/README
00 Jun 06 04:42:13       420 m.. -rwxr-xr-x root      root
/etc/init.d/umountnfs.sh
```

```
00 Jun 06 04:42:14        430 m.. -rwxr-xr-x root      root
/etc/init.d/umountfs
                          601 m.. -rwxr-xr-x root      root
/etc/init.d/mountall.sh
00 Jul 27 23:05:51        927 m.. -rwxr-xr-x root      root      /etc/init.d/ipx
01 Jan 28 01:29:37        800 m.. -rwxr-xr-x root      root      /etc/init.d/mt-st
01 May 11 20:03:54       1007 m.. -rwxr-xr-x root      root      /etc/init.d/kerneld
                          197 m.. -rwxr-xr-x root      root      /etc/init.d/reboot
```

Notice that files are first listed in order from oldest to newest using the date format specified, and then by the time. The next column provides the size of the file in bytes, and then the action on the file (m for modified, a for accessed, and c for changed). Following that are permissions and ownership, similar to running ls -l.

In this listing, it's very easy to determine whether files were perhaps altered within a specific time span. If you see a file that has been altered, and you don't remember changing it, tampering may be indicated. The mactime command can help you identify files that should get your attention. With that in mind, it might be nice to run it regularly with a cron job and have the output emailed to you for possible follow up later.

Looking at Unrm and Lazarus

The other two major programs in TCT—unrm and lazarus—are run separately from grave-robber. This discussion won't walk you through all the details of these programs, but it provides an overview so you'll know what they are and how to use them.

Be aware that unrm has one very large limitation: At this time, it works only on Linux systems formatted with the ext2 filesystem. Because more and more Linux distros ship with journaled filesystems such as ext3, reiserfs, and even XFS by default, this greatly limits the usefulness of unrm.

Suppose that you accidentally delete a file on your computer, or that you're trying to see whether any bad guys took over a machine and attempted to delete evidence of their presence. In those cases, the combination of unrm and lazarus will help. Run unrm first; it makes a copy of all free disk space. Then lazarus analyzes the data in the copy created by unrm and tries to figure out what the data is.

Understanding Unrm

Think about what unrm does for a second before you run it. It makes a copy of all free disk space. In other words, if you have a 60GB filesystem drive, and 19GB are used on that filesystem, unrm is going to make a bit-by-bit copy of everything not occupied by those 19GB (and then lazarus is going to process those files, and in so doing create another copy). Hmmm . . .

This means you need to consider two things before running unrm. First, unrm is going to copy 41GB—everything not used by the 19GB of data—and lazarus is going to generate another 41GB. Second, just where are you going to put those 82 (41 + 41) GB? You can't put them on the same filesystem you're running unrm against, or you'll be busily overwriting the very things you're trying to recover! You must send unrm's output to a different filesystem.

To check the deleted space on /mnt/hda2 using Knoppix, for example, you boot Knoppix and run the following:

```
$ df -h
```

The output is something like the following (your results will obviously differ):

```
Filesystem         Size  Used Avail Use% Mounted on
/dev/root          3.4M   13K  3.4M   1% /
/dev/hdc           695M  695M     0 100% /cdrom
/dev/cloop         1.9G  1.9G     0 100% /KNOPPIX
/ramdisk           392M   75M  318M  19% /ramdisk
/UNIONFS           6.1G  5.6G  477M  93% /UNIONFS
/dev/hda2           27G   25G  1.7G  94% /mnt/hda2
/dev/hda1          9.8G  5.2G  4.7G  53% /mnt/hda1
```

You can see that hda2 is a 27GB file system, with 1.7GB free. Fortunately, hda1 has 4.7GB free, so it's going to be close but not a problem. You can send the unrm output to hda1 for safekeeping.

Before running unrm, you must umount the filesystem against which you want to run unrm:

```
$ umount /mnt/hda2
```

Check that you've mounted hda1 with writing allowed, or this process won't work. Now run the unrm command, sending the output to a file on the still-mounted hda1:

```
$ unrm /dev/hda2 > /mnt/hda1/hda2_unrm_results
```

The unrm command can take a while to run, depending on the amount of free space on a device. Once it finishes, it's time to go to work with lazarus.

Understanding Lazarus

Lazarus analyzes the data dug up by unrm and tries to bring anything it can find back to life. Be warned: lazarus can take twice as long to complete its job as it took unrm to work, so this may be one of those commands that you start and then go to bed. Here's how to run it:

```
$ lazarus -h /mnt/hda1/hda2_unrm_results
```

The -h option tells lazarus to produce a report in HTML that you can load in a browser and use. That report is composed of three files: hda2_unrm_results.html, hda2_unrm_results.menu.html, and hda2_unrm_results.frame.html; the last one is the one you need to open in your Web browser, and it takes care of loading the others.

Lazarus tries — emphasis on the word "tries" — to figure out whether recovered data is binary or text, and then it tries to figure out what kind of text or binary data it is: HTML, mail, logs, executable, sound, and so on. A key is available in the HTML files that lazarus displays in your browser. Most of the Web page is taken up with a list of those keys, one for each file that lazarus recovered. Click the link, and you can see the contents of the file.

This is very similar to looking for a needle in a haystack, of course, so you may want to speed things up by using grep. For example, if you're looking for a file having to do with the McGillicuddy account, you could try grep McGillicuddy /mnt/hda1/hda2_unrm_results/*. Try long enough, and you may just find that file you so desperately need.

Note For further info about grep, try man grep. For more information about TCT, see Clarke L. Jeffris' "The Coroner's Toolkit—In depth," a PDF available at www.sans.org/rr/ whitepapers/incident/651.php. For an excellent overview of unrm and lazarus, see www.antioffline.com/TCT/help-recovering-file, written by the folks behind the two programs, or CERT's "Using The Coroner's Toolkit: Rescuing files with lazarus" at www.cert.org/security-improvement/implementations/i046.03.html.

For more on computer forensics, see Timothy E. Wright's "A Method for Forensic Previews" at http://securityfocus.com/infocus/1825. Another good piece, which also contains some great info on TCT, is Derek Cheng's "Freeware Forensics Tools for Unix," at http://securityfocus.com/infocus/1503. There's a massive list of whitepapers, FAQs, and other great links at http://forensics.nl/links, and a nice list of forensics software at http://forinsect.de/forensics/forensics-tools.html.

Wiping a Hard Drive

Probably anyone reading this book is a bit paranoid when it comes to computers, most likely because you have an idea how computers really work. For instance, you know that sending an unencrypted email is pretty much like sending a postcard through the mail—anyone can read it along the way—and you also know that deleting a file doesn't really delete it.

In fact, in a well-publicized report published in 2003, tech writer Simson Garfinkel looked at 150 hard drives purchased at sales. Many of those hard drives were supposedly erased, yet Garfinkel and his team were able to recover data—including credit card numbers, bank account numbers and balances, sensitive corporate memos, email messages, and pornography—from 64 percent of them.

If you're getting rid of a computer, or just a drive, it's a good idea to really remove the data on that drive. If you don't care about the drive any longer, take a ball-peen hammer and beat it until you've destroyed the drive (be sure to wear safety goggles!), or take a drill with a strong bit and run through that sucker a number of times until your drive resembles Swiss cheese. No one— not even Jack Bauer at CTU—could recover any data off that drive.

If, however, you want to pass the drive along to someone else to use, but you don't want anyone to be able to recover any of the data on it, you have two options available on Knoppix: employing dd and using wipe. No matter which technique you use, do not mount the partitions you want to wipe. Leave them unmounted. If you're not sure which partitions are on your machine, or what Knoppix thinks they are, go to the K menu and select System → QTParted to display your drives and their partitions.

Caution Be very careful when using QTParted because you can accidentally format or delete a partition. (For more about this great program, see the discussions in Chapters 4 and 5.)

When QTParted opens, select a drive in the Device panel at the upper left. Most likely, you'll be interested in /dev/hda, your first hard drive. QTParted takes a few seconds to analyze the drive, and then you see something like what is shown in Figure 6-12 (remember, though, that your drives and partitions may vary).

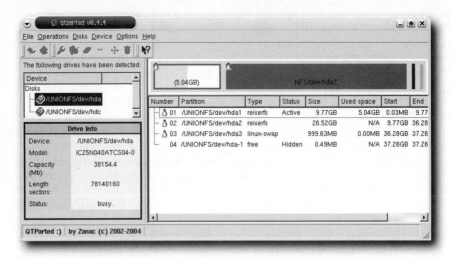

FIGURE 6-12: QTParted shows you a graphical representation of your drives and partitions.

Make note of your drives and their partitions. In this example, there are two drives on the machine: a hard drive at `/dev/hda` and a CD-ROM (the one currently holding the Knoppix disk!) at `/dev/hdc`. The hard drive at `/dev/hda` has three partitions and some free space, and you need to take care of all three of those.

Employing dd

The first method involves running a script that uses the built-in `dd` command that comes with Knoppix (and every other Linux distro in the world, for that matter). `dd` duplicates disks, among other wonderful things, enabling you to make perfect copies of a hard drive, for instance. However, that's not what you're going to do now; instead, you're going to do something much sneakier. Take a look at this code:

```
for (( i = 0;i<11;i++ )); do
  dd if=/dev/random of=/dev/hda && dd if=/dev/zero of=/dev/hda
done
```

The `dd` command takes two parameters — `if`, for input file, and `of`, for output file — and then takes the input and writes it to the output. In this code example, `dd` uses the contents of `/dev/random` (random data generated by the system) and `/dev/zero` (a string of never-ending ASCII zeros generated by the system) to overwrite your hard drive located at `hda` 11 times!

Why 11 times? The U.S. Department of Defense 5200.28 standard states that a file must be overwritten at least seven times to be considered securely wiped, but I always take my file wipe command beyond seven to 11, which means that drives are just a bit more wiped than drives wiped only 10 times. (I got the 11 from the movie *This Is Spinal Tap*.)

Note Peter Gutmann, a security researcher, contends that a disk must be overwritten at least 22 times, with different patterns, before it is securely wiped. You can read his argument at `http://wipe.sourceforge.net/secure_del.html`.

To use the `dd` command, boot Knoppix but don't mount the disk you want to wipe. Open Konsole and enter the following:

```
for (( i = 0;i<11;i++ )) ; do dd if=/dev/urandom of=/dev/hda ⤸
   ; dd if=/dev/zero of=/dev/hda ; done
```

Press Enter, and then get up and leave the computer. It's going to take a long, long time (many hours, perhaps days) for that command to finish, unless you're trying to erase a pretty dinky hard drive. It's worth it to know that your data is safely — and permanently — erased, isn't it?

Employing Wipe

The other method for securely erasing drives (or partitions) utilizes the `wipe` command. With Knoppix, it's pretty easy. To nuke the second partition on your hard drive, for example, boot with Knoppix and then invoke the `wipe` command as follows:

```
$ wipe -fik /dev/hda2
```

The options do the following:

- `f`: You will not be asked for confirmation (if that makes you nervous, don't use the option).

- `i`: Print information about the command's progress on the command line. If you don't need to see this, don't use the option.

- `k`: Don't get rid of the file (in this case, a device).

Caution If you use Wipe to nuke an entire hard disk instead of just a partition (if you wipe `/dev/hda` instead of `/dev/hda1`, in other words), you will erase the Master Boot Record on the drive, which means that all of your partitioning data will be gone and you will not be able to boot using the drive any longer. This may not be a bad thing if you're planning to reinstall an OS from scratch on that drive, or if the drive is not used to boot your machine, but you should at least know about it. Besides, you can recover the MBR — maybe — if you read the "Restoring a Missing MBR" section in Chapter 4.

`wipe` is a pretty powerful command; by default, it overwrites files with random data 34 times. If that number is too high for you and you want to use 11 instead, for example, change it with `-Q 11` as an option to the `wipe` command (make sure you use a capital Q). If you're really impatient and you don't mind a superficial job, you can use `-q` as an option, which just wipes the drive four times (not recommended, but it's your data).

You can also wipe directories, if you'd like, instead of entire drives, by first mounting the partition containing the directory and then using this command:

```
$ wipe -fickr /mnt/hda2/secretstuff/
```

The c option uses the chmod command to set write permissions so that everything can be written over, while the r recourses through the directory structure, wiping everything in its path. The command taken together with its options writes over the contents of the secretstuff directory 34 times, but leaves the directory itself alone. If you want the directory to go bye-bye as well, omit the k option.

Now don't you feel safer? Go ahead and donate those old computers to charity with a clean conscience, assured that no one will ever find your collection of . . . whatever it is that you have on your hard drive.

Note   For more on wipe, try man wipe or check out the project's Website at http://wipe. sourceforge.net.

Summary

Security is one of those things you are forced to think about, whether you really want to or not. Fortunately, Knoppix makes it easy not only to check the security status of your network but also to learn about security and have fun while you're doing so. You can use Knoppix to encrypt your data, check for vulnerabilities, sniff packets streaming by on a network, perform forensic analysis on a compromised system, and wipe a hard drive. All of these are key tasks, and even if you don't know how to do them right now, Knoppix helps you learn so that you can protect not just your own networks, but those of your clients, family, and friends as well.

Knoppix Variants

part

Clustering with Knoppix

Knoppix and Knoppix-derived distributions can be used for large computational problems that would benefit from the use of multiple computers. This chapter introduces the concept of a *cluster,* which, for the sake of this discussion, is a group of systems networked together to run a single computational task.

A cluster is the opposite of a shared system whereby multiple users run concurrent tasks. Clusters are used to run tasks, frequently called *jobs,* that are computationally intensive (often called expensive), such as the ones that scientists and mathematicians often need. This chapter focuses primarily on ParallelKnoppix, which is by far the easiest of the clustering setups, but it shows most of the problems you might run into with a Knoppix-based ad hoc cluster. ParallelKnoppix is perfect for the basement supercomputer, which is a great hack. If your problem can be solved using MPI (Message Passing Interface, an industry standard for parallel computing), ParallelKnoppix is for you. If it can't, ParallelKnoppix is a good learning experience. It presents a very gentle learning curve for handling all the basic components of clustering.

☑ Exploring cluster concepts

☑ Using ParallelKnoppix

☑ Understanding ClusterKnoppix

☑ Surveying other science-oriented Knoppix distros

Note Another type of cluster—the high-availability or fail-over cluster—involves pooling multiple computers, each of which is a candidate server for your filesystems, databases, or applications. In the event of failure in one of the cluster members, the others take over its services, usually in a way that makes it transparent to client systems accessing the data. That's a subject for another book. This chapter covers only parallel clusters.

Clustering is of special interest to system administrators, whose job is to configure the cluster with the libraries and services needed and then to maintain the system. Parallel programming would be another book entirely. The administrator's task in and of itself can be complex, and this chapter can only begin to cover it.

This chapter assumes that you're using Knoppix and its derived distros as a development platform, so, for example, $PATH values will be the default on Knoppix. Code will be written, whenever possible, as bash (Bourne Again Shell) shell scripts. The chapter also assumes that the purpose of your cluster is to do real work in an environment similar to a research group, in which the task of maintaining the cluster isn't the job of just one system administrator but several. The intent is to ensure that you have a maintainable system that doesn't depend on just one knowledgeable person. (It almost goes without saying that your system should be behind a firewall and be generally secure.)

After examining the basic concepts of clustering, you'll explore ParallelKnoppix and ClusterKnoppix distros and then take a look at some other science-related Knoppix derivations.

Understanding Basic Clustering Concepts

Clusters are meant to run "jobs" exclusively for a single user and often without interaction. A job scheduler manages the tasks, and libraries and programs manage the behavior of the task. It's basically that simple.

Why cluster systems? Some tasks are just too large not to have multiple systems calculate some aspect of a sizeable project or problem. Here is a simple example: I built a six-system (12-processor) cluster. The systems have Intel Pentium III 866MHz processors and 512MB of RAM per processor (not a fast system by today's standards). ClusterKnoppix was configured the first time on the entire cluster in about 15 minutes. As a test, a graphic rendering package called POV-Ray was used to render a benchmark file called `skyvase.pov`. (POV-Ray rendering is often referred to as an embarrassingly parallel application; it easily runs on a cluster because there aren't any cross-communication and other complexities associated with the process.) Running the benchmark on a single system took 1 minute, 24.5 seconds. Running the same benchmark across all 12 processors took 34 seconds. The point is pretty obvious: If the problem that you're trying to solve fits into the parallel computer model, you'll see a dramatic increase in computational speed and power.

A Linux cluster is a bunch of systems that share nothing; you can't read the memory on processor 0 on machine foo from processor 0 on machine bar. You could equivocate and say, "No, but there is fancy hardware MemFooBar that will do shared memory" (often called *shmem*), or "But I have a massive 64-way SMP system running Linux and I can see all the memory from any processor . . . some expert you are, Mr. Numbskull." That's not the kind of cluster that's being discussed here. This chapter is tackling cheap, ubiquitous PC-quality systems networked together with Ethernet. The most you're going to share is an NFS filesystem.

This sort of cluster, one made up of independent machines, was once complicated to set up and maintain. Now, thanks to Knoppix-derived distributions, you can set one up in a matter of minutes. In this chapter, you set up clusters using ParallelKnoppix and ClusterKnoppix, and then run various applications on them.

Understanding ParallelKnoppix

ParallelKnoppix is a live CD designed to make setting up ad-hoc clusters quick and easy. It's ideal for getting started with parallel computing; it only takes a few machines. It uses a form of clustering known as MPI (Message Passing Interface), which enables applications specifically designed for parallel computation to be run on several different processors or computers.

Note ParallelKnoppix was developed by Michael Creel at the Universitat Autonoma de Barcelona. Its homepage (`http://pareto.uab.es/mcreel/ParallelKnoppix/`) has links to ISO images you can download, and much more useful information.

Download an ISO image and burn it to a CD before continuing.

Setting Up ParallelKnoppix

ParallelKnoppix has pretty basic requirements:

- A master node, with CD-ROM, keyboard, mouse, network card, and a hard disk partition on which you can write. This machine can be a stock Windows installation using FAT32, or a Linux installation using ext3, ReiserFS, or any other filesystem. It just needs to be writable from Knoppix.

- From 1 to 200 slave nodes, with kernel-supported network cards and the capability to PXE boot. (PXE booting enables your computer to boot off the network instead of a hard drive or CD-ROM. You can find out more at `http://en.wikipedia.org/wiki/Pxe`.) You want these to all take the same boot-time arguments for Knoppix because they'll be booted homogeneously by default. You also need to know which kernel driver supports the network card.

- A reasonably fast network

- A single copy of the ParallelKnoppix CD, which enables you to create a cluster from 2 to 200 nodes

One thing to note right up front: ParallelKnoppix clusters are, by design, very insecure. You really don't want to run on an open network such as a campus computer lab. In addition, they depend on being the only DHCP/netboot server on the network, so pull the uplink to the outside network before you begin (just remember to plug it back in after you're finished with your crunching!). An astute reader might notice that there is no way to get your programs and data into the cluster; you'll deal with that in a second.

After you have all your equipment together, you're about 10 minutes from having your very own computer cluster. First, boot the master node with the ParallelKnoppix CD, just like you would if you were running Knoppix on the machine. Leave all the slaves off—they need to boot up after the master is configured. When the master node is up, you'll be at a normal KDE desktop, with a copy of the ParallelKnoppix home page on the screen. From the KDE menu, select ParallelKnoppix → Setup ParallelKnoppix. A series of windows appear to guide you through configuring your cluster.

This is where you'll need a list of required network drivers (I just accept the default list, and haven't run into any problems). Given how fast this process is, it's probably easier to just run through once to find any kinks, and then resolve them in the second pass. It's worth noting that your network will be configured as 192.168.0.0/255.255.255.0: If this conflicts with your existing network setup, you won't be able to use the network, which means you won't be able to set up a cluster. Unfortunately, there's no way to work around this, short of remastering the ParallelKnoppix distribution CD.

After the network is configured, you need to decide which existing partition on the master node to use. The setup program creates a directory named `parallel_knoppix_working` in the root of the partition unless the directory already exists. If it does exist, ParallelKnoppix just leaves it in place, creating a great place to stash things you want to keep across sessions. This directory is NFS-exported with relatively open permissions.

 Caution

Did I mention that this setup is insecure by design and that you want to be on your own private network segment? It really is, and you really do.

Further into the setup, a dialog box pops up informing you that "Now would be a good time to boot the slave nodes." Go ahead and do so. If you have machines in your cluster that require their own boot arguments, make sure they have keyboards and a monitor. Boot all your homogeneous machines, and then boot these special machines one by one. If you don't have monitors on all your nodes, be sure to wait a few minutes for the boot process to complete. After they're all booted, click OK in the dialog box. The setup program then SSHes into each slave machine as root to mount the NFS share. If you find that one of your machines isn't quite booted yet, you'll have to start the setup process over or try to limp along without that machine.

After all your slave nodes are booted, you return to the KDE desktop on the master node. From here, you can run one or two of the included demos to get a feel for things and then settle into a semi-permanent cluster.

Exploring ParallelKnoppix Demo Applications

ParallelKnoppix ships with a few good demo programs on the CD. These programs are a fine way to test a new cluster to make sure it's working. They're also a good learning experience: You can use them as bases for your own clustering applications.

Using Octave for Kernel Regression

GNU Octave is a numeric computation program, used to solve systems of equations. One of the unique features of ParallelKnoppix is an MPI-enabled version of Octave, which makes it a great environment for doing numeric analysis when your processing lends itself to parallelization. As a general rule of thumb, if you have multiple large, mostly independent steps in your processing, then you can parallelize your process. It might take some creativity, but it can (probably) be done.

Take a look at a kernel regression implemented in GNU Octave. If you're not a mathematician, this probably isn't the kernel you're thinking of: Octave is a numeric computation environment. In this context, a "kernel regression" is a fancy way of saying "curve fitting." If this is new to you, don't worry: It's still a good example of running an MPI program under ParallelKnoppix. That said, this problem is of special interest to math nerds.

First get things into shared space. You can do this really easily: On the KDE desktop is a link, named `parallel_knoppix_working`, that points at the working space. The example programs can also be found on the desktop, in the `ParallelKnoppix` directory. (That directory's icon isn't a folder, but a white square.). Open `ParallelKnoppix`, go into the `Examples` directory, and copy the `Octave` folder into the `parallel_knoppix_working` folder. Then open a shell window, and cd into the copied `Octave/kernel_regression/` directory. From there, run `octave` to start the Octave interpreter. Once you reach a new prompt, type **kernel_example1** and press Enter.

After a little while, you get a graph and its fit. Okay, it isn't the most visually stunning example, but it is a good test to ensure that your cluster is functional.

Calculating Pi

In the same vein, the pi sample program is an instructive case if you have an MPI application you'd like to compile on ParallelKnoppix. It's a simple demonstration of compiling an MPI application for use on a ParallelKnoppix cluster.

The pi example contains a neat technique for estimating pi: Instead of trying to do a lot of calculations, it simulates the "dartboard" technique, which is elegant in its own right. Imagine you have a square dartboard. Now, draw a circle centered on one of the corners with a radius equal to the side length of the square. This leaves a quarter-circle that covers the majority of the square's surface. Next, you throw darts at this board, keeping track of how many hit inside the quarter-circle and how many hit outside. Compare the areas and you see that there's a $(\pi r2/4)/r2 = \pi/4$ probability of a dart landing inside the circle. Just multiply the percentage of darts landing inside the circle by four, and you have an estimate of π! In a moment, you'll see just how accurate the estimate is.

As with the Octave example, begin by copying the `pi` directory into the shared working space. The `pi` folder is found in `ParallelKnoppix/Examples/C/pi/`; just copy that directory into the working folder. Switch to a console window, cd into the newly copied directory, and run `mpiCC -o pi pi_send.c dboard.c`. This command should create a pi binary.

Run the binary with `mpirun -np 4 ./pi`, a command that handles all the MPI-related voodoo that gets nodes to start running the application. All of these steps are shown in Figure 7-1.

FIGURE 7-1: A sample run of pi.

/dev/hdc1 was used for mounting in this example, so it became /mnt/hdc1 in the prompt. You need to replace it with the appropriate partition on your setup.

Getting Data into a ParallelKnoppix Cluster

You have source code and real datasets to move in and crunch, which is why you're interested in clustering, right? With the master node booted off a CD, and without a network, you face a problem: getting your data into the cluster. There are three basic methods, each with its own benefits and drawbacks.

First, Knoppix has excellent removable storage support: You can just schlep your material in on a USB or IEEE1394 drive. Plug the drive in, it is detected and mounted, and you just need to manually move things off the disk before you start (don't forget to move your results back onto the disk!). The removable storage method is a very simple, low-overhead way to get things into and out of your cluster. If your data is large, or you're stuck with USB 1.x devices, however, it might be too slow.

The second technique is the most obvious: Slap the data on a drive in the master node before you get going. This allows really fast access and makes it less likely that you'll forget to save your results after you finish. Unfortunately, it also requires opening the master node, or at least a lot of planning work with the master node. If you are using a computer lab in the middle of the night, you might not have time to do all that planning, but if you are in the lab, you thoughtfully removed the uplink, right? That should leave you a place to plug into the network, which leads to the third option.

The last technique is a nice compromise between the first two. Because ParallelKnoppix only supports 201 nodes, but practically requires its own /24 netblock, you have more than 50 free IP addresses to play with. Just bring in a fileserver laptop or desktop containing your data. You can then use CIFS/SMB to access your data on the master node. This enables you to do all your staging up front without worrying about the speed of the USB on your master node. As long as the network is reasonably fast, you can copy your working set to the master node in a matter of minutes, crunch your data, and then offload your results in a few minutes. If you need Internet access, adding a second network card to the fileserver enables you to set it up as a fire-wall of sorts. Not only does this protect your cluster from the network; it protects other nodes on the network from your master node (I use this technique, although I typically use my lap-top's wireless card as the upstream).

Creating a Semi-Permanent Cluster for Using ParallelKnoppix

The next challenge you face with ParallelKnoppix is settling in. If you're doing any long-term projects, you will invariably want to use the cluster for more than just one or two runs. Instead of compiling your application every time, it would be nice to just fire things up, load in your data, and run.

One option available is the new UnionFS support, which enables you to put new data onto the Knoppix CD, assuming that it's a CD-RW and that your master node has the appropriate CD-RW device. This is a good first attempt, but it has one minor drawback: It would be even better if your applications would work with any new version of the ParallelKnoppix CD. Then you could upgrade your cluster by just burning a new CD image. This would require some stor-age that won't change out from under you.

There are two obvious candidates: the storage you're carrying around in which your data resides and the hard disk you're using for your working directory. If your working directory won't dis-appear on you, it's a good first choice. In addition, because that path is the only shared space on the cluster, it's the best place to put any libraries, shared data, and so on, required by your soft-ware. Even if you need to use external storage to guarantee persistence, you will probably be putting your "constant stuff" into your working directory anyway.

After your ParallelKnoppix habits have settled in a bit, so that you use the same partition each time and know what applications you need, you can start firming your installation to match. Software can be downloaded and installed in the usual ways. For instance, the following exam-ple builds a new MPICH installation from ANL. You don't actually need the new MPICH, but there is a really neat demo program embedded, and it's typical of third-party build and installation. Here's what to do:

1. Go to the MPICH home page at `www-unix.mcs.anl.gov/mpi/mpich/`.

2. Go to the download page and download the source code (`mpich.tar.gz`) into a loca-tion on your hard disk.

3. Untar the file and go through a standard build process, but with the installation directory being the working directory. First, to set things up:

```
configure --prefix=/mnt/hdc4/parallel\_knoppix\_working/
```

Then, to build it:

```
make
```

Finally, to install the new MPICH:

```
make install
```

After all that, you can go on to build a very cool parallel-processing demo. Figure 7-2 shows the payoff: building and running `pmandel`, a parallel-processing Mandelbrot set viewer. There's hardly a more appropriate problem for a cluster. Because a fractal is computed pixel by pixel, you can just break the field of view into a bunch of independent rectangular regions. Each of those regions is sent to a cluster node, which then sends back the appropriate values to the master, which draws it in. If your cluster is slow enough, you can watch the output window as it splits into white rectangles, which are then filled in sequentially. To see just how much your cluster helps, try `mpirun -np 1 ./pmandel` to run a single process instead of the usual four. It's a stunning presentation of the power of parallel processing, perfect for demonstrations (when you're applying for funds, for example).

FIGURE 7-2: Beautiful results from a `pmandel` run

Now you should be able to use your cluster however you want. Even if you're not using ParallelKnoppix, the experience gained here gives you a good idea of how to proceed with another clustering setup.

Understanding ClusterKnoppix

ClusterKnoppix provides an easy-to-use openMosix master node and enables you to PXE boot your slave nodes. It was developed by Wim Vandersmissen and is available via its home page at `http://bofh.be/clusterknoppix/`.

OpenMosix is a clustering technology that enables a set of nodes to transparently share processes. If you start a bunch of processes that swamp one node, it passes them out to other nodes to share the load. This includes passing around IPC (Inter-Process Communication) file descriptors. You may know already just how involved this is. If you don't, just realize that it's really, really tricky.

Because openMosix enables any arbitrary process to be migrated, it provides a lot more power for general use. This lowers the bar for parallel programming: Any program that can split itself up into multiple processes can now take advantage of the cluster.

Are you ready to tackle this more powerful, slightly more complicated clustering technique? Then read on.

Setting Up ClusterKnoppix

ClusterKnoppix, once it boots up, drives much like any other Knoppix. Begin by starting the OpenMosix Terminal Server (from the KDE menu, select KNOPPIX → Services → Start openMosix Terminal Server). This starts a set of prompts, much like the setup for ParallelKnoppix. Following the defaults is a good choice, but don't start the client nodes just yet — there's a bit of command-line work to do first.

When running openMosix under ClusterKnoppix, you must do more manual bookkeeping up front. You need to run several commands to get the master node's openMosix setup running before you bring up the slave nodes. Otherwise, you'll have a cluster with no detected nodes (and a cluster of a single machine won't do you much good!). Start either `omdiscd` or `tyd`. These are openMosix discovery daemons that enable openMosix slave nodes to be "discovered" by the master node. `omdiscd` is a broadcast discovery daemon; it sends out broadcast packets to any machine on the network, asking "Are you my peer?" This can lead to some (serious) security problems, but on a private network it's not an issue. `tyd` uses (I am not making this up) the Terrence and Phillip protocol to ensure security. Basically, it uses unicast (directed) packets to keep things in sync. It also encrypts your data before it is sent, ensuring that nothing sensitive is visible on the wire.

Because `tyd` is more security conscious, it insists on a couple of things that you may or may not have in your network: a default gateway that works and a good grasp of `iptables` (the Linux kernel's software firewall and general packet-mangling framework). The latter is a real problem because the default rules `tyd` wants to use are overly restrictive. They make PXE booting slave nodes nearly impossible. To avoid the problem, always start `tyd` by telling it to initialize the packet filtering rules, and then to turn them off. This is done with the single command `sudo tyd -f init -f off`, as shown in the following steps.

I can see every foot of every network cable between my switch and my machines at home, so I just use `omdiscd`, with my laptop plugged in to the network, acting as a gateway. I use its wireless card as my outward-facing interface. Because I trust my network, and I control the firewall between my network and the outside world, I feel very safe using `omdiscd`. If I were running ClusterKnoppix in a computer lab, though, I would opt for the more secure, but more complicated, `tyd` setup.

You can use `omdiscd` and `tyd` together, which means there are no real problems with running one right after the other. Whichever you use, the following instructions should work for you. With the openMosix Terminal Server open, perform the following steps:

1. Open a new shell terminal.

2. Enter the following command:

   `sudo omdiscd or sudo tyd -f init -f off`.

3. After the daemon starts, open the openMosix Monitoring application (click on the little white penguin on the KDE panel). Your screen should look similar to the one shown in Figure 7-3.

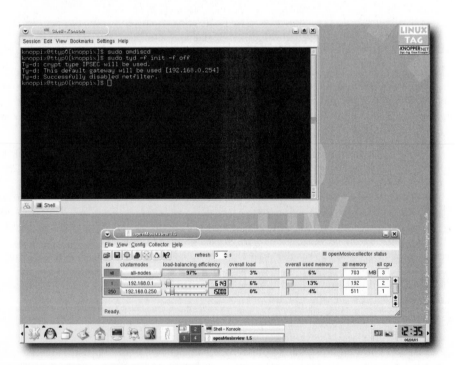

FIGURE 7-3: After booting the slave nodes

4. Boot up the slave nodes. As they join the cluster, they're appended to the list of available nodes.

After all the nodes are up and in the list, you can move on to the fun part: running applications on the cluster.

Note One quick aside on monitoring here. My kitchen cluster is made up of less-than-ideal hardware. I don't like running the overhead of the GUI monitor all the time, so I use `mosmon` on the command line. You can see it peeking out of the background in some of the screenshots; it's a great tool, and gives you a quick idea of your cluster's CPU utilization.

Exploring ClusterKnoppix Applications

Several ClusterKnoppix applications are available, although this chapter only introduces you to two: POV-Ray and John the Ripper. Search for others on your own and determine whether they'd help you out.

Using POV-Ray

POV-Ray is a ray-tracing computer rendering program. That is, it takes text files describing scenes, and renders them as three-dimensional spaces. Ray tracing is really neat because it works by simulating rays of light emanating from a light source, and tracks them as they bounce off surfaces. This creates stunningly realistic results by modeling real-world physics. Keeping track of all those light rays is also stunningly expensive in computational terms, which makes the program an attractive candidate for parallel processing.

To run POV-Ray as a parallel program, first start the PVM (Parallel Virtual Machine) daemon by running `pvm` and then `quit` out of the console it opens. Run your parallel POV-Ray ray-trace with this command:

```
povray -i /usr/share/doc/povray/povscn/level2/skyvase.pov +v1 ⤶
    +ft -x +a0.300 +r3 -q9 -mv2.0 -w1600 -h1200 -d +NT16
```

The last parameter, `+NT`, is the number of processes to begin. In general, try out a few smaller runs with different numbers of processes; I find that using a couple more threads than CPUs usually works best. In addition, you might want to change `-w` and `-h`, which are the width and height (in pixels) of the output image; processing time increases quickly as the image gets larger. The remaining parameters are settings for POV-Ray's rendering engine and are beyond the scope of this chapter. For more information on what they do, check out the POV-Ray manual (man `povray`).

Using John the Ripper

John the Ripper is a well-known password-auditing utility. It uses a brute-force attack to crack passwords, which is a great tool for making sure that your users are picking good ones. Because John the Ripper enables you to obtain users' passwords, you should be aware of any privacy, policy, or legal issues with the use of this tool in your jurisdiction or place of employment.

John the Ripper, while not a "scientific" application, is a good example of clustering. It too is from an earlier generation of software, with a slightly convoluted build process. If you've ever compiled scientific software, you've probably run into these sorts of things. If you haven't, this program is a good, gentle introduction to the kinds of issues you'll have to deal with.

Understanding John

First, a bit of background on what John the Ripper does, for those who are new to it. Passwords are typically stored in hashed form, meaning that the original, plaintext password isn't available in a file anywhere — only a hash and a salt value are stored. Whenever someone types in his or her password, the system gets the salt value, and combines it with the password given in a hashing process. The computer then compares the output to what's stored in the password file. If they match, it's almost certainly the correct password, so the user is authenticated. In its brute-force attack, John the Ripper tries a bunch of possible passwords in sequence. It starts with "a", then "b", "c", and so on, working its way up to long, arbitrary strings of characters. Needless to say, this exhaustive search takes a long, long time. Take a ballpark figure of 40 character options available for each password character of an 8-digit password, and that's 40^8 possible passwords — 6.5×10^{12} unique strings to check!

One way to speed up the process is to keep a dictionary of possible passwords, and work through that. Even with a dictionary, brute-force password discovery is a very computationally intensive process. Thankfully, each guess is totally independent of the other guesses, making this a perfect candidate for parallelization. John the Ripper doesn't include an explicitly parallel mode, but it does come with a built-in rule language and a rule that enables you to split up a cracking session.

Setting Up John

John the Ripper isn't included with ClusterKnoppix, so you need to download and compile the program, and download a dictionary to start from as well. First, create a build directory to work in. Because you typically want to audit passwords every few months, creating the build directory on a hard disk is recommended, so you won't have to rebuild John the Ripper every time you want to run it. If you usually have more than one program installed, make a generic src directory on your disk:

```
mkdir /mnt/hdc4/src/
```

Follow that with the following:

```
cd /mnt/hdc4/src
```

Then fetch a new copy of the John source code:

```
wget http://www.openwall.com/john/c/john-1.6.tar.gz
```

After the file downloads, unpack the source code:

```
tar xzvf john-1.6.tar.gz
```

John is an older UNIX application, and it doesn't have a configure script. Instead, you must use a slightly old-fashioned build interface. First change directories (cd john-1.6/src/), and then run make, which will give you a list of options for build targets. This example uses Linux x86 with MMX, so the following command compiles the program:

```
make linux-x86-mmx-elf
```

You're going to see a bunch of errors, which is perfectly normal. Don't worry about installing the software: It's best to leave it in the src directory and use it from there, ensuring that you won't lose the program later. If you plan to use a more permanent master node, you can install it there, but the rest of this example assumes the binaries are left where John's makefile created them.

After the program compiles, download a dictionary to use. The de facto standard dictionary is all.gz, available at ftp://ftp.openwall.com/pub/wordlists/all.gz. Use the following to fetch it into the John directory:

```
cd /mnt/hdc4/src/john-1.6/
wget ftp://ftp.openwall.com/pub/wordlists/all.gz
```

Configure your copy of John the Ripper to tell it how many nodes you have. By default, John assumes you have two nodes: If this is the case for you, skip this paragraph. To change the number of nodes in the cluster, you need to manually edit the john.ini config file in the run/ directory. Open the file in your favorite text editor. Toward the bottom is a line reading total = 2;. Change the number 2 to the number of nodes you have.

With John the Ripper compiled, a dictionary installed, and the number of nodes configured, the installation is finished. Next you'll create a password, extract its hash, and finally crack that password.

Running John

Begin cracking by setting a new password for user knoppix on the ClusterKnoppix machine. For this example, choose something relatively simple, such as bottle, to ensure that you won't spend hours waiting for John to stumble across it. To set the password, run the following:

```
sudo passwd knoppix
```

Enter the new password twice when prompted. Then create an unshadowed version of the password file. In modern UNIX and Linux systems, the /etc/passwd file doesn't actually contain the password hashes. Those are stored in a *shadow* of the password file, which is readable only by root or the shadow user. To crack the password without running John as root, you must create a password file containing hashes that you, a normal user, can read. To store the unshadowed results in /tmp/unshadow, run the following:

```
john-1.6/run/unshadow /etc/passwd /etc/shadow > /tmp/unshadow
```

This gives you a set of hashes to work with, and you can now begin cracking passwords. From within the john-1.6/run/ directory, run the following:

```
./john -rules -external:parallel -wordfile:../all /tmp/unshadow
```

As shown in Figure 7-4, processing is distributed nicely among the nodes.

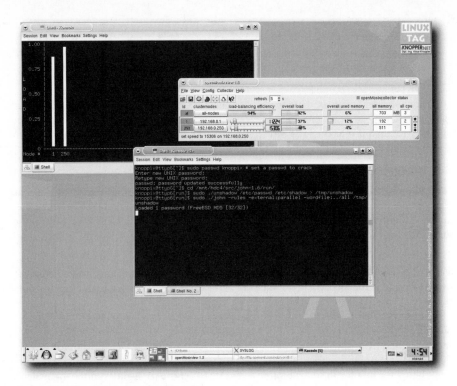

FIGURE 7-4: Running John on two nodes

The results should be displayed in the window from which you ran John. If you miss them for any reason, don't worry; John creates and saves a file containing the password and hash pairs it found in the directory from which it ran so that it can just look up hashes during future runs — a real time-saver. If you miss John's output or need to review your session, you can always use the -show option to get a copy of your results.

It is hoped that you're now comfortable building and running custom software on your openMosix cluster. Between this and the MPI system covered with ParallelKnoppix earlier in the chapter, you have the base knowledge required to set up many common parallel applications for your research or hobby. (If nothing else, you've got some bragging rights: How many people can say they've got a compute cluster at home?)

A Glance at Other Science-Oriented Knoppix Variants

Scientists can always use good operating systems. We've examined ParallelKnoppix and ClusterKnoppix, which are both extremely useful for computationally heavy science and math research. Following are some other Knoppix-derived, science-oriented distributions that may be helpful to you.

BioKnoppix

BioKnoppix is a Knoppix-derived distribution that includes many biology tools, such as Artemis, Bioconductor, Bioperl, BioPython, ClustalX, Cn3D, EMBOSS, ImageJ, Jemboss, and Rasmol. It is a product of the University of Puerto Rico's High Performance Computing facility, and its home page is `http://bioknoppix.hpcf.upr.edu/`.

DistCCKnoppix

DistCCKnoppix is a tiny Knoppix derivative developed by James Greenhalgh of Open Door Software. At the time of writing, it is just 50MB, but it can boot a computer into distcc slave mode, allowing for distributed compilation of programs. Its home page is `http://opendoorsoftware.com/cgi/http.pl?cookies=1&p=distccKNOPPIX`.

Morphix-NLP

Morphix-NLP is a Morphix-derived LiveCD containing many Natural Language Processing tools, created by Zhang Le of China's Northeastern University NLP Lab. It includes many packages at all levels of language processing, from tokenization to machine learning. Its home page is `http://morphix-nlp.berlios.de/`.

It includes the following applications: AntConc, Brill's TBL Tagger, CMU-Cambridge Statistical Language Modeling Toolkit v2, Collins Parser, Festival, fnTBL, fnTBL tagger, ICTCLAS, Link Grammar, LoPar, Maximum Entropy Modeling Toolkit, Memory Based Tagger, MXPOST, MXTERMINATOR, Ngram Statistics Package, N-gram tools, QTag, Qtoken, SNoW (Sparse Network of Winnows), SVM-light, Tilburg Memory Based Learner, Tree-Tagger, Trigger Toolkit, and unaccent.

PaiPix

PaiPix is a general science-oriented Knoppix derivative. It includes the usual suspects (Grass GIS, R, and LaTeX), as well as an MPI implementation. Most interestingly, it also supports AFS, enabling you to access data stored in an AFS cell. It was developed by the Post-Graduate Course of Applied Programming and Instrumentation of the College of Sciences of the University of Lisbon, and its home page is `http://aamorimsrv.fis.fc.ul.pt/`.

It includes the following applications: AMIDE, Ant, Dia, Festival, freeFem, freeFem3D, GCC Version 4 (including FORTRAN and Java support), GEANT3, gEDA, Gmsh, GMT, GrADS, Grass, HERWIG, ISAJET, Jikes, Kaffe (pthreads), Kile, KPovModeler, LAM4, LAPACK, LaTeX, Maxima, MPI (MPICH), MySQL, NGSPICE, Octave, omniORB, OpenAFS, Opensched, PAW (CERN), pcb, PostgreSQL, PVM, PYTHIA, QMTest, R, RTAI, Scilab, TeXmacs, Umbrello, Verilog, Vis5d, VTK, and XMedCon.

Quantian

Quantian is a ClusterKnoppix-derived distribution with a strong focus on numeric analysis. It comes with many mathematical packages installed by default, including a full LaTeX environment. It can also be used to create OpenMosix clusters. It was created by Dirk Eddelbuettel, and its homepage is `http://dirk.eddelbuettel.com/quantian.html`.

It includes the following applications: Axiom, BioConductor, BioPERL, Biopython, Blast2, Bochs, Cernlib, ClustalW, EMBOSS, FreeFem, GAP, GGobi, GiNaC, GMT, Grass, GSL, HMMER, Inline::Octave, Kile, Lyx, Maxima, Mayavi, MPI (MPICH), Numeric Python, Octave, OpenDX, Pari/GP, QEMU, QuantLib, R (including most of CRAN), SciPy, TeXmacs, Wine, and YaCaS.

Summary

This chapter includes the design for a cluster using Knoppix and Knoppix-derived cluster distros. With the advent of UnionFS and other tools, Knoppix is a good alternative for building a quick cluster system. Because Knoppix is a live-CD distro, its performance won't be as good as other architectures, but for speed of development and flexibility, it's straightforward to configure, can be designed to be dynamic, and is growing in popularity. With a little planning, a Knoppix cluster integrates well into an existing environment.

Checking Out
Security Distros

O
ne of the great things about Knoppix is that it's a general-purpose distro. You can do a gazillion different things with it, and that's one of its strengths. However, there's also something to be said for specialization, and the distros in this chapter are single-minded about one thing: security. Each of these distros focuses solely on security, but that doesn't mean they're all the same. Granted, there is a lot of overlap here (each distro has Nmap and SSH, for instance), but each distro also has a different focus and a unique set of tools.

In the same way that Knoppix is free, making it worth your while to try out, each of these distros is free for the download. Grab 'em, burn 'em, and boot 'em — you have no excuse!

Inspecting Auditor

When you first boot Auditor, you're going to be blown away by the amazingly well-structured K menu. The folks behind Auditor have done a simply incredible job organizing the various tools they provide so that everything is easy to find and presented in a logical fashion. Figure 8-1 shows an example of Auditor menus.

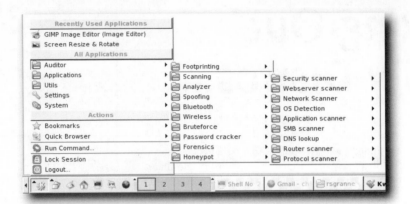

FIGURE 8-1: Now that is good menuing!

As you can see, everything is broken down into the major tasks you'd want in a distro focused on security checking, which is Auditor's goal. It wants to be the Live CD you use when you need to check out a network or machine to figure out what's going on. In particular, it has a lot of good scanning tools, especially wireless scanning tools, and 64 million entries in word lists that you can use for brute-force password cracking. Best of all, the main developer — a guy named Max Moser — seems to work hard to keep Auditor up-to-date, with regular changes and tweaks. He details his progress at http://new.remote-exploit.org/index.php/Auditor_devlog. Bookmark that page and view it often to see what's new and different.

Note If you find that you like Auditor and want to help the developers out, you can give them money by visiting their Website and clicking the Make a Donation button.

To acquire Auditor, head over to the project's home page, http://new.remote-exploit.org/index.php/Auditor_main; scroll down to the Downloads section; and click the link for the list of download mirrors. Download the zipped ISO (about 525MB) from one of the sites, unzip it, burn the ISO, boot with it, and you're ready to go.

Following are three tips that will come in handy when you start to use the feature-packed Auditor distro:

■ How to not run Konsole as root: When you open a terminal in Auditor, it always opens as root. Generally this is fine with Auditor because most of the useful command-line tools you need should be run as root anyway. However, if you mount your local drive to write data to it, you may want to take safeguards. To become a nonroot user in Konsole, just type su knoppix and press Enter. You're now running without root privileges; to become root again, enter **exit** and press Enter.

- Why won't your wireless card work? If you want to get online wirelessly, and especially if you want to use the cool wireless security tools that Auditor provides, you're going to need a supported wireless card. Auditor supplies a list of recommended wireless cards (both WiFi and Bluetooth) at http://new.remote-exploit.org/index.php/Auditor_FAQ; a longer list of devices known to work, including laptops, USB wireless adapters, PCMCIA wireless adapters, mini-PCI wireless cards (the ubiquitous Intel Centrino falls into this category), Bluetooth adapters, and even GPS devices can be found at http://new.remote-exploit.org/index.php/Auditor_dev_list1.

- So that you don't go crazy . . . If you want to view the files on your system using a GUI, don't bother selecting the Home icon on the panel because it doesn't work. This should be fixed, it is hoped by the time you're reading this book, but if it isn't, here's what to do: Instead of the Home icon, select the Konqueror icon, and then click the Home icon on the toolbar. Bang! Konqueror goes into file manager mode, and you can browse your files.

There are many, many tools on the Auditor distro, so you really must play with it at length, spending some time trying out all the myriad software options. The following sections describe a few of those tools, just to whet your appetite.

Scanning Your Web Servers with Nikto

Nowadays it seems like everyone is running a Website; unfortunately, it also seems like another Website gets broken into and defaced just about every day. It's important to try to prevent embarrassing and potentially dangerous Website hacks, and Nikto helps do the job. Nikto is a constantly updated open-source tool that, as its Website describes, tests for "over 3,200 potentially dangerous files/CGIs, versions on over 625 servers, and version-specific problems on over 230 servers." Run it against your Web server, and you may just find holes about which you knew nothing.

Caution

Do not run Nikto against any ol' server that you feel like scanning because you could be the subject of an unpleasant visit from the authorities. Instead, confine it to Websites and servers that are under your control. When in doubt, ask first.

To start Nikto, from the K menu select Auditor → Scanning → Webserver scanning → Nikto. Konsole opens, and the various options available for Nikto appear. Take a look through them if you're interested, but to get started, just enter the following in the terminal, substituting your Website's domain name for www.webserver.com.

```
# nikto -h www.webserver.com
```

Author's Experience

I used a Lucent Orinoco Gold (yes, I know it's ancient, but it's my Old Faithful because it works with virtually any Linux distro), and although Auditor saw the card, I didn't get an IP address automatically. I first ran `ifconfig` to find out which device Auditor thought my Orinoco was. Once I saw that it was eth0, I ran `pump -i eth0` to ask my router to assign the card an IP address using DHCP. After another `ifconfig` command to ensure that yes, I was now 192.168.0.102, I was ready to go. If you can't get online with your wireless card, and you know that Auditor supports it, try that sequence of commands and see whether that fixes your problem.

Be patient as you let Nikto do its work. It'll take some time, but you eventually get some interesting results. For instance, here's what came back from one scanned Web:

```
- Nikto 1.32/1.23      -     www.cirt.net
+ Target IP:      [IP address redacted]
+ Target Hostname: [Domain name redacted]
+ Target Port:      80
+ Start Time:      Fri Apr 28 04:52:05 2005
---------------------------------------------------------------
- Scan is dependent on "Server" string which can be faked, use -g to override
+ Server: Apache/1.3.33 (Darwin) PHP/5.0.1 mod_ssl/2.8.22 OpenSSL/0.9.7b
+ /robots.txt - contains 7 'disallow' entries which should be manually viewed
(added to mutation filelists) (GET).
+ Allowed HTTP Methods: GET, HEAD, POST, PUT, DELETE, CONNECT, OPTIONS, PATCH,
PROPFIND, PROPPATCH, MKCOL, COPY, MOVE, LOCK, UNLOCK, TRACE
+ HTTP method 'PUT' method may allow clients to save files on the web server.
+ HTTP method 'CONNECT' may allow server to proxy client requests.
+ HTTP method 'DELETE' may allow clients to remove files on the web server.
+ HTTP method 'PROPFIND' may indicate DAV/WebDAV is installed. This may be used
to get directory listings if indexing is allowed but a default page exists.
+ HTTP method 'PROPPATCH' may indicate DAV/WebDAV is installed.
+ HTTP method 'TRACE' is typically only used for debugging. It should be
disabled.
+ Apache/1.3.33 appears to be outdated (current is at least Apache/2.0.47).
Apache 1.3.28 is still maintained and considered secure.
+ OpenSSL/0.9.7b appears to be outdated (current is at least 0.9.7c) (may depend
on server version)
+ 2.8.22 OpenSSL/0.9.7b - TelCondex Simpleserver 2.13.31027 Build 3289 and below
allow directory traversal with '/.../' entries.
+ mod_ssl/2.8.2 - mod_ssl 2.8.7 and lower are vulnerable to a remote buffer
overflow which may allow a remote shell (difficult to exploit). CAN-2002-0082.
+ /~root - Enumeration of users is possible by requesting ~username (responds
with Forbidden for realusers, not found for non-existent users) (GET).
```

There's a lot more than this. Consider it just a taste of all the great info you can get with nikto. For more pointers on using Nikto, be sure to read man `nikto` and visit the project's home page at `http://cirt.net/code/nikto.shtml`.

Sniffing Packets with the Snarfs

This story really happened, and it explains just how you can use various tools that come with Auditor to sniff packets on a wireless network, potentially to devastating consequences. I was at my buddy Ben's house, using his wireless network and writing the portion of this chapter about Auditor. Ben and his fiancée were talking in his office and looking at Ben's computer screen. Ben's machine was also wirelessly connected to the Net.

From the dining room, I asked, "Hey, Ben! Mind if I eavesdrop on what you're doing for my book?" He gave his assent, and so I started by firing up Mailsnarf, part of the excellent dsniff package, opening the K menu, and selecting Auditor→Analyzer→Applications→Mailsnarf. A Konsole window opened, and in it I typed the following command:

```
# mailsnarf -i eth0 . "tcp"
```

I used eth0 with the -i (interface) because I knew that Auditor had assigned that device ID to my wireless card by running the ifconfig command. "tcp" tells dsniff what kind of traffic to sniff, using the same terminology that tcpdump and ethereal use. Finally, the . (period) in the command looks for all emails going by; if I wanted to limit Mailsnarf's activity to certain emails, I could use a search word or phase instead, like this:

```
# mailsnarf -i eth0 password "tcp"
```

After a few minutes, the following email popped up in Konsole (I redacted the domain names for privacy's sake):

```
From mailsnarf Sat Apr 30 00:40:41 2005

Return-Path: <Jans@DOMAIN.com>

Delivered-To: jans-DOMAIN:com-Ben@DOMAIN.com

X-Envelope-To: ben@DOMAIN.com

Received: (qmail 6440 invoked from network); 30 Apr 2005 00:39:19 -0000

Received: from relay03.pair.com (209.68.5.17)

  by chanas.pair.com with SMTP; 30 Apr 2005 00:39:19 -0000

Received: (qmail 91563 invoked from network); 30 Apr 2005 00:39:18 -
0000

Received: from unknown (HELO ?192.168.1.3?) (unknown)

  by unknown with SMTP; 30 Apr 2005 00:39:18 -0000

X-pair-Authenticated: 69.155.165.22

Mime-Version: 1.0 (Apple Message framework v622)

Content-Transfer-Encoding: 7bit
```

Continued

Continued

```
Message-Id: <79fa9de385e470b11d6f0d585d388caf@DOMAIN.com>

Content-Type: text/plain; charset=US-ASCII; format=flowed

To: Ben Jones <Ben@DOMAIN.com>

From: Jans Carton <Jans@DOMAIN.com>

Subject: Wedding plans

Date: Fri, 29 Apr 2005 19:39:17 -0500

X-Mailer: Apple Mail (2.622)


Ben, I forgot when your wedding is (sorry!)

Can you tell me the date again?

Thanks.

Jans
```

Well, that explained what Ben and his fiancée were doing on Ben's computer: looking at wedding stuff. I thought I'd use URLsnarf to see what Websites they were checking out. I opened the K menu and selected Auditor→Analyzer→Applications→URLsnarf. Another Konsole window opened, and I entered the following command:

```
# urlsnarf -i eth0 . tcp
```

In a few seconds, the URLs accessed by my friends began to stream by, including the following:

```
192.168.1.107 - - [30/Apr/2005:00:07:12 -0400] "GET
http://www.modestapparelchristianclothinglydiaofpurpledressescustom
sewing.com/wedding_dresses_topaz_backview.jpg HTTP/1.1" - -
"http://www.modestapparelchristianclothinglydiaofpurpledressescustom
sewing.com/wedding_dresses.htm" "Mozilla/5.0 (Windows; U; Windows NT
5.1; en-US; rv:1.7.7) Gecko/20050414 Firefox/1.0.3"

192.168.1.107 - - [30/Apr/2005:00:07:12 -0400] "GET
http://www.modestapparelchristianclothinglydiaofpurpledressescustom
sewing.com/wedding_dresses_melissa.jpg HTTP/1.1" - -
"http://www.modestapparelchristianclothinglydiaofpurpledressescustom
sewing.com/wedding_dresses.htm" "Mozilla/5.0 (Windows; U; WindowsNT
5.1; en-US; rv:1.7.7) Gecko/20050414 Firefox/1.0.3"

192.168.1.107 - - [30/Apr/2005:00:07:12 -0400] "GET
http://www.modestapparelchristianclothinglydiaofpurpledressescustom
sewing.com/wedding_dresses_melissa_small.jpg HTTP/1.1" - -
"http://www.modestapparelchristianclothinglydiaofpurpledressescustom
sewing.com/wedding_dresses.htm" "Mozilla/5.0 (Windows; U; Windows NT
5.1; en-US; rv:1.7.7) Gecko/20050414 Firefox/1.0.3"
```

```
192.168.1.107 - - [30/Apr/2005:00:07:12 -0400] "GET
http://www.modestapparelchristianclothinglydiaofpurpledressescustomsewi
ng.com/favicon.ico HTTP/1.1" - - "-" "Mozilla/5.0 (Windows; U; Windows
NT 5.1; en-US; rv:1.7.7) Gecko/20050414 Firefox/1.0.3"
```

Now, before you ask, the engaged couple were not intending to head to the Website with the longest URL I've ever seen—www.modestapparelchristianclothinglydiaofpurple dressescustomsewing.com—but instead stumbled across it after a Google search. They found the site interesting, and began to surf around. I heard them exclaim at several of the dresses they saw, so I thought I'd view just what was inspiring their noise. I fired up Driftnet by opening the K menu and selecting Auditor → Analyzer → Applications → Driftnet. A command-line window opened, and I entered the following:

```
# driftnet -i eth0
```

Another window opened, and in it began to shoot by the images Ben and his fiancée were seeing on his computer, as the following figure shows.

Driftnet in action, showing a variety of wedding dresses.

Continued

Continued

Driftnet's display window doesn't include a scrollbar, so if a picture zooms past, you can't scroll up to see it. Fortunately, Driftnet wants to save the pictures that it captures, in addition to displaying them to you, but there's a problem: The default directory you're in when the Driftnet Konsole window opens is `/root`, which is actually in your RAM and will fill up quickly. If you really want to save the images Driftnet sees, tell the program to use another directory (on your hard drive or a USB flash drive) by using the following command:

```
# driftnet -i eth0 -d /mnt/hda2/driftnet_pix
```

I quietly left Ben and Tracy at the computer, happily planning their wedding. (Congratulations, you two!)

Remember, Ben and Tracy knew that I was watching them the whole time, so this little story isn't as creepy as it might seem. They actually found it kind of funny yet worrisome that their wireless Internet access was so wide open. Your average wireless coffeehouse is just as wide open, and virtually none of the patrons realizes it.

Note   To learn more about Mailsnarf, try `man mailsnarf`; for URLsnarf, try—you guessed it!— `man urlsnarf`. Both tools are part of the dsniff suite, and a visit to the dsniff home page provides a bit more info, but not much: `http://monkey.org/~dugsong/dsniff`. A longer look at dsniff can be found at `http://ouah.org/dsniffintr.htm`. Definitely look into dsniff—I only covered a fraction of what it can do.

For more on Driftnet, a separate tool from dsniff, use `man driftnet` or `driftnet -h`, and be sure to visit the home page, at `http://ex-parrot.com/~chris/driftnet/`.

Detecting and Sniffing Wireless Networks with Kismet

Ever wonder how you could discover a wireless network? Enter Kismet.

To start Kismet, open the K menu and select Auditor ➔ Wireless ➔ Scanner/Analyzer ➔ Kismet tools ➔ GKismet (gkismet is a GTK GUI for Kismet). Choose a data directory, in which Kismet will store the packet database it's going to create. Select a folder on your hard drive if you can (make sure you can write to it), or point at a mounted USB flash drive. When you're asked about a file prefix, leave the default in place and click OK.

Gkismet opens, and it immediately detects any wireless networks in the area. Figure 8-2 shows quite a few—the gkismet user is probably near an apartment building.

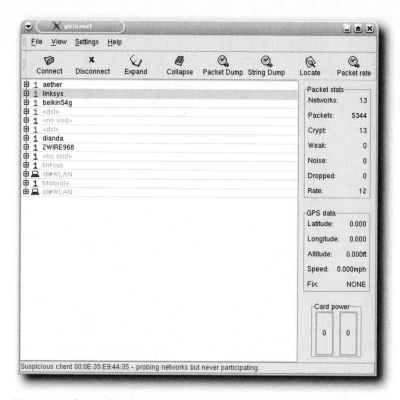

FIGURE 8-2: Gkismet has found quite a number of wireless networks near me.

Kismet is such a rich tool that it could easily be the subject of its own book. The Locate button, for example, actually maps the physical location of each Wireless Access Point (WAP) it discovers, if you have a working GPS device installed. This capability obviously makes Kismet perfect for wardriving.

Expand one of the nodes (see Figure 8-3), and you find a wealth of detail about that WAP.

There is an almost infinite list of things you can do with Kismet. It's one of those tools that you really need to learn how to use if you want to become a wireless security master. One of the coolest things about Auditor is that is makes it easy to start learning how to use this wonderfully powerful software.

Note Kismet's Website (http://kismetwireless.net/) is a gold mine of useful information about this software. If you have any questions about Kismet, start there. Of course, man kismet doesn't hurt either.

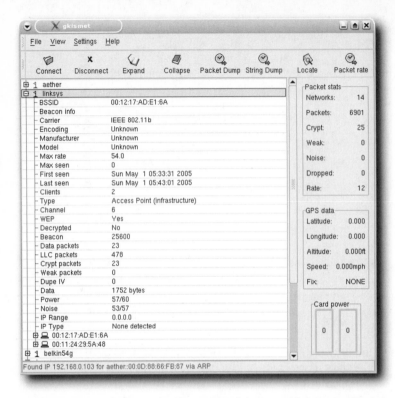

FIGURE 8-3: You can find out a lot about a Wireless Access Point using Kismet.

Tip

Auditor is unique among the distros examined in this chapter in that it has been reviewed, and many of those reviews contain interesting and useful tidbits of information. In particular, read "Product Review: Moser Informatik Auditor Security Collection (Auditor)" at www.tomsnetworking.com/Reviews-154-ProdID-AUDITOR.php, WindowsITPro's "The Auditor Security Collection," at http://windowsitpro.com/Windows/Articles/ArticleID/44648/pg/1/1.html, and TheSecure.Net blog, which has posts discussing Auditor at http://thesecure.net/blog/archives/2004_05.html (be sure to scroll down and read all the posts about Auditor and some of the other Live CDs discussed in this chapter). And here's a final tip: I didn't have space here, but if you start playing with Auditor, make sure you check out hotspotter.

Exploring Helix

Helix has two claims to fame: a sharp focus on Incident Response and Forensics, and that it is used by the world famous SANS (SysAdmin, Audit, Network, Security) Institute during training in "System Forensics, Investigation, and Response." Because it's used by SANS, Helix is kept up to date; as of this writing, the latest release is March 2005.

Helix has been carefully calibrated so that it does not touch the host computer in any way, leaving the machine and its contents forensically sound. In other words, Helix does not automount the host machine's swap space, and it does not automount devices such as hard drives and USB flash drives.

Another cool feature of Helix is that it contains a lot of neat tools for working with Windows computers in addition to the infinitude available for *nix boxes. Getting Helix is easy: Just head over to www.e-fense.com/helix/downloads.php and grab the ISO image using HTTP, FTP, or BitTorrent. Burn the ISO image to a CD, boot your computer with it, and you're ready to use Helix.

Helix uses the Xfce window manager (yes, yet another window manager . . . remember, no one said that consistency was an overriding goal of these different distros). A taskbar along the top of your screen displays open applications and files, while the bottom contains the Xfce menu, which is a Startlike menu; a clock; various system diagnostic tool; and links to common programs.

Tip

For some reason, the default color scheme for Konsole in Helix produces unreadable text. The solution is to select Settings → Schema, and change from Transparent, Dark Background to White on Black. Ah, much better!

If you need more aid with Xfce, select Xfce → Help for an HTML-based manual that covers all of basics and then some.

Helix comes with hundreds of extremely useful security tools (the full list is at http://e-fense.com/helix/contents.php), organized into the following categories:

- Incident response and forensics
- Network utilities
- Servers
- Packet sniffers and assemblers
- Vulnerability assessment
- Wireless tools

Keep in mind that many tools run via the command line, so they won't show up on the Xfce menu. Check out the complete list of software, and then investigate everything that interests you. It's a feast, so dig in, and don't worry about being gluttonous. The next few sections discuss some of the available tools.

Imaging a Hard Drive with GRAB

When you're performing a forensic analysis of a compromised machine, one of the first things you usually need to do is make an image of the hard drive that you can examine. Although the command-line tool dd can be used, GRAB — a program created by e-fense, the developers of Helix — has several nice features, including the following, which are listed in the Helix manual:

- Autodetection of IDE and SCSI drives, CDROMs, and tape drives
- Choice of using either dd, dcfldd, or sdd
- Image verification between source and copy via MD5 or SHA1
- Image compression/decompression via gzip/bzip2
- Image over a TCP/IP network via Netcat/Cryptcat, or SAMBA (NetBIOS)
- Support for SCSI tape drives
- Wiping (zeroing) drives or partitions
- Splitting images into multiple segments
- Detailed logging with date/times and complete command line

To start GRAB, just click the program's icon, located on the Xfce panel at the bottom of your screen. Once it opens (see Figure 8-4), you'll see that GRAB isn't hard to use at all.

In particular, GRAB makes it easy to copy your disk image over a network to another machine. For more details about this feature, and many of the other nice things that GRAB can do for you, refer to the Helix manual, available at http://e-fense.com/helix/HELIX-Manual.pdf.

Finding All the Images on a Drive with Retriever

Helix comes with Retriever, a tool unique to its distro, which finds certain kinds of files and gathers them together so that you can look them over at your leisure. To start the program, just click the Retriever icon (which looks like a close-up of a dog's nose) on the Xfce panel. When it opens, you're immediately given more details about the program. Just click OK to close that alert. You choose whether to have Retriever place the files it finds when it scans the hard drive on a USB flash drive or /images/retriever, a hard-coded path. If you choose the latter, Retriever does not actually copy the files, but simply creates soft links pointing back to the files it finds. Choosing /images/retriever makes things easy.

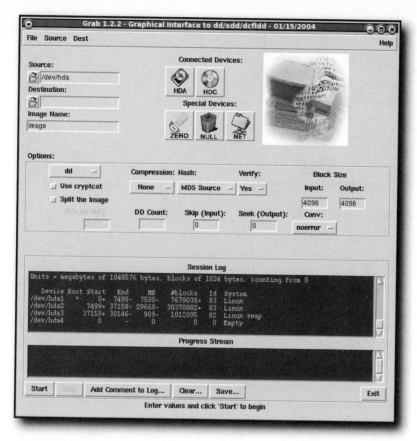

FIGURE 8-4: GRAB gives you a simple way to image a hard drive.

Caution

No matter what you choose, make sure you have enough storage, whether on the USB drive or in RAM, to hold everything that Retriever discovers.

Now choose where you want Retriever to look. For this example, a test directory called `/mnt/hda2/rsgranne/retriever_test` was created and then populated with files of the following types: `.jpg`, `.doc`, `.xls`, `.pdf`, and `.avi`. After `retriever_test` (or whatever your directory is named) is loaded, you can tell the program to look there.

Finally, you select the kinds of files you want to find, as shown in Figure 8-5.

FIGURE 8-5: What kinds of files do you want
Retriever to find today?

Retriever will look for images, movies, office documents, and email. Make your choice, click
OK, and Retriever begins to work.

Note

Retriever doesn't depend on file extensions, which can be completely off base, but instead actually looks at the file type (equivalent to using the `file` command) to determine what kind of
files it's examining. Unfortunately, Retriever doesn't yet look for files that have been deleted, but
that's supposedly coming in a future version.

When a file is found, Retriever lists it in a results window, and also displays a thumbnail of any
images in the file manager. Once it completes its task, you can view what it has found (see
Figure 8-6).

If you had Retriever copy everything to a USB flash drive, you now possess exact copies of the
files that Retriever located, which you can examine at any time. As you can see, Retriever is
quite useful now, and it should continue to improve as the Helix developers work on it further.

Working on a Live Windows Machine

Helix offers a feature that is incredibly powerful, useful, and cool: the capability to use the distro on a live Windows system, without rebooting. That's right — just stick the Helix CD in,
and in a few seconds Helix is running (see Figure 8-7).

Note

If you have automount turned off — a wise choice — you will need to open the CD manually by
going to My Computer, your CD-ROM, and then double-clicking `helix.exe`.

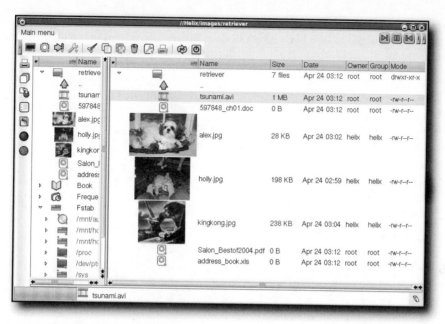

FIGURE 8-6: Retriever displays its finds.

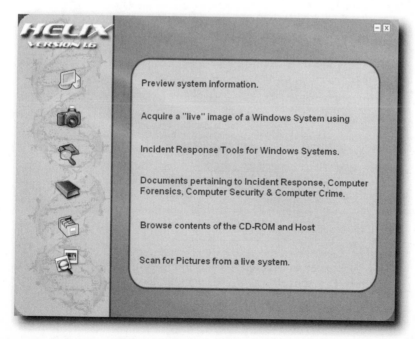

FIGURE 8-7: Helix enables you to perform several tasks on a running Windows machine.

Gathering Information

There's a lot you can do with Helix on a Windows machine, but the most interesting—and fun!—things are found when you click the third icon from the top, the one that reveals Incident Response Tools. The first screen is shown in Figure 8-8.

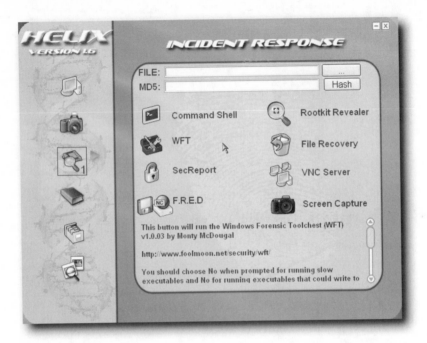

FIGURE 8-8: Eight invaluable tools for recovering computers running Windows

Create a security report about your Windows machine by selecting SecReport from the list. Choose where the report's files should go. A: is the default, but you really don't want to do that unless you enjoy waiting for floppies to slooooowly write their data. Better to choose a USB flash drive, or a folder on the machine's hard drive, such as C:\secreport.

Caution Make sure the directory you enter actually exists, or SecReport will not write any files. (Yes, that is annoying and something that should be fixed.)

Click OK. Do you want to update information on hotfixes? If you think that's important, choose Yes; otherwise, leave the default, No, and click OK. You're asked one final time if you want to run the report, so click OK here too. A command prompt window opens, SecReport does its work, and you then press any key to close the command prompt.

In C:\secreport (or wherever you saved the report's files), you'll find two files: security report.xsl and VIRGIL_20050426.xml (the second filename is a concatenation of your machine's name and the date). Open the XML file (VIRGIL_20050426.xml in this example) in a modern Web browser such as Mozilla Firefox, Netscape 6.2+, or Internet Explorer 5.5+, and a report like the one shown in Figure 8-9 will be displayed.

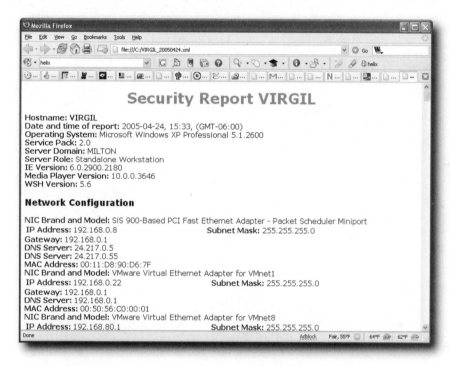

FIGURE 8-9: Helix generates a very useful security report about your Windows machine.

Beyond the data visible in the figure, SecReport provides you with the following information about a machine:

- Network configuration
- Audit policy
- Event log configuration
- Services (including start type and status)
- Applications (name and version numbers)
- Hotfixes (but nothing is listed unless you chose Yes when running SecReport)
- Ports open (including protocol, PID, program, and program's path)
- Pagefile settings
- Hardware (including brand and model, BIOS, RAM, processors, and drive letters)

This is a great report to print out and file away in case you ever need to review changes made on a computer. It's also a good way to take a quick gander at a machine to determine whether anything pops out at you as suspicious. In particular, take a look at running services, applications, and open ports. If something causes you to raise an eyebrow, examine it further.

Viewing IE History

Here's another cool thing you can do with Helix on a Windows box: Look at the history of all the URLs and paths that Internet Explorer has accessed. To get to the tool that enables that function, you need to click the little arrow to the right of the Incident Response Tools icon. The other tools Helix provides in this area are displayed, as shown in Figure 8-10.

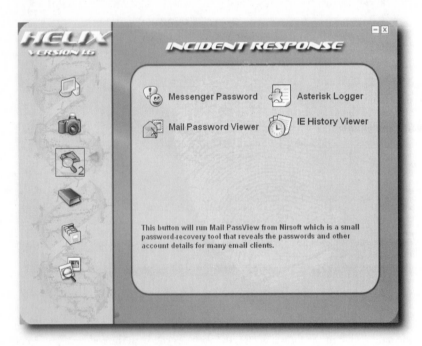

FIGURE 8-10: Four more invaluable tools

Select the IE History Viewer icon. IE History Viewer opens, displaying all the URLs visited with Internet Explorer . . . and all the paths accessed in Windows Explorer. Why? Well, remember how Microsoft linked the Web browser and the file manager together in Windows 98? Now that bad decision pays off for you. If you just want to see local filesystem paths, filter the data IE History Viewer shows you by choosing Edit → Select By URL, and then enter file: as your filter. The results will be similar to what's shown in Figure 8-11.

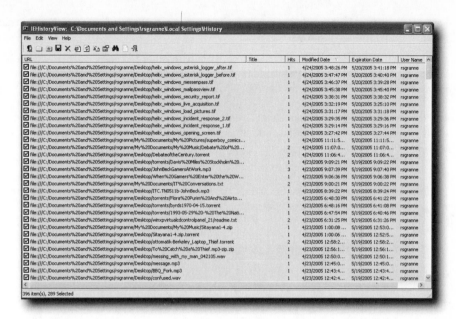

FIGURE 8-11: Directories and files that have been accessed on a Windows machine

Want to see even more stuff? Select View → Display Typed URLs. How about a nice report, suitable for viewing in your Web browser? Try View → HTML Report, and pick either Horizontal or Vertical. Want to see another user's history? Select File → Select User Profile.

Betcha never knew that snooping could be this easy, did you?

Viewing Passwords

One final item for Windows data recovery is actually several different tools — the other three on the second Incident Response Tools screen in addition to the IE History Viewer you just examined:

- Messenger Password
- Mail Password Viewer
- Asterisk Logger

Together, these three tools enable you to find out many of the key passwords used on a Windows system, which can be helpful when someone has forgotten his password, or when you suspect that an unauthorized user has created a new account for herself and you want to track her down.

Messenger Password (MessenPass) reveals the usernames and passwords used with any Instant Messaging programs in Windows.

I've used GAIM, which enables you to communicate with other IM users no matter what IM protocol they have, and MessenPass had absolutely no trouble revealing the usernames and passwords. The same holds true for the AIM, MSN, and Yahoo! IM clients.

Note If you're interested in learning more about GAIM, head to `http://gaim.sourceforge.net`. If you IM, you really should try it out, especially if you IM with people on different IM networks.

Mail Password Viewer (Mail PassView) does the same thing as Messenger Password, but for email programs. Figure 8-12 shows an example result.

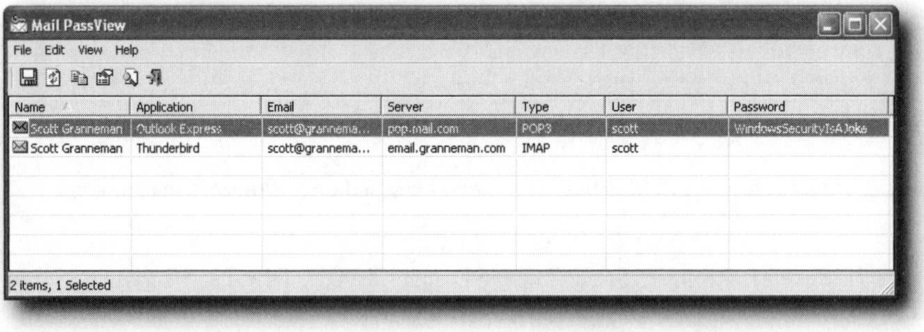

Name	Application	Email	Server	Type	User	Password
Scott Granneman	Outlook Express	scott@grannema...	pop.mail.com	POP3	scott	WindowsSecurityIsAJoke
Scott Granneman	Thunderbird	scott@grannema...	email.grannema.com	IMAP	scott	

2 items, 1 Selected

FIGURE **8-12: Think your email username and password are secret? Guess again.**

Outlook Express on Windows is an underpowered program that's not very secure; MailPassView doesn't have the slightest problem showing that program's username and password. When you use Windows, you could use Mozilla Thunderbird, because it's far more secure than either Outlook Express or Outlook. Interestingly, it appears that MailPassView is unable to show Thunderbird's password, even though it's a supported program. This is a bug that will be fixed shortly; don't assume that Thunderbird is invulnerable to MailPassView.

Finally, Asterisk Logger enables you to view the passwords hidden behind the asterisks or dots that Windows normally uses to hide things. For example, Figure 8-13 shows a mail account from Outlook Express before Asterisk Logger is opened.

FIGURE 8-13: What's the password?

Figure 8-14 shows the same window, after Asterisk Logger is up and running.

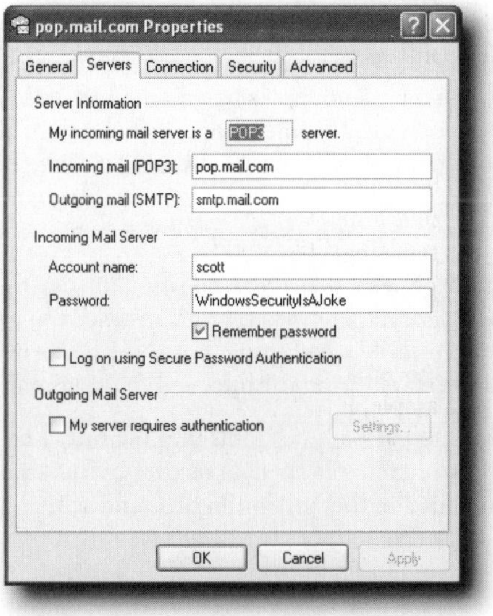

FIGURE 8-14: Not a very secure password

Meanwhile, the Asterisk Logger window remains open, logging all of the programs whose passwords have been revealed. When you've gathered all the passwords you need, select them all in Asterisk Logger and go to File → Save Selected Items, and you can create a text file containing the passwords. Very handy!

These are just a few of the Windows tools you can find in Helix. Take your time and try them all out. You'll find many that will prove useful.

Note

Helix comes with a small help file that covers a few issues, such as getting FireWire devices to work, creating and mounting Samba shares, and the good news that Intel Centrino wireless cards should work fine and dandy with the distro. Access that information by clicking the Manual button on the panel, the one that looks like a book. A few of the forensics programs have help files available as well, under Xfce menu → Forensics → Manuals. Of course, man pages for most of the apps exist and should be consulted.

The Helix manual is 48 pages of valuable information; you can download the PDF from `http://e-fense.com/helix/HELIX-Manual.pdf`. If you want to look online, Helix has a short FAQ available at `http://e-fense.com/helix/faq.php` that can help you with a few installation issues, but the real meat and potatoes can be found on the Helix forum, at `www.e-fense.com/helix/forum/index.php`. It's not the busiest online forum in the world, but folks have posted around 700 items and that number keeps growing, so it's an excellent resource for Helix users.

Using INSERT

INSERT (Inside Security Rescue Toolkit) is designed to fit on a credit-card-sized CD, so when you boot it, don't expect anything fancy. Whereas Knoppix is based on KDE, the K Desktop Environment, a feature- and eye-candy-rich GUI (some would say too much, but not me!), INSERT is instead built around the FluxBox window manager. As such, it's bare bones, with no obvious K menu to click on to get started. The solution? Right-click on the bare desktop, and menus of sorted security tools open up before your eyes, ready for use.

In addition to the possible strangeness of FluxBox, realize that INSERT contains mostly command-line-based apps. For example, don't expect Firefox, or even Mozilla; instead, you get the links-textmode Web browser to use. This isn't necessarily a bad thing, but INSERT is most definitely designed for folks who already know their way around Linux and the terminal.

Although it's a small package, INSERT manages to pack a lot of tools into the mix. The distro's focus is on rescuing a damaged system, so there are tools for data recovery, virus scanning, forensics, and more. The full list of software included in this distro can be found at `http://inside-security.de/applicationlist.html`.

To get INSERT, head to `http://sourceforge.net/projects/insert/`, follow the Download link and grab the 50MB ISO image in either English or German. Once it's on your computer, burn the ISO to either a credit-card-sized CD if you have one or to a regular CD-R/W if that's all you have. Both will work just fine. Boot from your new CD, and INSERT loads.

INSERT is a good, lightweight Knoppix-based distro centered on recovery and analysis. For more information about the program, be sure to visit the project's home page, at `http://inside-security.de/insert_en.html`, or the Freshmeat page about INSERT, at `http://freshmeat.net/projects/insert/`.

Note If you find anything to be a bit confusing in INSERT, visit `http://ubcd.sourceforge.net/insert/ostart.html` and look through the long list of hints. The answer to your question can probably be found there, along with a tip for using the default Web browser links, a way to download and install Firefox, a method for installing INSERT to run in RAM so that you can burn CDs, and how to configure your network cards.

Unfortunately, there does not seem to be a forum or any other public help available at this time. It is hoped that this will change because a high-quality project such as INSERT deserves a place where users can come together online and help each other.

Scanning for Viruses with ClamAV

If you think a machine might be infected with any of the countless viruses that now scamper about the Internet, it's not a difficult matter to check for them and then do something about the little beasties if any are found. INSERT comes with a free anti-virus checker — ClamAV — and it does a good job.

To run the ClamAV tool, right-click on the Desktop and select Applications → Security → Virus scanner GUI avscan — super user. When it opens, click on the Database tab, shown in Figure 8-15.

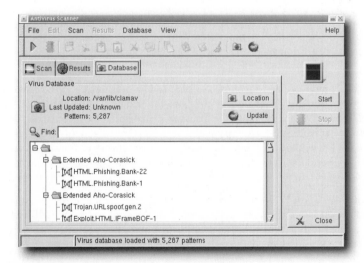

FIGURE 8-15: Update ClamAV's anti-virus database.

The first thing to do is update the AV database so that Clam can detect the latest nasties. Click the Update button, and Clam connects via the Internet to download any new patterns (in one case, Clam went from the capability to recognize 5,287 virus patterns to seeing more than 6,143!). When the process has finished, the screen indicates the last update time and the new number of virus signatures. Now select the Scan tab, shown in Figure 8-16.

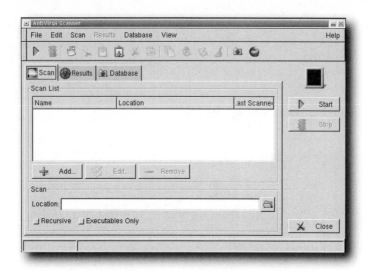

FIGURE 8-16: Tell ClamAV where you want to scan for viruses.

To give ClamAV something to scan, open a root terminal by right-clicking on the Desktop and then choosing Terminal session ➔ Rxvt — super user. When the shell opens, enter mount /mnt/hda2 (or whatever partition you use) to mount the partition on the hard drive that holds your data.

Now that the partition is mounted and therefore available to ClamAV, return to the program, and click the open folder icon just to the right of the Location text box. Select /mnt/hda2 and click the Select button. At the bottom of the Scan tab, check both Recursive (so the scan looks at every folder on /mnt/hda2) and Executables Only (so the scan doesn't waste its time on text files and the like). Click the Start button, and go for a cup of coffee. You could continue to work on other things, of course, but you might as well leave the computer alone so it can focus on one task.

As soon as you click Start, ClamAV switches to the Results tab. If anything is flagged, it shows up here. Just to give you an idea about how much time ClamAV needs to run, a 30GB partition on a 2GHz Pentium 4 with 512MB of RAM takes about five minutes or so (no viruses were flagged, but of course it was a Linux machine).

ClamAV is a good tool to have available for virus detection and cleanup. It's really easy to run it in scripts using its command-line tools, but that's left as an exercise for you.

For more information on ClamAV, check out the project's home page, `http://clamav.net/`, where you can access a wide variety of information, documentation, a wiki, and a whole lot more.

Reading and Writing NTFS Partitions

Out of the box, INSERT comes with support for an incredible variety of filesystems, including Ext2, Ext3, Minix, ReiserFS, JFS, XFS, FAT, DOS, NFS, SMBFS, NCPFS, UDF, UFS, HFS, and HFS+. Nowadays, however, if you're using INSERT to rescue a damaged Windows machine, you need support for at least reading partitions formatted with NTFS. Fortunately, INSERT supports that filesystem as well. You can definitely read data from an NTFS volume; if you're feeling brave, you can also write to that volume.

Caution If you're going to write to an NTFS-formatted volume, either back that data up first or commit yourself to not caring much if everything gets corrupted and goes bye-bye.

To read and write NTFS, use the Captive virtual driver, which requires certain files from a Windows XP install. If you've booted INSERT on a Windows XP box, just copy `C:\WINDOWS\system32\ntoskrnl.exe` and `C:\WINDOWS\system32\drivers\ntfs.sys` to `/var/lib/captive`. If you haven't booted over Windows XP, you'll need to copy those files from another machine onto your computer, using either a USB flash drive or the network. In fact, if you plan to use INSERT (or any of the other distros in this chapter that support reading and writing to NTFS) a lot, you'll probably want to keep copies of those Windows drivers on some storage mechanism so that you can get to them anytime.

Tip If you just don't have a Windows box around, you can download Windows XP Service Pack 1 from `http://download.microsoft.com/download/9/7/6/9763833d-bd58-41e2-9911-50f64c7252a3/xpsp1a_en_x86_CHK.exe`, save it, and then extract the files you need. Keep in mind that it's a 144MB download and rather a pain, so it's much easier to find those drivers, copy them to a USB flash drive, and keep it close by.

Now that the Windows drivers have been copied to the correct location, run the following in a terminal window (this assumes that you're trying to mount `/mnt/hda1`, which is your Windows partition formatted with NTFS; if it's not, adjust as necessary):

```
# mkdir /mnt/hda1
# mount /dev/hda1 /mnt/hda1 -t captive-ntfs
# ls /mnt/hda1
```

That last command should show you the contents of your Windows partition. You can now read and write to the NTFS partition. Be careful!

Tip

There is a script on INSERT that somewhat automates this process: `/usr/sbin/use captive`. If you don't want to use Captive manually, try running that script first. For further info on Captive, visit the project's home page at `http://jankratochvil.net/project/captive/`. Captive is no longer under active development by the original author, but others have evidently taken up the cause and are still working on it. If you Google for "captive ntfs," you'll find a lot of other good resources as well.

Changing a Windows Administrator Password

Now that you have read/write access to a Windows NTFS partition, you might as well do something cool with it, such as change the Administrator's password—without having to know the original password.

To change the password, you need to know where the SAM database file is. On Windows XP, it's located at `C:\Windows\System32\Config\SAM`; for Windows 2000, look at `C:\WINNT\System32\Config\SAM`. Assuming a Windows XP machine, you'd run the following command:

```
# chntpw /mnt/hda1/Windows/System32/Config/SAM
```

Enter the new password you want to use, click OK, and you're finished. Now the Administrator on that box has a new password. Pretty easy, eh?

Tip

If you want to learn how to change the passwords of other users, take a look at `man chntpw` or visit `http://home.eunet.no/~pnordahl/ntpasswd/`.

Testing Your System's RAM

Sometimes a computer acts flaky, but it has nothing to do with the software at all. One user's Linux laptop, for example, constantly locked up on him, with no apparent cause. He tried three or four different distros, with no discernable change—eventually, and sporadically, his laptop would lock up, no matter what apps he was running at the time. He finally emailed a local Linux users group and asked for help. Another user suggested what perhaps should have been obvious: bad RAM.

To test that hypothesis, the first user booted INSERT and then ran Memtest as follows:

```
# memtest all -l /mnt/hda1/memtest.log
```

This told Memtest to look at all available memory and to log to a file on a mounted drive. (If you don't want to use a logfile, you can leave that off and STDERR would instead be used.)

Memtest can take a long time to run, depending on the amount of RAM you have and the speed of your machine, so you need to be patient. Start it and then leave the computer alone. Don't try to use the machine for anything else, or you'll just prolong the agony.

After running Memtest, the user did indeed find that one of his DIMMs was bad. He contacted the vendor for a free replacement, popped it in, and his problems were solved. Insanity was staved off again, all thanks to INSERT and Memtest.

Tip

For more on Memtest (although there's really not a lot to the program), try running man memtest or refer to its home page, http://.memtest86.com/.

Tracing That Route

Sometimes your network connection is slow as all get out and you can't figure out why. Traditionally, two of the first tools a network-savvy user runs is ping, which tells you whether a machine is up and running, and traceroute, which informs you of the path packets are taking from your machine to another. INSERT comes with a cool little software program that combines the two functionalities into one: mtr.

For example, suppose I noticed a slowdown getting to my Website, http://granneman. com. To check, I run the following command:

```
$ mtr www.granneman.com
```

Within a few seconds, I get the output shown in Figure 8-17.

```
INSERT                                                                     _ □ ×
                           My traceroute  [v0.67]
insert (0.0.0.0)(tos=0x0 psize=64 bitpattern=0x00)           Mon May  2 18:58:36 2005
Keys:  Help   Display mode   Restart statistics   Order of fields   quit
                                        Packets              Pings
Host                                  Loss%  Snt   Last   Avg  Best  Wrst StDev
 1. 192.168.0.1                        0.0%   38    1.8   2.2   1.8  11.9   1.6
 2. 10.29.64.1                         0.0%   38   12.5  12.3   8.1  25.1   4.3
 3. 24.217.2.165                       0.0%   38   16.5  13.7   8.6  28.3   4.5
 4. 12.124.129.97                      0.0%   38   11.3  14.0   9.7  52.8   7.2
 5. gbr6-p40.sl9mo.ip.att.net          0.0%   37   11.8  14.2   8.9  38.1   6.4
 6. tbr2-p013601.sl9mo.ip.att.net      0.0%   37   11.6  21.2  10.5  84.8  17.9
 7. tbr2-cl7.cgcil.ip.att.net          0.0%   37   18.4  27.4  17.6  83.0  15.5
 8. ggr2-p390.cgcil.ip.att.net         0.0%   37   20.6  29.8  16.5  92.1  18.2
 9. att-gw.chi.gblx.net                0.0%   37   18.2  21.9  18.1  44.5   5.8
10. so0-0-0-2488M.ar3.LAX1.gblx.net    0.0%   37   75.6  82.5  74.8 135.8  12.0
11. Intelenet-Communications-Intelenet-Communications.so-6-0-  0.0%  37  82.7  85.4  82.3  98.0   3.3
12. v9.core2.irv.intelenet.net         0.0%   37   97.3  89.7  82.4 142.2  11.6
13. 216.23.180.5                       0.0%   37  152.4  91.8  82.1 186.7  22.5
```

FIGURE 8-17: Mtr hard at work, pinging constantly along the route to my host.

mtr figures out the route from my laptop to my Web server, and then begins constantly pinging every step along the way, giving me an up-to-the-second look at the network path from point A to point B. It's actually kind of hypnotic, watching the changes endlessly cycle by . . .

Note If you want to learn more about `mtr` (it, too, is a pretty simple little program), use `man mtr` or visit `http://bitwizard.nl/mtr/`. Another good way to learn what the program can do is to run it, and then press H for the in-program help.

Summary

This chapter explored several very good distros — Auditor, Helix, and INSERT — all based on Knoppix and all focused on security. As mentioned in an article for *SecurityFocus* (`http://securityfocus.com/columnists/323`) that focused on these fantastic tools, "These are bootable Linux CDs . . . that give you a wealth of security tools in one convenient package." Whether you're learning about security tools or you're already a security pro who wants to carry everything you need to do your job on one CD, the distros examined in this chapter should become a regular part of your computing life.

If you're looking for another hardcore security-focused distro, check out Knoppix-STD, available at `http://knoppix-std.org`. STD basically attempts to cram as many security tools as possible onto one disc, tools that enable you to perform an almost dizzying variety of tasks. For a big list of Live CDs that includes many others that can be used for security research and testing, head over to Frozen Tech's LiveCD List at (`http://frozentech.com/content/livecd.php`) and filter on Security, Diagnostics, Firewall, Forensics, or Rescue.

Customizing Knoppix and Live CDs

part
IV

Changing Knoppix to Fit Your Needs

Knoppix comes bundled with a bucket of tools, and although 1.7GB of uncompressed space goes a long way, you might encounter the problem of having to use software that Knoppix doesn't include by default. Additionally, you may make changes in configurations that you want to keep when you reboot, or store data between Knoppix sessions. Thankfully, there are a few different ways to solve this problem, some being easier to use and more successful than others. This chapter shows you how to use and modify Knoppix to save your data and install new software.

Although most of these techniques can be done without using a terminal, it's assumed that you know the command-line basics of Linux and bash.

Using apt-get and KPackage to Install New Software

In the latest versions of Knoppix, you can use the Debian package management utilities directly. The most important of these utilities is `apt-get`, a software package retrieval and installation tool that provides access to the more than 16,000 packages available in Debian. KPackage is a front-end to `apt-get` for the KDE desktop in Knoppix, making it easy to find and install new software packages available in Debian.

This section shows you how to use KPackage to install KPDF, a PDF viewer for KDE. (KPDF is normally part of the KDE desktop but it doesn't come with Knoppix.) Depending on the version of Knoppix used, you might have to first set the user password from a terminal:

```
sudo passwd knoppix
```

Enter a new password for the user knoppix. (If you're asked for a root password, use `sudo passwd root` instead.)

To start KPackage, choose KNOPPIX ➔ Utilities ➔ Manage Software in KNOPPIX (kpackage). After KPackage starts, update the package lists by opening the KPackage menu and selecting Special ➔ APT: Debian ➔ Update.

With the package lists updated, you're ready to install new software packages. Search for the KPDF package and select it. A description of it appears in the right pane (see Figure 9-1).

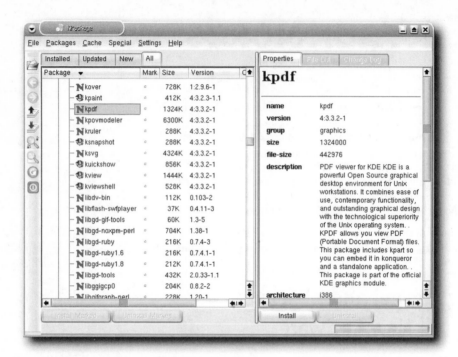

FIGURE 9-1: KPackage, showing the details of KPDF

Click the Install button below the description to begin installing KPDF. A detailed overview of the actions KPackage takes displays in a new window. Click the Install button to commence the retrieval and installation of KPDF.

After KPDF has been installed, you can start it from a terminal simply by entering the command kpdf. KPDF opens (see Figure 9-2) and is ready for your PDF viewing enjoyment.

Do experiment with KPackage and apt-get. Thanks to Debian and UnionFS, a vast collection of software is available at the touch of a button.

UnionFS Opens New Doors

The main problem with using new software used to be coping with the fact that the Knoppix filesystem for the most part was read-only, with /usr, /lib, and large parts of /etc and /var not being writable and the rest of the filesystem residing on a RAM disk. There were techniques that could be used to work around this limitation, but they were somewhat clumsy to use. Recent versions of Knoppix have removed this limitation, thanks to the UnionFS overlay filesystem. UnionFS enables you to write to read-only directories as if they were writable, while transparently placing the changes into memory and rerouting requests to the new file. This greatly eases the task of installing new software and opens up a lot of new possibilities for Live CDs.

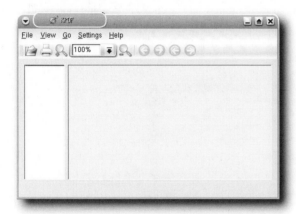

FIGURE 9-2: KPDF, ready to open PDF files

Changing Knoppix Without Remastering

Remastering — the rebuilding of a Live CD — is a complicated and time-consuming process, as you'll see in Chapter 10. Although plenty of fun, it is overkill for minor modifications because there are ways to save your Knoppix changes on floppy disk, USB flash drive, or one of your hard disk partitions. You can run the saveconfig script, which uses knoppix.sh to unpack an archive of modified configuration files on one of those writable media, for instance, or you can run the knoppix-mkimage script, which is much like the older mkpersistent home script that saves the files in your home directory, using a writable image or a whole partition. Let's take a closer look at those two methods.

Using the saveconfig Script

The `saveconfig` script, written by Klaus Knopper, is a graphical tool for saving the configuration of your Knoppix Live CD on a floppy, USB flash drive, or hard disk partition. You can either run it as root from the Live CD via a terminal or you can start it from the KDE menu: select Knoppix ➔ Configure ➔ Save Knoppix configuration.

When you start `saveconfig` (see Figure 9-3), you can choose to save the following:

■ Personal configuration (all your dot files in the `/home/knoppix` directory that have been changed)

■ Desktop files (everything that has changed in `/home/knoppix/Desktop`)

■ Network configuration files, including dial-up and ISDN files

■ X Window system configuration, defining your screen resolution and video card driver

■ Any other files from `/etc` that have been changed

FIGURE 9-3: The saveconfig script shows the selection of save options.

Choose what you want to save and then specify where you want to store your files (see Figure 9-4). The script saves the selected files, wraps them together, and saves the resulting archive on the selected media.

For Knoppix to find your saved files, you need to use a cheatcode at boot time. Use `knoppix myconfig=scan` to have Knoppix search all your inserted media for the saved configuration files, or use `knoppix myconfig=/dev/hda1`, where `hda1` is the device on which you saved your files. The second command skips searching all your devices, which speeds up the time required to boot Knoppix. After you've booted Knoppix, you can use `saveconfig` again to overwrite your changes on the same writable media.

FIGURE 9-4: Specify where your files should be stored.

saveconfig seems like quite a bit of magic. How does it work? It creates two files — knoppix.sh and configs.tbz. These files are saved on the media specified. Knoppix searches for the knoppix.sh shell script at startup and runs it when it's found. That script extracts configs.tbz, which is a bzip2-compressed tarball containing the modified files. If you know a bit of shell scripting, it's easy to modify and extend the knoppix.sh script to do more complicated or location-specific tasks.

The configs.tbz file contains the files from the home directory (/home/knoppix) and certain files from /etc that were writable. Its contents are extracted by knoppix.sh onto the writable portions of the Knoppix Live CD, which has certain directories loaded on a RAM disk. You can modify this yourself if you want to add more files in different locations; just remember that the whole tarball is extracted into RAM. This works fine for smaller files, but you don't want to save your entire home directory in this tarball because you can quickly run out of RAM, leaving your Knoppix Live CD unbootable when using the myconfig cheatcode.

Using the knoppix-mkimage Script

The knoppix-mkimage script is similar to saveconfig, but it is more useful for saving larger files in your home directory when booted from the Knoppix Live CD.

knoppix-mkimage is opened from the KDE menu: Select Knoppix ➔ Configure ➔ Create a Persistent Knoppix Home Directory. The script starts, showing an introduction screen (see Figure 9-5) with all the details.

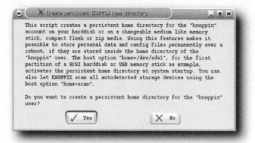

FIGURE 9-5: The introduction screen

Choose the writable media on which you want to store your files (see Figure 9-6).

FIGURE 9-6: Specify where your files should be stored.

Then decide whether you want to use the entire filesystem (see Figure 9-7). Select yes only if you want to remove all existing files on the partition! Even if you have an existing Linux partition set up on the selected media, using the entire partition removes all your files.

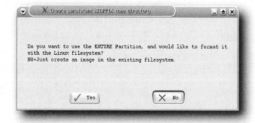

FIGURE 9-7: Warning! Don't click Yes right away!

Click No and you get the option to create a file on the writable media that contains all the files in your home directory, and you can specify how large the persistent home directory should be (see Figure 9-8).

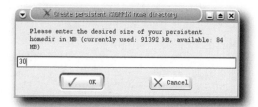

FIGURE 9-8: Make sure you have enough free space before continuing!

`knoppix-mkimage` then either makes the home directory file or formats the selected partition and then copies over all the files in `/home/knoppix`. You can choose to encrypt your home directory file, which is useful if you run the risk of losing your media or if you are paranoid.

To use your new persistent home directory, you again need a cheatcode at boot time: `knoppix home=scan` has Knoppix search for your persistent home directory at boot time; `knoppix home=/dev/hda1` tells Knoppix to use the persistent home directory on the `hda1` partition. If you are using the whole partition, Knoppix detects this and mounts the partition as the knoppix user's home directory; otherwise, it finds the persistent home directory file and makes that the knoppix user's home directory.

`knoppix-mkimage` enables you to save applications that have been downloaded and installed as described earlier. If you save your home directory, those programs are available upon reboot — you won't have to redownload the applications every time.

Summary

This chapter showed you how to work with `apt-get` and KPackage to install applications. `apt-get` and UnionFS are making the creation of Live CDs much easier for you. `apt-get` and front ends such as KPackage remain a powerful combination for more advanced users who know what they are looking for. Using `saveconfig` and `knoppix-mkimage` scripts, you can easily modify Knoppix without having to remaster it.

Remastering Knoppix

chapter

10

in this chapter

☑ Preparing Knoppix

☑ Customizing your Distro

☑ Booting with different kernels

☑ Mastering your CD

Saving your home directory isn't enough? Not satisfied with merely saving some configuration files? Then welcome to the wonderful world of Knoppix remastering. Leading to numerous Live CDs of all different shapes and sizes, modifying Knoppix seems to have become an epidemic. This isn't all that strange because it only takes a single motivated user with some time on his hands to modify Knoppix until what is left can hardly be traced back to Knoppix at all.

Remastering Knoppix can be highly addictive, but it does have some prerequisites. First, remastering Knoppix is usually done from a normal GNU/Linux install, be it Knoppix, Debian, Fedora, or Gentoo. Remastering while running the Knoppix Live CD, although possible, isn't recommended. Booting the Knoppix Live CD consumes a healthy amount of memory, so install Knoppix to your hard disk first — it will save you plenty of headaches in the long run. Second, to remaster Knoppix, you'll likely want to have fairly recent hardware, as rebuilding does take some time. Depending on the amount of RAM in your machine, you will also likely want to have around a gigabyte of swap space available. Other Live CDs use compression types and tools that make this unnecessary, but Knoppix doesn't.

 Note Appendix B explains how to install Knoppix on your hard drive.

Also, check www.knopper.net/knoppix/index-en.html for the latest Knoppix version. This book's CD-ROM includes a version of Knoppix 4.0, the latest version to date. Still, you'll likely want to grab a newer release if it is available because it will save you plenty of time when updating and will give you the latest and greatest Knoppix magic. Ready? Start warming up that CPU.

Preparing Knoppix

To access the files in Knoppix, you first must uncompress them. You've already mounted the Knoppix CD at /cdrom, so now create a directory in which you can store the files from the CD. Substitute the directory names with the location of your home directory: mkdir /home/knoppix/knoppixiso. Note that some commands will need to be executed as the root user.

Copy all files from the Knoppix CD except for the KNOPPIX/KNOPPIX file:

```
$ cp -r /cdrom/[a-z]* /home/knoppix/knoppixiso
$ mkdir /home/knoppix/knoppixiso/KNOPPIX
$ cp -r /cdrom/KNOPPIX/*.* /cdrom/KNOPPIX/images /home/⏎
   knoppix/knoppixiso/KNOPPIX/
```

The KNOPPIX/KNOPPIX file contains the compressed contents of the Knoppix Live CD and is quite large, which is why you're extracting it separately. There are two different ways to uncompress the KNOPPIX/KNOPPIX file: by mounting it manually or by using the cloop utilities. Both are discussed in the following sections. If you have installed Knoppix or a similar distribution, choose the former because it is quicker.

Mounting the KNOPPIX/KNOPPIX File

To mount the KNOPPIX/KNOPPIX file, your current install needs the cloop kernel module driver. Load this kernel module first just to be sure:

```
# modprobe cloop file=/cdrom/KNOPPIX/KNOPPIX
```

If this command succeeds, you're in luck: Your system has the cloop kernel module. If this command fails, you can retrieve the cloop package from http://altlinux.com/index.php?module=sisyphus&package=kernel-modules-cloop-std26-up or http://morphix.org/debian/cloop-2.6/ (or search the Web for other sources) and compile the kernel module against your current kernel. Alternatively, you can uncompress the KNOPPIX/KNOPPIX file with the cloop command-line utilities, as discussed in the following section.

```
$ mkdir /tmp/mountdir
# mount -o ro -t iso9660 /dev/cloop /tmp/mountdir
```

If all goes well, the Knoppix files are now available in /tmp/mountdir. However, the files are read-only. Copy the files to a writable directory:

```
$ mkdir /home/knoppix/knoppixuncompressed
# cp -a /tmp/mountdir/* /home/knoppix/knoppixuncompressed/
```

Then clean up the remaining files:

```
# umount /tmp/mountdir
# rmdir /tmp/mountdir
```

Now you have access to all the Knoppix files and can modify them at will. Skip the following section and head straight to "Installing and Removing Software."

Using the cloop Command-Line Utilities

If you don't have the cloop kernel module, don't worry: There is another way that will just take more time. To extract the KNOPPIX/KNOPPIX file, you must have the extract_ compressed_fs command-line tool. This is always the case when using a Knoppix install. Check whether it exists:

```
# whereis extract_compressed_fs
```

If nothing comes up, you'll need to install the cloop-utils package. If you are running a Debian or Debian derivative, this is easily done using apt-get:

```
# apt-get install cloop-utils
```

Otherwise, retrieve the latest cloop tarball package (version cloop_2.01-5.tar.gz at the time of this writing) from http://morphix.org/debian/cloop-2.6/ or a Website of your own choosing. Download the package to /tmp and uncompress it:

```
$ cd /tmp
$ tar zxvf cloop_2.01-5.tar.gz
```

Now compile and install the cloop utilities:

```
$ cd cloop-2.01
$ make
# cp create_compressed_fs extract_compressed_fs /usr/local/sbin/
```

The key to extracting the KNOPPIX/KNOPPIX file is, you guessed it, extract_ compressed_fs:

```
# /usr/local/sbin/extract_compressed_fs /cdrom/KNOPPIX/⤵
KNOPPIX > /tmp/knoppix.iso
```

This command takes some processing time, so grab some coffee. You'll see feedback as cloop does its job, showing you each block as it is extracted. On a Pentium III 1GHz system, it takes about five minutes to extract 30,728 blocks.

Now the KNOPPIX/KNOPPIX file is extracted as an ordinary iso9660 file. It can be mounted using a loopback device:

```
$ mkdir /tmp/mountdir
# mount -t iso9660 /tmp/knoppix.iso /tmp/mountdir -o loop
```

Finally, copy over all the files over to your writable directory:

```
$ mkdir /home/knoppix/knoppixuncompressed
# cp -a /tmp/mountdir/* /home/knoppix/knoppixuncompressed/
```

When you've finished, clean up the remaining files:

```
# umount /tmp/mountdir
# rm /tmp/knoppix.iso
# rm /tmp/cloop*
```

Installing and Removing Software

You can use the extracted files to install and remove software from Knoppix. All files from the Knoppix ISO are now available via /home/knoppix/knoppixiso, and the files that were in the KNOPPIX/KNOPPIX file are available in /home/knoppix/knoppixuncompressed.

To begin, chroot (change the root directory) into the extracted filesystem:

```
# chroot /home/knoppix/knoppixuncompressed
```

This means that you will see the /home/knoppix/knoppixuncompressed directory as your new root filesystem. You now have a shell that has access only to the files in /home/knoppix/knoppixuncompressed.

To install certain packages, you need to mount the proc filesystem inside the chroot:

```
# mount -t proc /proc proc
```

You will get a warning (warning: can't open /etc/fstab: No such file or directory.), which you can safely ignore.

Test whether your Internet connection works by pinging a server:

```
# ping slashdot.org
```

If you receive replies, congratulations! You have a connection with the Internet from within the chroot and can start using apt-get to install new software.

If you didn't get a reply, you'll have to add your DNS nameservers to /etc/resolv.conf. Open the file using vim or a different text editor:

```
# vim /etc/resolv.conf
```

For each nameserver, add an entry:

```
# nameserver 0.0.0.0
```

where 0.0.0.0 is your nameserver. Save the file and try pinging again to make sure your connection works. You need it if you want to install new software from the Internet using apt-get.

Using apt-get

First, update apt-get's package lists so it will know which new packages are available:

```
# apt-get update
```

Now you can install packages at will. For example, use this to install the latest version of AbiWord:

```
# apt-get install abiword
```

Similarly, use the following to install the newest Firefox Web browser:

```
# apt-get install mozilla-firefox
```

Naturally, you can also remove packages, which is necessary if you want to install additional packages. If you don't free up enough space for your new packages, your final Live CD won't fit on a CD! The following removes OpenOffice:

```
# apt-get remove openoffice.org*
```

Adding * to the command catches all of the packages.

Afterward, you have to clean up inside the `chroot`:

```
# apt-get clean
# umount /proc
```

After you are done, simply exit the `chrooted` shell.

Other Customizations

You can make several other common modifications to a Knoppix Live CD. The following sections explore some of them.

Setting Passwords

Setting the initial passwords of the knoppix and root users is simple. To set the knoppix user password, execute the following in the `chroot`:

```
# passwd knoppix
```

To set the root user password, execute the following:

```
# passwd
```

Enter and confirm the password. Setting these passwords on a Live CD that is distributed and used "in the wild" isn't as good an idea as it might seem. In Knoppix, with the knoppix user able to execute commands directly using `sudo`, you want to avoid anyone being able to log into Knoppix remotely over a network. Although Knoppix itself can't be tampered with permanently by a remote user, it is possible for such a user to access the hard disk or other media on the computer that is running Knoppix.

Picking a Different Background

Changing the default background is easy once you have uncompressed the KNOPPIX file. The location of the background used in Knoppix is `/usr/local/lib/knoppix.jpg` in the `chroot`. You can overwrite this file simply by overwriting this image:

```
# cp mybackground.jpg /home/knoppix/knoppixuncompressed/↵
    usr/local/lib/knoppix.jpg
```

You can overwrite this image with an image of any format.

Changing the Boot Screen

The Knoppix boot screen is set up in the `/home/knoppix/knoppixiso/boot/isolinux` directory. Three files are of interest:

- `isolinux.cfg`: The configuration of the isolinux bootloader. Isolinux provides the initial boot screen and starts the Knoppix boot process. This file can be edited directly using any editor.

- `boot.msg`: The text section of the boot screen. You can use any editor to modify this file, too.

- `logo.16`: The image shown at boot time. It is more difficult to modify. `logo.16` in the LSS16 image format, which is designed especially for isolinux and its counterpart, syslinux. To convert an image to this format, you must first save the image in the Gimp as a `.ppm` file. Then:

```
# ppmtolss16 < myimage.ppm > /home/knoppix/knoppixiso/⤵
   boot/isolinux/logo.16
```

`myimage.ppm` must be a 640 × 480 16-color image. Any other image, and isolinux refuses to show an image, so getting this right will take some practice.

Setting Languages

In the `isolinux.cfg` file, introduced in the preceding section, you can define the default cheatcodes used for booting Knoppix. These cheatcodes are the ones that can normally be entered on the command line right before Knoppix boots from the Live CD and displays the boot screen.

Open the `isolinux.cfg` file with your favorite text editor and locate the lines that start with APPEND. On these lines you'll see a cheatcode in the form `lang=us` or `lang=de`. Changing this to another language's two-letter abbreviation changes the default language used on the Live CD.

Note that setting the cheatcode doesn't always work. Certain programs, such as KDE, OpenOffice.org, Mozilla, and Mozilla Firefox, don't have all language packs installed by default. If you want to have a completely translated Live CD, you will have to install these, similar to installing new software as described in the section "Installing and Removing Software" earlier in the chapter. For example, if you want to install the Dutch language package for KDE, you'd execute the following in the `chroot`:

```
# apt-get install kde-i18n-nl
```

Similarly for Mozilla Firefox:

```
# apt-get install mozilla-firefox-locale-nl-nl
```

Creating translated Knoppix Live CDs isn't very complicated after you've mastered the installing of software in Knoppix; however, language package names differ per software package. If you aren't sure, start synaptic to search for software package names and their language package counterparts. Not every language will be available.

Choosing a Different Desktop Environment

A lot of simple hacks are possible using the Knoppix cheatcodes. Knoppix comes with a number of desktop environments pre-installed, and you can use the desktop cheatcode for altering the desktop environment Knoppix starts.

Say, for example, that you want to start with icewm, a quick desktop environment suited for older machines, by default. Change the isolinux.cfg file APPEND lines to include desktop=icewm.

If you don't want to use the cheatcodes to easily modify your Live CD, you have to modify the Knoppix startup files. In that case, open from within the chroot the /etc/init.d/ knoppix-autoconfig file with a text editor. This shell script contains the largest part of the boot process and starts a lot of other programs for hardware detection and the like. On line 483 of this file is a case statement defining the way the desktop cheatcode is used in Knoppix. If you want to change the default in this way, modify

```
DESKTOP="kde"
```

to

```
DESKTOP="icewm"
```

Modifying the default desktop environment is, of course, more complicated if that desktop environment isn't installed in Knoppix to begin with! In that case, you also have to install the environment you want. For example, to install the XFCE4 desktop environment, simply execute

```
# apt-get install xfce4
```

from within the chroot. This installs the XFCE4 desktop environment and all the dependencies it requires. Remember to free up a corresponding amount of space or your Live CD won't fit on a CD! One of the largest challenges in remastering Knoppix is making sure the Live CD contains everything you need and is still small enough to fit on the CD.

Booting with a Different Kernel

One of the more complicated areas of Knoppix remastering, swapping the Linux kernel is not for the faint of heart. There are three ways you can go about exchanging the kernel:

- The Debian way, by installing a pre-made kernel
- By using make-kpkg to create your own kernel package, which can be installed manually
- By manually downloading, configuring, compiling, and installing your kernel

This section discusses the first two; doing everything manually doesn't offer any advantages over using make-kpkg.

The first step in all three processes is removing the installed kernel in the chroot of the KNOPPIX/KNOPPIX file. As with everything in Knoppix, you can easily remove the kernel by using apt-get:

```
# apt-get remove kernel-image-2.6.12
```

You get a warning when running this command if your host system is running the same kernel. Because you are removing the kernel from the chroot, you can safely ignore the warning. Type **Yes** to continue.

You should also remove any existing kernel module packages for the 2.6.12 kernel. They won't function with a different kernel, so keeping them installed doesn't serve any purpose:

```
# apt-get remove *modules-2.6.12
```

When replacing the kernel, the most work involves ensuring that all the kernel modules you want are included in your Live CD. Different kernel modules need to be built in different ways, as you'll see later in this chapter.

Installing a Pre-Made Kernel from the Debian Archive

In Debian, a large number of kernels are available for a variety of systems. The kernels are generic enough to work on as many different machines as possible and are a good bet if you aren't acquainted with configuring and compiling your own kernel. The advantage is that this process is relatively easy to do; the drawbacks are a lack of choice as to which kernels you can use and a lack of control over which kernel module and options are chosen — these already have been chosen for you.

To begin, you have to find the kernel that suites your purposes. Use synaptic to search for kernel image packages (their names start with kernel-image). Say, for instance, that you want to use an older 2.4 Linux kernel; execute the following in the chroot:

```
# apt-get install kernel-image-2.4.27-2-386
```

There you have it, your new (albeit old) kernel. Don't think that you're done this quickly, though, because each kernel also needs kernel module packages in order for all functionalities to be available. The following command installs the pcmcia modules, which are required if you want your Live CD to function properly with removable hardware in laptops:

```
# apt-get install kernel-pcmcia-modules-2.4.27-2-386
```

If you want to support wireless network cards, install the linux-wlan-ng package:

```
# apt-get install linux-wlan-ng-modules-2.4.27-2-386
```

To be able to compile kernel modules that aren't pre-packaged for your kernel, it's a good idea to also install the accompanying kernel-headers package:

```
# apt-get install kernel-headers-2.4.27-2
```

Using make-kpkg to Create Your Own Kernel Package

If you prefer more control over choices made regarding what kind of kernel goes onto your Live CD, you still can use the flexibility that Debian provides. It's highly recommended that you do this on your host system and save the resulting packages in a separate directory, so that you don't have to worry about losing all your hard work. You'll also be able to make small changes without having to start from scratch.

On your host system, do the following:

```
# apt-get install kernel-source-2.6.11
```

This downloads the kernel source from the Debian repository; it ends up in /usr/src. Unpack the source:

```
# cd /usr/src
# tar jxvf kernel-source-2.6.11.tar.bz2
```

This command extracts the kernel source into /usr/src/kernel-source-2.6.11. Enter that directory:

```
# cd kernel-source-2.6.11
```

Now you have two options: use a default configuration supplied by Debian or create your own. If you want to create your own configuration, you can use one of the following commands:

```
# make menuconfig
# make xconfig
# make gconfig
```

All three configuration tools provide an interface in which you can select the various kernel options for the intended systems. You can use the existing Knoppix configuration by loading in the configuration from /usr/src/linux/.config; this is possible in all three configuration tools. Unless your kernel is very different from the existing Knoppix kernel or the intended usage is restricted, it's a good idea to start with the existing Knoppix kernel configuration, so that you only have to tweak the settings for situations in which your usage differs.

After you have configured your kernel, you're ready to create the kernel packages for your Live CD. Execute the following:

```
# make-kpkg kernel_image
```

This command starts compiling your new kernel. It takes a while, but afterward four new files are in the /usr/src directory: a kernel-image package, a kernel-source package, a kernel-headers package, and a kernel-doc package. Copy the kernel-image package and kernel-headers packages into your chroot and install them there using dpkg. For example:

```
# dpkg -i kernel-image-2.6.11_10.00.Custom_i386.deb ⤵
    kernel-headers-2.6.11_10.00.Custom_i386.deb
```

If everything went well, you have replaced your kernel successfully. Congratulations! However, you aren't out of the woods yet.

Adding the cloop Linux Kernel Module

There is one kernel module a Knoppix-based Live CD can't function without: the cloop driver. You used the cloop utilities for extracting the /KNOPPIX/KNOPPIX file at the beginning of this chapter, and in a few moments you'll use them to compress it again. For your Live CD to actually use the compressed data, however, the cloop driver has to be on that CD. The cloop package isn't pre-compiled for any kernels, so you have to make your own.

First, make sure you either have the kernel headers installed or the kernel source. If you followed the directions in either of the preceding sections, this should be the case. Now do the following outside of the chroot:

```
# apt-get install cloop-src
```

The cloop-src package contains the source you need to compile. It is placed in /usr/src/cloop.tar.gz:

Unpack the cloop source in /usr/src/modules/cloop:

```
# cd /usr/src
# tar zxvf cloop.tar.gz
```

If you have installed the kernel headers, make sure you have the same kernel headers installed on your host system. Then do the following:

```
# cd /usr/src/modules/cloop
# debian/rules KSRC=/usr/src/↩
   kernel-headers-2.4.27-2 KVERS=2.4.27-2 kdist_image
```

The package required is built and placed in /usr/src/modules.

Otherwise, use the following if you still have the source of the kernel you made on your host system:

```
# cd /usr/src/kernel-source-2.6.11
# make-kpkg modules_image
```

The package required is built and placed in /usr/src.

Now, copy either the cloop-module-2.6.11 or the cloop-module-2.4.27-2 package into the chroot:

```
# cp ../cloop-module-2.6.11_2.01.5-3_i386.deb /home/↩
   knoppix/knoppixuncompressed/
```

Inside the chroot, install the package:

```
# dpkg -i cloop-module-2.6.11_2.01.5-3_i386.deb
```

If all goes well, your new cloop kernel module exists as /lib/modules/2.6.11/kernel/drivers/block/cloop.ko. Make sure it exists, because you'll need it for the next section.

Updating the Initial RAM Disk

When booting up, Knoppix first loads a small compressed image into memory. That image is called the *initial RAM disk;* it contains just enough information (drivers and scripts) to start up the Linux system and hand the boot process off to another set of scripts located elsewhere that are responsible for bringing up services on a machine. Using the files on that image, Knoppix accesses the larger compressed /KNOPPIX/KNOPPIX file. On the ISO, this image is at /boot/isolinux/minirt.gz. To have Knoppix use your updated kernel, you have to update the image file, too, because it contains a number of kernel modules.

Use the following to uncompress the RAM disk:

```
# cd /home/knoppix/boot/isolinux
# gunzip minirt.gz
```

To access its contents, you have to mount the image:

```
# mkdir /home/knoppix/minirt
# mount -o loop minirt /home/knoppix/minirt
# cd /home/knoppix/minirt
```

Now comes the ugly part. You need to copy quite a few kernel modules, and if you are doing this more than once (which you probably will), you should make a shell script to automate the process. To make matters worse, the directories, names, and extensions of those kernel modules are all hard-coded and in a different location than they normally are. If you are remastering a newer version of Knoppix, check the locations of these modules in the modules/ directory. If you have a different kernel, you check its location in the /home/knoppix/knoppixun compressed/lib/modules/KERNEL_VERSION/kernel/drivers directory, replacing KERNEL_VERSION with the version you are using.

Copy the new/custom kernel modules into the new RAM disk:

```
# cp /home/knoppix/knoppixuncompressed/lib/modules/2.6.11/lib/⤸
    modules/2.6.11/kernel/drivers/block/cloop.ko /home/knoppix/⤸
    minirt/modules/cloop.ko
# cp /home/knoppix/knoppixuncompressed/lib/modules/2.6.11/lib/⤸
    modules/2.6.11/kernel/drivers/scsi/BusLogic.ko /home/⤸
    knoppix/minirt/modules/scsi/BusLogic.o
# cp /home/knoppix/knoppixuncompressed/lib/modules/2.6.11/lib/⤸
    modules/2.6.11/kernel/drivers/scsi/NCR53c406a.ko /home/⤸
    knoppix/minirt/modules/scsi/NCR53c406a.o
# cp /home/knoppix/knoppixuncompressed/lib/modules/2.6.11/lib/⤸
    modules/2.6.11/kernel/drivers/scsi/a100u2w.ko /home/⤸
    knoppix/minirt/modules/scsi/a100u2w.o
# cp /home/knoppix/knoppixuncompressed/lib/modules/2.6.11/lib/⤸
    modules/2.6.11/kernel/drivers/scsi/advansys.ko /home/⤸
    knoppix/minirt/modules/scsi/advansys.o
# cp /home/knoppix/knoppixuncompressed/lib/modules/2.6.11/lib/⤸
    modules/2.6.11/kernel/drivers/scsi/aic7xxx/aic7xxx.ko /⤸
    home/knoppix/minirt/modules/scsi/aic7xxx.o
```

```
# cp /home/knoppix/knoppixuncompressed/lib/modules/2.6.11/lib/↩
  modules/2.6.11/kernel/drivers/scsi/dtc.ko /home/knoppix/↩
  minirt/modules/scsi/dtc.o
# cp /home/knoppix/knoppixuncompressed/lib/modules/2.6.11/lib/↩
  modules/2.6.11/kernel/drivers/usb/host/ehci-hcd.ko /home/↩
  knoppix/minirt/modules/scsi/ehci-hcd.o
# cp /home/knoppix/knoppixuncompressed/lib/modules/2.6.11/lib/↩
  modules/2.6.11/kernel/drivers/scsi/fdomain.ko /home/↩
  knoppix/minirt/modules/scsi/fdomain.o
# cp /home/knoppix/knoppixuncompressed/lib/modules/2.6.11/lib/↩
  modules/2.6.11/kernel/drivers/scsi/gdth.ko /home/knoppix/↩
  minirt/modules/scsi/gdth.o
# cp /home/knoppix/knoppixuncompressed/lib/modules/2.6.11/lib/↩
  modules/2.6.11/kernel/drivers/scsi/ieee1394/ieee1394.ko /↩
  home/knoppix/minirt/modules/scsi/ieee1394.o
# cp /home/knoppix/knoppixuncompressed/lib/modules/2.6.11/lib/↩
  modules/2.6.11/kernel/drivers/scsi/initio.ko /home/↩
  knoppix/minirt/modules/scsi/initio.o
# cp /home/knoppix/knoppixuncompressed/lib/modules/2.6.11/lib/↩
  modules/2.6.11/kernel/drivers/scsi/mptscsih.ko /home/↩
  knoppix/minirt/modules/scsi/mptscsih.o
# cp /home/knoppix/knoppixuncompressed/lib/modules/2.6.11/lib/↩
  modules/2.6.11/kernel/drivers/usb/host/ohci-hcd.ko /home/↩
  knoppix/minirt/modules/scsi/ohci-hcd.o
# cp /home/knoppix/knoppixuncompressed/lib/modules/2.6.11/lib/↩
  modules/2.6.11/kernel/drivers/scsi/pas16.ko /home/knoppix/↩
  minirt/modules/scsi/pas16.o
# cp /home/knoppix/knoppixuncompressed/lib/modules/2.6.11/lib/↩
  modules/2.6.11/kernel/drivers/scsi/psi240i.ko /home/↩
  knoppix/minirt/modules/scsi/psi240i.o
# cp /home/knoppix/knoppixuncompressed/lib/modules/2.6.11/lib/↩
  modules/2.6.11/kernel/drivers/scsi/sbp2.ko /home/knoppix/↩
  minirt/modules/scsi/sbp2.o
# cp /home/knoppix/knoppixuncompressed/lib/modules/2.6.11/lib/↩
  modules/2.6.11/kernel/drivers/scsi/seagate.ko /home/↩
  knoppix/minirt/modules/scsi/seagate.o
# cp /home/knoppix/knoppixuncompressed/lib/modules/2.6.11/lib/↩
  modules/2.6.11/kernel/drivers/scsi/sym53c8xx_2/↩
  sym53c8xx.ko /home/knoppix/minirt/modules/scsi/sym53c8xx.o
# cp /home/knoppix/knoppixuncompressed/lib/modules/2.6.11/lib/↩
  modules/2.6.11/kernel/drivers/scsi/t128.ko /home/knoppix/↩
  minirt/modules/scsi/t128.o
# cp /home/knoppix/knoppixuncompressed/lib/modules/2.6.11/lib/↩
  modules/2.6.11/kernel/drivers/scsi/tmscsim.ko /home/↩
  knoppix/minirt/modules/scsi/tscsim.o
# cp /home/knoppix/knoppixuncompressed/lib/modules/2.6.11/lib/↩
  modules/2.6.11/kernel/drivers/scsi/u14-34f.ko /home/↩
  knoppix/minirt/modules/scsi/u14-34f.o
# cp /home/knoppix/knoppixuncompressed/lib/modules/2.6.11/lib/↩
  modules/2.6.11/kernel/drivers/scsi/ub.ko /home/knoppix/↩
  minirt/modules/scsi/ub.o
```

```
# cp /home/knoppix/knoppixuncompressed/lib/modules/2.6.11/lib/↩
   modules/2.6.11/kernel/drivers/scsi/ultrastor.ko /home/↩
   knoppix/minirt/modules/scsi/ultrastor.o
# cp /home/knoppix/knoppixuncompressed/lib/modules/2.6.11/lib/↩
   modules/2.6.11/kernel/drivers/usb/storage/usb-storage.ko /↩
   home/knoppix/minirt/modules/scsi/usb-storage.o
# cp /home/knoppix/knoppixuncompressed/lib/modules/2.6.11/lib/↩
   modules/2.6.11/kernel/drivers/usb/host/usb-uhci.ko /home/↩
   knoppix/minirt/modules/scsi/usb-uhci.o
# cp /home/knoppix/knoppixuncompressed/lib/modules/2.6.11/lib/↩
   modules/2.6.11/kernel/drivers/core/usbcore.ko /home/↩
   knoppix/minirt/modules/scsi/usbcore.o
# cp /home/knoppix/knoppixuncompressed/lib/modules/2.6.11/lib/↩
   modules/2.6.11/kernel/drivers/scsi/wd7000.ko /home/knoppix/↩
   minirt/modules/scsi/wd7000.o
```

If you make it through all these commands and all goes well, you've now replaced all the kernel modules on the Knoppix RAM disk. You might have noticed that in addition to SCSI and the cloop driver, the USB and FireWire kernel modules were included. All these kernel modules enable your Live CD to also boot from SCSI, USB, and FireWire devices!

Now you can umount the RAM disk and finalize your modifications to your Live CD:

```
# cd /home/knoppix/knoppixiso/boot/isolinux
# umount /home/knoppix/minirt
# gzip minirt
```

The updated RAM disk now resides at
/home/knoppix/knoppixiso/boot/isolinux/minirt.gz.

Copying the Kernel

The last step is to replace the actual kernel on your Live CD ISO. Copy it from the /boot directory in your chroot in your knoppixiso directory, overwriting the one previously used to boot Knoppix. For example:

```
# cp /home/knoppix/knoppixuncompressed/boot/↩
   vmlinuz-2.6.11 /home/knoppix/knoppixiso/boot/isolinux/linux
```

If you have installed a different kernel, check the /boot directory of your chroot for the correct name; the kernel name will start with vmlinuz and typically have the kernel version appended.

Survived until this point? Everything work as planned? Well done, because you have successfully replaced the Knoppix kernel! If something went wrong retrace your steps: Replacing the Knoppix kernel is an error-prone process and is likely to take a few tries before success is achieved.

Mastering the CD

Once you are done with your changes, it is time to compress the KNOPPIX/KNOPPIX filesystem and make the burnable CD ISO:

```
$ mkisofs -iso-level 4 -R -U -V "My LiveCD" -hide-rr-moved
    -cache-inodes -no-bak -pad /home/knoppix/
    knoppixuncompressed | nice -5 create_compressed_fs
    - 65536 > /home/knoppix/knoppixiso/KNOPPIX/KNOPPIX
```

Please be aware that this command should be executed on a single line, and it will take a long time to run, depending on the size of the /home/knoppix/knoppixuncompressed directory and the speed of your machine.

When the command is finished, you create the final ISO:

```
$ mkisofs -pad -l -r -J -v -V "My LiveCD" -b boot/
    isolinux/isolinux.bin -c boot/isolinux/boot.cat -no-emul
    -boot -boot-load-size 4 -boot-info-table -hide -rr -moved
    -o /home/knoppix/my-livecd.iso /home/knoppix/knoppixiso
```

If everything goes well, the final ISO should exist at /home/knoppix/my-livecd.iso.

Testing!

QEMU is an excellent tool for testing your ISO. It's a machine emulator that enables you to test your Live CD without having to (re)burn an actual Live CD. There is no reason not to use it—it will save you a lot of time and coasters. You can either apt-get it:

```
# apt-get install qemu
```

Or you can download it from http://fabrice.bellard.free.fr/qemu.

Using QEMU is very simple. It is a command-line tool, showing on your host system what would happen if you tried to boot your newly created Live CD. Here's the command:

```
$ qemu -cdrom /home/knoppix/my-livecd.iso
```

Once your Live CD works as planned, you can start burning the ISO using your favorite CD recording software. Knoppix comes with the excellent K3B CD/DVD burning suite that will make this easier.

Summary

This chapter explored the field of Knoppix remastering. It showed you how to extract the files from a Knoppix Live CD, how to install and remove software, how to do various other customizations, and how to put the pieces back together to create your very own Live CD based on Knoppix. The remaining chapters provide a couple of elaborate examples of customizing Knoppix for specific purposes.

Creating Archix,
Knoppix for Kids

In this chapter, you actually make your own Knoppix-based distro. The distro is targeted at kids between the ages of 6 and 13, for several reasons.

First, more kids should be using Linux and open source, and Knoppix is a great way to do that. Make it fun and easy to use and kids will start asking for Linux. Then, when they grow up, they'll take their preferences for Linux into the workplace, and Linux can achieve total world domination (cue maniacal laughter)!

Second, the distro can help harried parents. If your brother's kids are visiting, for example, and you don't want them messing around on your Windows machine because you don't want to clean spyware and other garbage off again (for the umpteenth time), boot with your customized Knoppix for kids and your worries are gone. They can have fun and maybe even learn something, and you don't have to spend hours after they leave cleaning off malware.

Third, the cool new distro could be a boon for schools. Microsoft and the Business Software Alliance have been making life miserable for several cash-strapped school districts in recent years. Nothing would be nicer than a switch to more open-source software so that those schools wouldn't have to spend what little money they have on software licenses.

in this chapter

☑ Preparing Knoppix

☑ Creating a new distro

☑ Customizing the look of your distro

☑ Mastering the CD

☑ Testing Archix

Note For information about Microsoft's and the BSA's actions against schools, see `http://dir.salon.com/tech/feature/2001/07/10/microsoft_school/index.html?sid=1039938`.

Finally, making a version of Knoppix for kids is fun, and once you get the basics down, you can customize it to meet the needs of the kids you know. Follow along with the instructions in this chapter, but then try your own thing. Change the software packages, use different images, and even change the name. Make this a version of Knoppix that your kids (or the kids you know) will enjoy!

Note Many of the commands in this chapter must be run as root, but many could be run as a normal user.

Preparing Knoppix

Before you can change Knoppix, you must get all the files on your Linux computer. Insert the Knoppix CD and mount it at /cdrom. Then run a command to create a subdirectory in your home directory that you'll use to store the CD's files:

```
$ mkdir /home/scott/knoppixiso
```

Now copy all the files from the Knoppix CD except for KNOPPIX/KNOPPIX:

```
$ cp -r /cdrom/[a-z]* /home/scott/knoppixiso
$ mkdir /home/scott/knoppixiso/KNOPPIX
$ cp -r /cdrom/KNOPPIX/*.* /cdrom/KNOPPIX/images /home/scott/⤶
  knoppixiso/KNOPPIX/
```

Note The author's directories are used in this project; you should substitute your own.

Now for the big boy: the compressed KNOPPIX/KNOPPIX file. As discussed in the preceding chapter, you can use the cloop kernel module if you've installed it. If Libranet, a Debian-based distro, did not come with that particular module, you can use the second method: the cloop command-line utilities. Are they on your machine?

```
# whereis extract_compressed_fs
```

Nope. If the whereis command can't find them, you need to install them. If you're using a Debian-based system, you can use APT, which makes it easy:

```
# apt-get install cloop-utils
```

After a minute or so, they're installed and ready to use. Then run the following command to extract the KNOPPIX/KNOPPIX file and get it on your hard drive:

```
# extract_compressed_fs /cdrom/KNOPPIX/KNOPPIX > /tmp/knoppix.iso
```

Note As cloop does its job, you'll see a lot of feedback on your screen, showing you each block as it's extracted. On a Pentium III 1GHz machine, it takes about five minutes to extract 30,728 blocks, which isn't too bad, except that the CPU has to run at nearly 100 percent the whole time, so you couldn't do a whole lot of other intensive work, other than read email. This might be a good time to get up and take a break.

When the extraction is complete, mount the KNOPPIX/KNOPPIX file as if it were a CD:

```
# mkdir /tmp/mountdir
# mount -t iso9660 /tmp/knoppix.iso /tmp/mountdir -o loop
```

The files are available at /tmp/mountdir, so now you can copy them to another subdirectory in your home directory.

```
$ mkdir /home/scott/knoppixuncompresssed
# cp -a /tmp/mountdir/* /home/scott/knoppixuncompressed/
```

Caution

You *must* run that `cp` command as root, or you will have problems later in this process! Yes, it's annoying to run one command as a normal user and one immediately thereafter as root; that's why you should use a terminal app such as Konsole, which provides tabs, or open two terminals, one as you and one as root, and switch between them with Alt+Tab.

After you've completed copying, clean up your filesystem before you move on to the fun stuff:

```
# umount /tmp/mountdir
# rm /tmp/knoppix.ixo
```

Creating a New Distro

It's almost time to craft a new distro based on Knoppix. There are a few things to do first to get your environment ready for the big changes in store, and then you need to get rid of as much unnecessary software as possible. Only then will you install new software for the kids, and wrap up by making some other changes designed to make your new distro kid friendly.

Preparing Your Environment

Tell your terminal that `/home/scott/knoppixuncompressed` (or whatever your directory is) is actually the root directory; otherwise, you won't be able to install and remove software correctly. To perform this magic, use the `chroot` command:

```
# chroot /home/scott/knoppixuncompressed
```

Your shell will change and will now think that `/home/scott/knoppixuncompressed` is actually `/`. In essence, the rest of your filesystem is hidden from this shell as long as you're inside it (if you type `exit`, you're back in a normal shell). Keep in mind that you're automatically running as root inside this `chroot` environment.

You also need to mount the `proc` filesystem inside your `chroot` jail, or things really won't work well:

```
# mount -t proc /proc proc
```

Note

Ignore the error message warning you that the system can't open the `/etc/fstab` file. No biggie.

Before you can install software, make sure that your Net connection is working by pinging a Website. For example:

```
# ping www.granneman.com
```

If it didn't work, you need to tell your chroot jail where your DNS servers are, so open `/etc/resolv.conf` with `vim` and then add the following line, pointing it to your router, the machine that handles DNS on your LAN:

```
nameserver 192.168.0.1
```

Note Don't remember how to use vim? Refer to Chapter 1.

Save the file and try pinging your server again. Success? Great! Time to remove some crud that kids don't need from the Knoppix disk!

Removing Software You Don't Need

Before adding or removing any software, tell APT to update the list of software available on repositories:

```
# apt-get update
```

You'll see a string of lines stream by as APT connects to the various repositories it knows about, thanks to the `/etc/apt/sources.list` file. When the process finishes, the great purge can begin.

First of all, how much space is currently used? To find out, use the `du` (disk usage) command:

```
# du -c
```

This command lists every directory and its size; and it can take a minute or two. When it's finished, take a look at the last line. Here's an example:

```
2804649 total
```

It says that out of the box, Knoppix is using 2.8GB of space. You need to jettison as much software as possible to make room for the packages you want to make available to the kids who will use your distro. Logically, it's a good idea to start with the stuff that's taking up the most space. To find out what packages are on Knoppix, sorted by size, with the largest at the end, run this command:

```
# dpkg-query -W --showformat='${Installed-Size} ${Package}\n' ⤶
   | sort -n
```

Try it out yourself, and look at the enormous list you've generated. Hmmm . . . it looks like the kde-i18n packages are pretty big, and if all the kids to whom you'll be giving your distro speak English, you could remove all the i18n packages. (i18n stands for internationalization: there are 18 letters between the i and the n.)

First you'd need to know the names of the i18n packages, so rerun the previous command, but this time pipe it through `grep` to show only packages with i18n in the name:

```
# dpkg-query -W --showformat='${Installed-Size} ${Package}\n' ⤶
   | sort -n | grep i18n
```

You could see quite a list, like this:

```
kde-i18n-tr
k3b-i18n
kde-i18n-ja
kde-i18n-pl
kde-i18n-ru
kde-i18n-nl
kde-i18n-es
kde-i18n-it
kde-i18n-fr
kde-i18n-de
```

Don't just remove these packages with APT; instead, purge them, which also removes any other files, such as configurations, from the machine. To do so, run this command:

```
# apt-get remove --purge kde-i18n-tr k3b-i18n kde-i18n-ja kde⤸
  -i18n-pl kde-i18n-ru kde-i18n-nl kde-i18n-es kde-i18n-it ⤸
  kde-i18n-fr kde-i18n-de
```

APT tells you what it's doing and then asks you a question:

```
Reading Package Lists... Done
Building Dependency Tree... Done
The following packages will be REMOVED:
  k3b-i18n* kde-i18n-de* kde-i18n-es* kde-i18n-fr* kde-i18n-it*
kde-i18n-ja* kde-i18n-nl* kde-i18n-pl* kde-i18n-ru* kde-i18n-tr*
0 upgraded, 0 newly installed, 10 to remove and 118 not upgraded.
Need to get 0B of archives.
After unpacking 196MB disk space will be freed.
Do you want to continue? [Y/n]
```

196MB removed? Do you want to continue? Why, yes! So type **Y**, press Enter, and watch as APT purges those packages from the machine.

What's next? Once again, run the following:

```
# dpkg-query -W --showformat='${Installed-Size} ${Package}\n' ⤸
  | sort -n
```

Here's an example of the result:

```
14076 scribus
15524 kstars-data
15548 libc6
15616 xserver-xfree86
15928 cupsys
16204 kcontrol
18048 enigma-data
18076 ethereal-common
19200 gimp-data
22988 kdevelop3-plugins
24372 mozilla-firefox
24552 kdelibs4
25980 libgcj4-dev
```

```
27129 kdelibs-data
33043 mozilla-thunderbird
34666 emacs21-common
38268 libwine
47168 kernel-image-2.6.11
```

Are kids really going to need emacs? Probably not. How many emacs packages are on Knoppix? Find out:

```
# dpkg-query -W --showformat='${Installed-Size} ${Package}\n' ⤶
    | sort -n | grep emacs
```

The results:

```
84 emacsen-common
338 emacs21-bin-common
5904 emacs21
34666 emacs21-common
```

No kid is going to use emacs (you might leave vim on your distro so that adults and really, really nerdy kids can edit config files). Purge emacs and related packages with this command:

```
# apt-get remove --purge emacs21-common emacs21 emacs21-bin⤶
    -common emacsen-common
```

APT tells you what it's going to do:

```
The following packages will be REMOVED:
  a2ps* emacs21* emacs21-bin-common* emacs21-common* emacsen-
common* gettext-el*
0 upgraded, 0 newly installed, 6 to remove and 118 not upgraded.
Need to get 0B of archives.
After unpacking 45.4MB disk space will be freed.
```

45MB gone? Sounds great!

This process can continue for a while. Here are other programs you could drop:

```
# apt-get remove --purge mozilla-thunderbird-offline mozilla⤶
    -thunderbird-locale-de mozilla-thunderbird
```

Any kid who needs to access email can use a Web browser to do so. Removing Thunderbird (which is a great program, just not for this particular distro) reclaims 34.3MB of space.

How about security tools? Does any kid need Ethereal or Nessus? And programming tools such as MySQL and KDevelop? If your child needs software like this, leave it, but most kids won't need it and you can use the space:

```
# apt-get remove --purge ethereal-common nessus-plugins ⤶
    mysql-server kdevelop3-data
```

APT lets you know that removing these packages also removes several others, including Ethereal, kdevelop3, kdevelop3-plugins, kismet, nessusd, startnessus-knoppix, and tethereal— 78.7MB of stuff.

Note While performing these actions, you are asked whether you want to completely purge some of the other components used by MySQL and whether you want to remove the entire Nessus directory. You can say yes to both. Just pay attention to questions like those while you're removing software, and you can get rid of even more unnecessary items.

Time for another check with du to see how you're doing in getting rid of unneeded packages:

```
# du -c
```

For this example, du reports that you're now down to 2503065KB — around 2.5GB. You've purged 301584KB from your distro — about 300MB or so. But there's more!

German Firefox files? They can go:

```
# apt-get remove --purge mozilla-firefox-locale-de mozilla ⏎
    -firefox-locale-de-de
```

This gets rid of 864KB.

How about OpenOffice.org?

```
# dpkg-query -W --showformat='${Installed-Size} ${Package}\n' ⏎
    | sort -n | grep openoffice
```

This presents some interesting results:

```
299508 openoffice-de-en
```

Keeping OpenOffice.org isn't a bad idea because kids can easily learn to use it, and it's good for them to have a good office suite for schoolwork. This particular one, however, is a combined German and English edition, and that doesn't make sense. Nuke it:

```
# apt-get remove --purge openoffice-de-en
```

That actually frees 307MB; but now install OpenOffice.org in just the English edition:

```
# apt-get install openoffice.org
```

Running this command means that you also have to install extra packages: libdb4.2++, libmyspell3, libneon23, libstlport4.6, openoffice.org-bin, openoffice.org-debian-files, and openoffice.org-l10n-en. A bunch of other packages are suggested and recommended, but you can ignore those. You need to download 55MB, and once that is unpacked and installed, it will take up 181MB of disk space. So removing the German and English version of OpenOffice.org and installing the English version saves you 127MB, which is still good.

Note Many of you may be thinking right now, forget OpenOffice.org! It shouldn't be in this distro at all! Remember, this is only an example distro, and you are free to do whatever you'd like with your distro when you remaster Knoppix.

There's yet another way you can squeeze some space. Remember that you've installed several software packages, and the installers are still sitting on your hard drive. To verify this, check how much space those installers are taking up:

```
# du -c /var/cache/apt/archives
```

The results come in quickly:

```
53812   ./var/cache/apt/archives
```

53MB of software you don't want. Tell APT to delete it:

```
# apt-get clean
```

Beautiful. What else? Well, a lot of times distros include several development packages designed for programmers or those who compile software. The kids using your distro don't need those, but how many are there? Here's how to check:

```
# dpkg-query -W --showformat='${Installed-Size} ${Package}\n' ⤵
    | sort -n | grep dev
```

The result shows 88 packages, totaling 135MB! Holy space waste, Batman!

Caution

You need to be careful while getting rid of the -dev packages, and read APT's warning closely because things may change in Knoppix between the time when this was written and when you're reading it.

Unfortunately, you can't just remove these packages all at once, or a lot more packages that depend upon them will be removed as well, like most of KDE. Instead, you'll need to remove them a bit at a time, paying careful attention to make sure you don't throw the baby out with the bath water. Following is an example of the process:

```
# apt-get remove --purge libxrender-dev libartsc0-dev ⤵
    libaspell-dev libbz2-dev pciutils-dev render-dev libwrap0 ⤵
    -dev libpopt-dev autotools-dev libesd0-dev libgpg-error ⤵
    -dev libxcursor-dev libfam-dev
```

18.8MB gone.

```
# apt-get remove --purge  libqt3-mt-dev libxft-dev libmad0 ⤵
    -dev xlibs-dev comerr-dev libxmuu-dev pm-dev libusb-dev ⤵
    libtasn1-2-dev libxrandr-dev libcupsys2-dev libxtst-dev ⤵
    libsm-dev libxp-dev libpam0g-dev libxpm-dev libxtrap-dev ⤵
    kudzu-knoppix-dev libopencdk8-dev libxv-dev libpcre3-dev ⤵
    libart-2.0-dev libjpeg62-dev libice-dev libogg-dev ⤵
    libexpat1-dev liblcms1-dev libaudiofile-dev
```

35.8MB outta here.

```
# apt-get remove --purge libglib1.2-dev libxmu-dev libpng12 ⤵
    -dev libxi-dev x-dev libsasl2-dev libgcrypt11-dev ⤵
    libjack0.80.0-dev libtiff4-dev libxext-dev libmng-dev ⤵
    libidn11-dev libgnutls11-dev libarts1-dev xlibmesa-glu ⤵
    -dev libxaw7-dev libjasper-1.701-dev libasound2-dev
```

7.5MB disappeared.

```
# apt-get remove --purge libglib2.0-dev libxml2-dev dietlibc ⤸
   -dev manpages-dev libaudio-dev libfreetype6-dev qt3-dev ⤸
   -tools libncurses5-dev binutils-dev libssl-dev ⤸
   libncurses5-dev binutils-dev
```

38.7MB bye-bye.

```
# apt-get remove --purge libgcj4-dev uudeview zlib1g-dev
```

27.6MB skidoo.

Amazing. What's left in this example are six dev packages that you can't remove without taking a lot of stuff you want to keep along with them, but that's acceptable. du -c reports that you've another deleted 112MB. Excellent!

That takes care of the dev stuff. Anything else? What about Apache? The kids you're targeting probably don't need a Web server:

```
# apt-get remove --purge apache2-utils apache-utils libapache ⤸
   -mod-ssl apache apache-common libapache-mod-php4
```

That sends 8MB to the bit bucket.

Here's another command that you can use:

```
# deborphan
```

The preceding command lists any libraries that aren't being used by any software packages on the system. Once you get the list, you can remove them:

```
# apt-get remove --purge libcvsservice0 libnas12 libzzip-0-12 ⤸
   libgmp3 libsvn0 libnspr4 libadns1 libkadm55 libtiffxx0
```

Another 3.2MB toodle-oo!

Installing the Software You Want

So far in this example, the only packages you installed were ones to make sure that you didn't lose some functionality you wanted to keep (OpenOffice.org). Mostly you've been streamlining your distro as much as possible. Now it's time to install stuff that you want kids to use.

How about some cool tools for learning how to type, discovering math, and painting on the computer:

```
# apt-get install tuxtype tuxmath tuxpaint
```

Now what? Well, Debian Jr. offers several different packages that you can use. To see the list, search the APT database:

```
# apt-cache search junior
```

It's quite a list:

```
junior-arcade - Debian Jr. arcade games
junior-art - Debian Jr. Art
junior-doc - Debian Jr. Documentation
junior-games-card - Debian Jr. Card Games
junior-games-gl - Debian Jr. 3D Games (hardware acceleration
required)
junior-games-net - Debian Jr. Network Games
junior-games-sim - Debian Jr. Simulation Games
junior-games-text - Debian Jr. Text Games
junior-gnome - Debian Jr. for Gnome
junior-internet - Debian Jr. Internet tools
junior-kde - Debian Jr. for KDE
junior-math - Debian Jr. educational math
junior-programming - Debian Jr. programming
junior-puzzle - Debian Jr. Puzzles
junior-sound - Debian Jr. sound
junior-system - Debian Jr. System tools
junior-toys - Debian Jr. desktop toys
junior-typing - Debian Jr. typing
junior-writing - Debian Jr. writing
```

Cool! Here's a quick-and-dirty way to install all of them at once:

```
# apt-get install $(apt-cache search junior- | awk '{print $1}')
```

Whoa, Nelly! That's going to install 183 packages that will require a 138MB download and then take up 347MB of space on the distro. You'd be back near where you started. Forget it!

A better method is to install only the Debian Jr. packages you actually want, or to just pick and choose the individual software items in each Debian Jr. metapackage.

For instance, if you want to check out Debian Jr. Internet packages, see what would happen if you installed it:

```
# apt-get install junior-internet
```

Here's what APT tells you:

```
The following extra packages will be installed:
  dillo libnspr4 mozilla mozilla-browser mozilla-mailnews mozilla-
psm
Suggested packages:
  mozilla-chatzilla xprt latex-xft-fonts
Recommended packages:
  myspell-en-us myspell-dictionary
The following NEW packages will be installed:
  dillo junior-internet libnspr4 mozilla mozilla-browser mozilla-
mailnews mozilla-psm
0 upgraded, 7 newly installed, 0 to remove and 83 not upgraded.
Need to get 12.7MB of archives.
After unpacking 39.1MB of additional disk space will be used.
```

If that looks good to you, go ahead and enter Y. Otherwise, enter N and be done with it, or install the individual packages that make up junior-internet, like mozilla-browser or dillo.

The Debian Jr. typing package is another in which you may be interested:

```
# apt-get install junior-typing
```

Find out what packages will be installed:

```
Reading Package Lists... Done
Building Dependency Tree... Done
The following extra packages will be installed:
  gtypist tipptrainer tipptrainer-data-de typespeed wamerican
wenglish wxwin2.4-i18n xletters
The following NEW packages will be installed:
  gtypist junior-typing tipptrainer tipptrainer-data-de typespeed
wamerican wenglish wxwin2.4-i18n xletters
0 upgraded, 9 newly installed, 0 to remove and 83 not upgraded.
Need to get 2037kB of archives.
After unpacking 6412kB of additional disk space will be used.
```

Look good? Go for it. Otherwise, ignore them, or feel free to pick and choose the software you want.

A distro for kids should be fun, don't you think? Check out the games:

```
# apt-cache search junior-games | awk '{print $1}'
```

These are the Debian Jr. metapackages that come up:

```
junior-games-card
junior-games-gl
junior-games-net
junior-games-sim
junior-games-text
```

Looks good. Here's how to install them the easy way:

```
# apt-get install $(apt-cache search junior-games | awk ⤸
   '{print $1}')
```

APT informs you that you're going to install 34 games, which will require a download of 33MB and 70.9MB of space on your drive. You've made room, and this should fit.

Of course, you could continue deleting and installing software, but it's time to move on. You need to perform any final clean-ups before proceeding.

```
# apt-get clean
```

That gets rid of 155MB you didn't need, but there's more. As you've been working, you may have been generating system mail. Use the following to remove it:

```
# rm -rf /var/mail/root
```

Finally, remove anything in the /tmp directory:

```
# rm -rf /tmp
```

Whew! Before leaving your chroot environment, unmount the proc filesystem:

```
# umount /proc
```

Caution Do not forget to unmount the proc filesystem, or your Knoppix may not function the way you want it to!

Now it's time to leave `chroot`:

```
# exit
```

You're now back in your normal shell, but, no, you're not finished yet.

Customizing the Look of Your Distro

You have the software you want, but you still need to make things look fun and inviting for the kiddies. You can make some changes that will improve the look of your new distro.

Getting a Desktop Background

The normal desktop background is OK, but the kids would get a kick out of something that's a bit cooler. First you need to find an image. If you're making this distro for a particular individual who has a favorite picture, by all means, use that; but if you would instead like to find something online, you'll find a few ideas in this section and the accompanying sidebar, "Searching for Cool Wallpaper." Just make sure that any images you decide to use are freely available or licensed in such a way that you can use them without any problems.

There's a particular image from the Astronomy Picture of the Day site that it is beautiful and thought-provoking, qualities you should always look for in a good photograph. Titled "Earth at Night," the photo (shown in Figure 11-1) was chosen as Picture of the Day in 2000. You can find it at `http://antwrp.gsfc.nasa.gov/apod/ap001127.html`.

FIGURE 11-1: Earth at Night

C. Mayhew and R. Simmon (NASA/GSFC), NOAA/ NGDC, DMSP Digital Archive

The composite photograph gives you a powerful sense of humanity's presence on the globe, perfect for a discussion with an intelligent kid. Where are there lights? Why? Where are there fewer lights? Why is that? Geography, history, environmentalism: It can all be taught using this one image.

The 386KB image's 2400 × 1200 dimensions won't work with Knoppix. Instead, it needs to be 1024 × 768. Open the image in the GIMP (examined in Chapter 1) and change the image's dimensions. Yes, the image will be a bit distorted, but it's not that bad, and it actually is closer to the Gall-Peters projection that some geographers find more accurate.

 Note For more information on the various ways to picture the spherical earth on a flat surface, see Gall-Peters projection (http://en.wikipedia.org/wiki/Gall-Peters_projection), Mercator projection (http://en.wikipedia.org/wiki/Mercator_projection), and Map projection (http://en.wikipedia.org/wiki/Map_projection).

Alternately, you can use the GIMP to change the size of the image's width, but keep your dimensions proportional. Then change the size of the image's canvas to 1024 × 768, center the image vertically, and give the blank areas at the top and bottom of the canvas a color, like the deep navy of the photo or black.

Once you have the image you want, copy it into the appropriate location in the Knoppix file system structure:

```
$ cp knoppix.jpg /home/scott/knoppixuncompressed/usr/local/lib/
```

Now when your distro finishes loading, the kids using it will have an amazing image in front of their eyes.

Changing the Boot Screen

Long before the desktop background screen shows up, the boot screen makes its appearance. That's where you can present the user with the name of your distro. This is clearly an important consideration: Your custom distro's name should be short, snappy, descriptive, and somehow cool. For example, St. Louis is the home of the world-famous Arch, and that's what sparked the name Archix for this chapter's example kid distro. It seemed like a fun name to use.

Creating a boot screen isn't nearly as easy as making a desktop background image. First, open the GIMP and create a blank image that's 640 × 480 pixels in size. Paste in a photo or some other graphic that you like (the example uses a photo of the Arch taken from one of its legs). Then use the Text tool to insert text blocks that describe your distro, welcome new users, and let them know to press Enter to boot the CD. Don't be afraid to use a little color to spice things up (a little orange, a popular color with kids, could give a little zing to the text showing your distro's name).

To finalize things for Knoppix, save your image as a PPM file (the example is, cleverly enough, archix.ppm). Then set it to use only 16 colors, which is required by Knoppix. This may chew up your image quite a bit, and greatly limit the quality of your boot screen, but you have no choice. It must be 16 colors. To limit the color palette, select Image → Mode → Indexed, choose Generate Optimum Palette, and then set Maximum Number of Colors to 16. The boot screen shown in Figure 11-2 isn't exactly a work of art, but it's clear and neat enough for kids to enjoy.

Searching for Cool Wallpaper

There are loads of Websites from which you can get terrific pictures to use as wallpaper for your distro. Here are some sites to check out:

- Creative Commons—`http://creativecommons.org/image/`. Creative Commons provides an alternative to copyright; instead of "All rights reserved," it's "Some rights reserved." It's brilliant.

- Common Content—`http://commoncontent.org/`. A catalog of works licensed using Creative Commons.

- Flickr—`http://flickr.com`. The best photo-sharing site in the world. In particular, see `http://flickr.com/creativecommons/`, which contains Flickr photos available under a Creative Commons license.

- Stock.XCHNG—`http://sxc.hu/`. 100,000+ stock photos taken by 9,000+ individuals

- The Open Photo Project—`http://openphoto.net/`. 2,395 photos taken by 2,158 users, and all photos are released under a Creative Commons license.

- Astronomy Picture of the Day—`http://antwrp.gsfc.nasa.gov/apod/`. Gorgeous, stunning astronomy photos available for personal, noncommercial, nonpublic fair use.

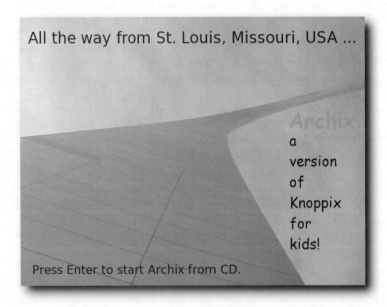

FIGURE 11-2: The boot screen for Archix utilizes the famous St. Louis Arch.

On the command line, convert the ppm to lss16, the format that Knoppix uses for a boot screen. The name must be `logo.16`, so don't use anything else:

```
$ ppmtolss16 < archix.ppm > logo.16
```

Now move the image to its correct location in the Knoppix filesystem:

```
# cp logo.16 /home/scott/knoppixiso/boot/isolinux/
```

You've customized the images that people will now associate with your distro. There's still more you could do, but this is enough to give you some ideas to tackle on your own.

Mastering the CD

You can now see the light at the end of the tunnel. All that's left is compressing your work, putting it onto a CD, and then final testing.

Begin by compressing the `KNOPPIX/KNOPPIX` filesystem:

```
$ mkisofs -iso-level 4 -R -U -V "Archix" -hide-rr-moved ⤶
   -cache-inodes -no-bak -pad /home/scott/knoppixuncompressed ⤶
   | nice -5 create_compressed_fs - 65536 > /home/scott ⤶
   /knoppixiso/KNOPPIX/KNOPPIX
```

This command can take a while, depending on the size of the `knoppixuncompressed` directory and the speed of your machine. When it's finished, it's time (finally!) to create your final burnable or loadable ISO image:

```
$ mkisofs -pad -l -r -J -v -V "Archix" -b boot/isolinux/ ⤶
   isolinux.bin -c boot/isolinux/boot.cat -no-emul-boot ⤶
   -boot-load-size 4 -boot-info-table -hide -rr -moved -o ⤶
   /home/scott/archix.iso /home/scott/knoppixiso
```

Again, this will take quite a while. It will finally finish, and `ls -l /home/scott` now shows the following:

```
-rw-r--r--  1 root     root       653142016 Jun 12 22:55 archix.iso
```

Awesome! Only 653MB! Archix is smaller than Knoppix itself, so there's plenty of room to add other software if the distro is ever re-remastered Archix.

There is one thing to fix before continuing. You don't want the ISO in your home directory to be owned by root, so you need to change the permissions (using your own info, of course), and then check it once again with `ls -l`:

```
# chown scott.scott archix.iso
# ls -l
-rw-r--r--  1 rsgranne    rsgranne     653142016 Jun 12 22:55
archix.iso
```

Now you can do whatever you want with your distro: burn it, test it, use it, or delete it and start all over.

Testing Archix

To test your ISO, you can use QEMU, an emulator that enables you to test the distro without burning it. To be honest, QEMU is slooooooooow. It would probably be quicker to burn the ISO file to a CD and test by booting with it, but it doesn't hurt to know how to use QEMU, and it is pretty cool.

If QEMU isn't already on your Debian-based system, you need to install it:

```
# apt-get install qemu
```

Once the program is on your system, you can test your distro with a simple command:

```
$ qemu -cdrom archix.iso
```

Booting Archix with QEMU took about 20 minutes from start to KDE (as they say in Missouri, slower than molasses running uphill in January). However, you will know for sure that your .iso is good and that your distro will boot. Time to burn that ISO to CDs and start handing them out to kids you know. It's going to be fun!

Summary

From preparing Knoppix to actually creating the new distro by removing and installing software, to customizing the look of your new distro and naming it, to mastering the CD image and testing it, remastering is a long process. Still, it's completely fascinating and you'll learn a lot about Knoppix, Linux, and all sorts of other items. Best of all, you'll have the satisfaction of knowing that you made something cool: a Linux Live CD distro that meets your needs and fulfills your creativity. Now how many people can say that? Not many. So why not get busy today and join them?

Creating Myppix, Your Personal Knoppix

I n this chapter, you apply what you learned in Chapters 9 and 10 to create your own Knoppix-based distro that is completely focused on you. It'll have all your settings, your favorite software, and everything "just so" — a Knoppix CD that's customized exactly the way you want it.

It's called Myppix because there's evidently a cosmic computing law stating that variants of Knoppix end with "ppix," or, if that's not possible, at least "ix," and because the name is descriptive and appropriate (literally "My Knoppix"). Of course, you can give yours any name you want.

The essentials of remastering Knoppix were explained in detail in the previous two chapters, so none of that needs to be repeated here. If you skipped ahead to this chapter and find yourself wondering what the heck you're doing, go back and read Chapters 10 and 11.

Before You Begin

Before you begin the whole remastering process that will eventually end with the unveiling of Myppix before the world, you need to perform a step that looks completely unrelated at first. Trust me, though — it will all become clear by the end of this chapter.

Configuring Your World

Start by booting using your favorite Knoppix disk, the one that you're soon going to use as a basis for Myppix. Once Knoppix has finished booting, change things to your liking. For instance, here are a few things you might do whenever you start out with a brand-new Knoppix:

- **Change the fonts:** See "Beautifying Knoppix" in Chapter 1. Set your font choices everywhere, so that all your programs, and even KDE itself, look nice, crisp, and readable.

- **Set up your printers:** Using the advice given in the section "Setting Up Printers" in Chapter 1, you can set up all of the printers you might use with your Knoppix — your home printer(s), your office printer, your friends' printers — ahead of time.

- **Choose your text editor:** If your text editor of choice is vim, for example, you probably have a `.vimrc` config file (and perhaps a `.gvimrc` file for those times when you use vim with a GUI). Copy those vim files into Knoppix. Do you have any scripts that reside in your `~/.vim` directory? You'll want to copy them, too, so you'll be ready to work with any text file.

- **Set up other key system files:** There are other important config files that you may want to have available whenever your custom Knoppix distro boots. Here are some examples: `~/.bashrc` (aliases galore!), `~/.gnupg` (be careful with this one — remember that it contains your private GnuPG keys!), `~/.mozilla` (actually the location of your Firefox bookmarks, settings, and extensions), and `~/.openoffice.org`. Again, copy any important or customized files and directories to your running instance of Knoppix.

- **Set your KDE preferences:** Your `~/.kde` directory contains several important files that control how your KDE apps work. If you're in a hurry, you could just copy the entire `~/.kde/share/config` directory from your usual Linux machine to the computer that's running Knoppix. If you want to go the slow 'n' steady route, once Knoppix is running, make all your changes by using the KDE Control Center and the Preferences found in the KDE programs you run.

  For instance, you may have very specific settings for KMail (and the rest of the Kontact suite, including KOrganizer and KAddressBook), Konqueror (both in file manager and Web browser mode), and Konsole (white text on a black background, perhaps?). It just won't be your distro until those apps are set up the way you like them.

- **Copy your `~/bin` directory:** If you're always writing (and finding) new scripts that make your life easier, you undoubtedly follow good Linux practice and keep them in `~/bin`, so you certainly want to copy that directory, too.

- **Rearrange your KDE panel:** When you first start KDE, it creates a default panel (see Figure 12-1) at the bottom of your screen.

Figure 12-1: The KDE default panel, just begging for improvement.

You can change it, too. For example, you can banish the Window List and the big Home, Konsole, and OpenOffice icons by right-clicking each and selecting Remove. (You can get them back, if you like.) Right-click on the panel, and choose Panel Menu→ Add to Panel, or just Add to Panel (it changes depending on the location of your right-click). Inside Add to Panel, select Applet→ Quick Launcher. This adds a collection of smaller icons, including Home and Konsole. Three others appear by default: Control Center, Help, and KWrite. (Because Help is accessible through the K menu, you can right-click the little icon and select Remove to clear it off your panel.) Then right-click in the Quick Launcher and select Add Application→ Office→ OpenOffice.org→ OpenOffice, followed by Add Application→ Editors→ GVim Text Editor. That puts small OpenOffice.org and GVim Text Editor icons into Quick Launcher. Now your panel should look more like the one shown in Figure 12-2.

FIGURE 12-2: A much cleaner, more efficient panel

If you've been paying attention, you've noticed that many of these files are very personal. Some of them contain unencrypted passwords, and others would enable someone to impersonate you online. The whole point of Myppix is that it's a distro made just for you, which means that you shouldn't be handing out copies of your Myppix willy-nilly to everyone you meet. The only person running Myppix should be you!

If you want to make any other changes, now is the time. Open the preferences, options, and settings of your favorite programs and configure everything to fit your needs. Close all your programs when you've finished. Done? OK, on to the next step: saving all your changes for eventual inclusion in Myppix!

Saving Those Changes

How to save your settings for later re-use was explained earlier in the book, and now it's time to put it to practice. From the KNOPPIX menu select→ Configure→ Save KNOPPIX Configuration. The Create KNOPPIX Configuration Archive window appears (see Figure 12-3).

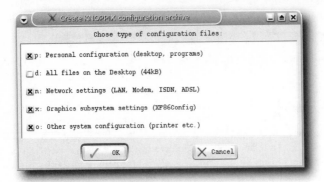

FIGURE 12-3: Which config files do you want to save?

If you want to preserve all the changes you just made, make sure that you check both Personal Configuration and Other System Configuration. If you left some files or data on the Desktop, check All Files on the Desktop as well. I don't recommend that you check Network settings or Graphics subsystem settings because you'll want those to change with the machine and network on which you're going to use Myppix. Click OK, and then choose where you want the config files to be saved (see Figure 12-4).

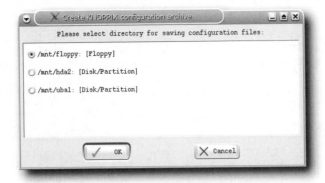

FIGURE 12-4: Pick where you want to save your configuration files.

You can choose a floppy, but that's so 2002. A USB flash drive (/mnt/uba1) will work, and so will a hard drive (/mnt/hda2 on my computer), as long as you can easily access the files once you begin the remastering process. Make your selection and click OK. Knoppix shows you a progress bar as it saves everything, and then displays a window indicating success. Click OK to close it, and verify that the files are where you can get to them in just a few minutes.

For example, there could be two files on your USB flash drive: `configs.tbz` and `knoppix.sh`. `configs.tbz` consist of changed files from `/etc` and `/home/knoppix`, which is exactly what you want.

That's it for settings and configurations. Soon you'll use the files you just created.

Preparing Knoppix

You must get all of the files onto your computer before you can change Knoppix. To do so, return to Chapter 11 and follow all of the instructions in the "Preparing Knoppix" section.

Creating Your New Distro

Now that preparations are completed, you can begin the fun part: making Myppix. Start thinking now, if you haven't already, about exactly what you want in a Knoppix built especially for you. What settings do you always alter? What software do you always install? What packages never get used? Fonts, colors, home pages . . . what do you like? Try to make a list of the things to go into *your* Linux.

Meanwhile, set up your remastering environment by returning to Chapter 11 and following all of the instructions in the "Preparing Your Environment" section.

All set? Good. Let's move on. In Chapter 11, you removed any software that didn't seem appropriate for the kiddies. For instance, you said bye-bye to internationalization packages, emacs, security tools, Thunderbird, Apache, development packages, and a whole lot more. You're not a kid, though, and you probably want to keep some of that stuff, so this time things are going to be a bit different. From your creation of Archix, you most likely have an idea of the things you want to remove from your own distro, but let's take another look at that procedure anyway.

As always, before adding or removing software, you need to tell APT to update the list of software available on repositories:

```
# apt-get update
```

Information appears on your terminal as APT connects to repositories listed in the `/etc/apt/sources.list` file. The first thing to do is update APT itself, just in case there's something new in there that you need, so enter the following on the command line:

```
# apt-get install apt apt-utils -t unstable
```

`unstable` in this command means, roughly, the beta set of Debian packages. APT asks whether you want to install the packages you indicated, as well as a few others. Enter **Y**, and, after that process completes, run the update command again. Then you can nuke some packages.

It's always vital to keep tabs on how much space is currently used in your distro, so run the disk usage command:

```
# du -c
```

Wait while this command lists every directory and its size, and then pay attention to the last line. For example, a last line that reads

```
2458927 total
```

tells you that Knoppix is using 2.45GB of space, and you'd need to get rid of as much software as possible so that you can install the packages you want to use when you run Myppix. It's helpful to first erase the packages that are taking up the most space. To find out what packages are on Knoppix, sorted by size, with the largest found at the bottom, run this command (actually, two commands, joined together by the pipe):

```
# dpkg-query -W --showformat='${Installed-Size} ${Package}\n' ⤸
  | sort -n
```

When you created Archix, the distro for kids, you dumped the kde-i18n ("internationalization") packages, and you can do the same now with Myppix if you're an English speaker and don't need Russian, Spanish, Italian, or Japanese translations of everything.

To elucidate the names of the i18n packages, rerun the previous command, but add another pipe followed by another grep so that you see only packages with i18n in the name:

```
# dpkg-query -W --showformat='${Installed-Size} ${Package}\n' ⤸
  | sort -n | grep i18n
```

Here's an example list of packages:

```
kde-i18n-tr
k3b-i18n
kde-i18n-ja
kde-i18n-pl
kde-i18n-ru
kde-i18n-nl
kde-i18n-es
kde-i18n-it
kde-i18n-fr
kde-i18n-de
```

You don't just want to remove these packages with APT; you want to purge them, which also removes any other files, such as configurations, from the machine. To do that, run this command:

```
# apt-get remove --purge kde-i18n-tr k3b-i18n kde-i18n-ja ⤸
   kde-i18n-pl kde-i18n-ru kde-i18n-nl kde-i18n-es kde-i18n ⤸
   -it kde-i18n-fr kde-i18n-de
```

APT lets you know what it's about to do and then asks you a question:

```
Reading Package Lists... Done
Building Dependency Tree... Done
The following packages will be REMOVED:
  k3b-i18n* kde-i18n-de* kde-i18n-es* kde-i18n-fr* kde-i18n-it*
kde-i18n-ja* kde-i18n-nl* kde-i18n-pl* kde-i18n-ru* kde-i18n-tr*
0 upgraded, 0 newly installed, 10 to remove and 118 not upgraded.
Need to get 0B of archives.
After unpacking 196MB disk space will be freed.
Do you want to continue? [Y/n]
```

If you want to remove 196MB of software you don't need, type Y, press Enter, and watch as APT purges those packages from the machine.

In the spirit of removing internationalization files, you can get rid of German Firefox files as well:

```
# apt-get remove --purge mozilla-firefox-locale-de mozilla
  -firefox-locale-de-de
```

That's another 864KB purged.

If you rely on OpenOffice.org and you've been dumping the internationalization files, purge the combined German/English version of OpenOffice.org that comes with Knoppix:

```
# apt-get remove --purge openoffice-de-en
```

Now install OpenOffice.org, and some other packages that OOo uses, but in just the English edition:

```
# apt-get install openoffice.org openoffice.org-mimelnk
    openoffice.org-kde openoffice.org-hyphenation-en-us
    openoffice.org-thesaurus-en-us openoffice.org-help-en
    -t unstable
```

By running this command, you have to install extra packages, but that's fine. You're still actually saving space; and more important, you're getting your toolkit in place just the way you want it.

If you like the vim text editor and never use emacs, you can gain a little more space with this command:

```
# apt-get remove --purge emacs21-common emacs21 emacs21-bin
    -common emacsen-common
```

Then update vim:

```
# apt-get install vim vim-common vim-gtk vim-scripts vimpart
    vim-doc -t unstable
```

You may recall removing the dev files from Archix in Chapter 11. That's a huge process, so if you'd like to delete those files from your distro, just follow the instructions in that chapter.

Now what? Well, at the time of writing, new versions of Mozilla Firefox and Thunderbird are out, and you probably want to upgrade to those. To find out whether they're available, run the following command, which tells APT that you want to upgrade to the Unstable (which means beta, roughly) set of Debian packages for that software. After the command, however, when you're asked if you in fact want to do the full, humongous upgrade of all packages to Unstable, immediately press n for No.

```
# apt-get upgrade -t unstable
```

Caution

I'm serious! Do not press **Y** here! Press **n**! Otherwise, you'll be installing about 50 gazillion packages.

Look through the massive list of packages for anything with "mozilla" in the name. Yup—there they are: mozilla-firefox, mozilla-thunderbird, and mozilla-thunderbird-offline. Just what you want, so use the following command:

```
# apt-get install mozilla-firefox mozilla-thunderbird ⮑
   mozilla-thunderbird-offline -t unstable
```

Some other packages come along for the ride, such as gcc-4.0-base, but that's okay.

If you want to upgrade KDE to the latest version available, again use apt-get upgrade -t unstable, and again press **n** so you can get a good look at the KDE packages that are there. Then upgrade with this command:

```
# apt-get install kate-plugins kdeaddons-kfile-plugins kdelibs ⮑
   -bin kdelibs-data kdelibs4 kernel-package kget kismet ⮑
   klogd konq-plugins kpf kphone kppp krdc krfb -t unstable
```

Cool. Now you're running the latest version of KDE. What else do you need? Well, Quanta, for example, is an excellent HTML editor that you can use to make Web pages and edit blog entries:

```
# apt-get install quanta -t unstable
```

What about security? If you use Knoppix to run security apps, you need to upgrade those, too:

```
# apt-get install ca-certificates chkrootkit ethereal ⮑
   ethereal-common ettercap-common ettercap-gtk gnupg nessus ⮑
   nessus-plugins nessusd nmap openssl tcpdump tethereal ⮑
   traceroute -t unstable
```

Want to use Myppix for multimedia? Update some of those related packages:

```
# apt-get install gimp gimp-data imagemagick xmms-cdread ⮑
   xmms-volnorm -t unstable
```

If you like nice fonts, try this:

```
# apt-get install msttcorefonts -t unstable
```

After that, run the deborphan command, which, you'll remember, lists libraries that are no longer in use by any other packages and therefore are safe to delete:

```
# deborphan
```

Then delete any packages that deborphan finds. That helps a bit.

You've installed a lot of software onto your system, and those installers are just taking up space that you need. How much space are the installers taking up? Check with this:

```
# du -c /var/cache/apt/archives
```

The results come in quickly; for example:

```
166429   /var/cache/apt/archives
```

Whoa. That's 166MB of software installers. Use APT to delete that stuff:

```
# apt-get clean
```

All gone. How big is your distro now?

```
# du -c
...
2449237 total
```

Excellent. You've got the software situation in hand. Time to perform final clean-ups.

All of this installing and uninstalling has been generating system mail that you need to remove:

```
# rm -rf /var/mail/root
```

Anything in the /tmp directory needs to go:

```
# rm -rf /tmp
```

Before exiting your chroot environment, unmount the proc filesystem:

```
# umount /proc
```

Do not forget to do this or your new Knoppix variant may not work the way you're expecting!

Finally, it's time to leave chroot:

```
# exit
```

You're now back in your normal shell, where you have some further customizations to perform.

Customizing the Look of the Distro

You have the software you want, but you might want to make things look cool.

In the preceding chapter, you learned how to set the desktop's background image to something a bit more interesting. The image used there — the earth at night, with all the lights in the world twinkling — is pretty cool. You can follow the instructions in Chapter 11 to change your desktop background to that image or to any other image you want.

Long before the Desktop background screen shows up, the boot screen make its appearance. That's where you usually present the user with the name of your distro and any other important information. Because the main user of Myppix is, well, *you*, there really isn't a huge need to change the boot screen. You know that this is your distro, after all, and you are the intended user, so a boot screen seems a bit superfluous.

OK, OK . . . if you really want to create your own boot screen, the entire process is covered in Chapter 11. Take a look there, and go crazy making a boot screen that absolutely screams *you*.

The Big Secret

Here's the big bad secret that you've been waiting for breathlessly: how to truly make this a distro that *exactly* meets your needs and wants. Since the beginning of this chapter, you booted Knoppix, customized things to your liking, and then saved your Knoppix config files. Now you'll include those files with your distro. Bingo! When you boot Myppix, you'll have in front of you all of your settings, your fonts, your bookmarks, and more! Is that cool or what?

Remember the files you created in the "Saving Those Changes" section? Named `configs.tbz` and `knoppix.sh`, these files contain, respectively, copies of key system config files and a script that automatically uses them when Knoppix boots. Find those files on your USB flash drive or hard drive — wherever you saved them — and copy them to the `knoppixiso/KNOPPIX` directory. For example, to copy the files from my USB flash drive, I use these commands:

```
$ cp /media/uba1/configs.tbz /home/scott/knoppixiso/KNOPPIX/
$ cp /media/uba1/knoppix.sh /home/scott/knoppixiso/KNOPPIX/
```

That's it! Now that those files have been copied into what will become the Myppix file structure, all you need to do is boot Myppix, and all your settings will be put into place. Man, that's easy . . . and really useful!

Mastering the CD

It's time to turn Myppix into an actual product! Start by compressing the KNOPPIX/KNOPPIX filesystem, using your own directories, of course:

```
$ mkisofs -iso-level 4 -R -U -V "Myppix" -hide-rr-moved -cache
   -inodes -no-bak -pad /home/scott/knoppixuncompressed |
   nice -5 create_compressed_fs - 65536 /home/scott/
   knoppixiso/KNOPPIX/KNOPPIX
```

Not surprising, this command can run for a long time, depending on the size of the knoppix-uncompressed directory and the speed of your machine. When the command finishes running, you can create the ISO image you're going to burn:

```
$ mkisofs -pad -l -r -J -v -V "Myppix" -b boot/isolinux/
   isolinux.bin -c boot/isolinux/boot.cat -no-emul-boot
   -boot-load-size 4 -boot-info-table -hide -rr -moved
   -o /home/scott/myppix.iso /home/scott/knoppixiso/
```

Again, this takes some time to run. When it finally finishes, `ls -l /home/scott` displays something like the following:

```
-rw-r--r--   1 root     root      664347215 Jun 13 12:55 myppix.iso
```

664MB. Not too bad, and there's still some space to add additional software to your distro if you ever want to re-remaster Myppix again.

There's one thing to fix before continuing. You probably don't want the ISO in your home directory to be owned by root, so you need to change the permissions to use your system's username, and then check it once again with ls -1:

```
# chown scott.scott myppix.iso
# ls -l
-rw-r--r--   1 rsgranne      rsgranne      664347215 Jun 13 ⤶
    12:55 myppix.iso
```

It's alive! It's alive! Myppix.iso is available for burning, testing, using, or whatever the heck you want to do with it.

Testing Myppix

As discussed in Chapter 11, QEMU is an emulator that enables you to test (albeit verrrrrrrry slooooooowly) the Myppix ISO without having to burn it first.

To test Myppix with QEMU, run the following:

```
$ qemu -cdrom myppix.iso
```

Booting Myppix with qemu took more than 20 minutes from start to KDE. That's a long time to wait, but you'll be certain that myppix.iso is good and that your distro will boot.

Summary

This chapter has focused on your specific needs as you create Myppix, a Knoppix-based distro just for you. One of the most important steps is at the beginning, when you boot Knoppix, configure everything to your liking, and then save those changes. Then you prepare Knoppix, remove and install software packages, customize the look of your new distro, copy over the saved config files, and finally master and test your CD image. The whole process takes a while, but the result is awesome: Myppix, a distro just for you. Enjoy!

Booting Knoppix

You are visiting a friend who just got the latest Knoppix CD. Excitedly, he puts it in the CD-ROM drive of his computer, boots up the PC, and a few minutes later you are both oooo-ing and ahhh-ing at the beautiful KDE Desktop. Life is good. After surfing the Web, writing some emails, and chatting with friends, he powers off and hands you the CD. You go home, put the CD in your PC's CD drive, power up the machine, and walk away to get a refreshing beverage from the fridge. When you get back, you look at the screen and see . . . nothing—nothing but a blank screen.

What happened? This same CD worked beautifully at your friend's house. To understand what might be wrong, you first need to understand how Knoppix boots.

Ideal Boot Process

Ideally, to boot Knoppix, you set your BIOS to boot from the CD-ROM, insert the Knoppix CD into your computer's CD drive, and then boot (either turn on the power or reboot the machine). After a few moments, the Knoppix splash screen displays. If you do nothing or press the Enter key, Knoppix boots using the default settings. After a few text messages go by, Knoppix displays the KDE splash screen followed shortly by the KDE Desktop.

That's what is supposed to happen, and while it sounds fairly simple, there's actually a lot more going on under the hood.

Booting: the Traditional View

The way Knoppix boots is not that different from any other Linux distribution. The BIOS loads the bootloader `isolinux` from the CD-ROM and turns control over to it. `Isolinux` locates and loads the Linux kernel and then mounts the initial ramdisk, `miniroot`, which contains the boot script `/linuxrc`. `/linuxrc` does all the heavy lifting by mounting the compressed system image on the CD and doing the primary hardware probing and setup.

Once /linuxrc finishes, it hands control over to /etc/init, which reads and parses /etc/inittab. With the default boot options, /etc/init runs the initial startup scripts in /etc/rc*, which tend to be soft links to files in /etc/init.d/. The most notable startup script is /etc/init.d/knoppix-autoconfig, which further probes and configures the system's hardware. When it finishes, init enters runlevel 5 and runs the script /etc/init.d/xsession, which starts X11 (the graphical user interface) with the KDE Desktop. (Runlevels are explained later in this appendix.)

Booting: The Knoppix View

Another way to look at the boot process is in terms of phases and stages, which are convenient breakpoints where you can interact with Knoppix. As Knoppix boots, it goes through the following four phases:

- Bootloader
- Text
- Graphics
- Shutdown (true, shutdown isn't really part of booting, but it does complete the cycle)

To see these phases in action, let's take a quick tour through the boot process. Insert the CD, boot the computer, and you should see the Knoppix boot splash screen, as shown in Figure A-1.

FIGURE A-1: Start with the Knoppix boot splash screen.

Notice the boot prompt, boot:. To see a list of some of the cheatcodes, press F2 for one page or F3 for the other. To return to the splash screen, press F1. (More on cheatcodes in a bit.)

Note Knoppix lists only a few of the cheatcodes when you press F2 or F3. You can find a more complete list on the CD. If your CD drive is letter D:\, the list is in D:\KNOPPIX\knoppix-cheatcodes.txt. If you boot with Knoppix, the list is in /cdrom/KNOPPIX/knoppix-cheatcodes.txt.

To move on to the text phase, enter

```
knoppix 3
```

at the boot prompt. A bunch of text flies by and then you see a shell prompt that looks like the following:

```
root@tty1[/]#
```

Now you're in textmode, with which you use your keyboard to interact with Knoppix via the command line.

To enter the graphics phase, enter init 5 at the shell prompt. After a few graphics services start up, the KDE Desktop (see Figure A-2) opens on your screen. In graphics mode, you use your mouse (and keyboard, especially your mouse) to interact with Knoppix via the graphical user interface.

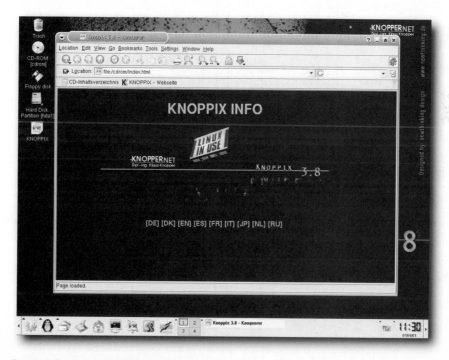

FIGURE A-2: Knoppix in graphics mode.

To enter the shutdown phase, open the K menu and select Logout → Turn off Computer. You can also shut down from within a virtual terminal by entering `shutdown` or `init 0`. When shutdown completes, Knoppix ejects the CD and gives you finishing instructions. Rebooting works similarly: open the K menu and select Logout → Restart Computer from within KDE, or enter `reboot` or `init 6` from a terminal window.

One important point about the Knoppix boot process is that each phase depends on the success of the previous phase. If you get into graphics phase, that means that Knoppix was able to get through the boot and text phases. Of course, that's if all goes well.

Although Knoppix does an excellent job at guessing your hardware and configuring the settings, it is still just that: a guess. Sometimes, Knoppix guesses wrong or makes the wrong assumption. When that happens you find yourself staring at a blank screen, a system that just seems frozen, or a screen full of odd-looking text with the word "Oops!" or "Panic!" So what do you do when that happens? That is, how can you nudge Knoppix so that it guesses correctly or makes different assumptions? Use cheatcodes.

Cheatcodes are options that you pass to Knoppix at boot time to configure various settings. In the earlier example, you used cheatcode 3 to tell Knoppix to stop the boot process in the textmode.

Note For a more complete list of cheatcodes and their descriptions, visit the KNOPPIX.net Website, `www.knoppix.net/wiki/Cheat_Codes`.

Booting: Knoppix Details

Let's go through the boot process again, this time examining each phase in a bit more detail and exploring some of the cheatcodes that are processed at each level.

Examining the Bootloader Phase

During the bootloader phase, the BIOS loads and runs the `isolinux` bootloader from the CD-ROM. At the end of the bootloader phase, the Knoppix splash screen displays. If you do not see the Knoppix splash screen, you might want to try out some of these fixes:

- Check your BIOS to ensure that your system can boot from a CD-ROM.
- Check the md5sum of the ISO to ensure that it was not corrupted during the download.
- Make sure that you burn the ISO to the CD as an image and not as a file.
- Make sure that you burn at a slow speed — less than 8x — to ensure that you get a good burn.
- Run `boot: memtest` to check your system's memory.
- Run `boot: knoppix vga=0 testcd` to check the CD.

If you've tried all of these options and Knoppix still does not display the splash screen, you may want to look into the Smart Boot Manager (http://btmgr.sourceforge.net/about.html), which automatically locates all bootable floppy, hard, and CD-ROM devices and enables you to boot from them even when the BIOS doesn't recognize them.

If you still have problems booting Knoppix, post a question to the knoppix.net forums (www.knoppix.net/forum). Be sure to include the Knoppix version, a brief description of your hardware, and any error messages.

At this stage of the boot process, there isn't much to look at. It pretty much either works or not. However, it is at the boot prompt that you type in cheatcodes that determine how the rest of the boot process progresses.

Examining the Text Phase

The text phase can be broken down into five stages. As Knoppix goes from stage to stage, it probes and configures more and more of your hardware. By pausing at each stage, you can examine what Knoppix has done and change it before moving on to the next stage.

Let's take a more detailed look at the stages in the text phase by using two additional cheatcodes, debug and -b, which tell Knoppix to pause and display a shell prompt at the end of each stage.

Exploring Stage 1

At the boot prompt, enter the following:

```
knoppix debug -b 3
```

This time, you see a lot more text fly by, and then the screen shown in Figure A-3 is displayed.

This stage is very important because it tells you a lot, including the following:

- Your machine can boot from the CD-ROM.
- The default Linux kernel works with your machine.
- Video mode is working.

At this stage, Knoppix is running a very stripped-down version of the ash shell. There's not a whole lot you can do except run the built-in ash commands and the few available external binaries. For example, you cannot type ls to get a listing of the files; there is no ls. Instead, use echo * or echo /proc/* to see a listing of files in the current directory or /proc, respectively. You can also do some simple looping to explore kernel settings or devices:

```
for i in /proc/* ; do echo $i ; done
```

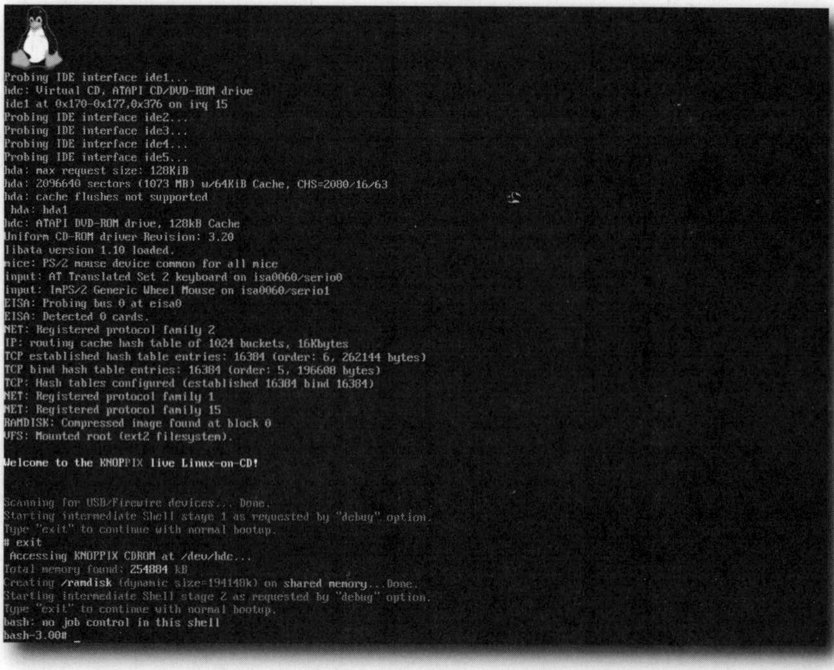

FIGURE A-3: Knoppix stopping at the end of the stage 1 boot process

The following cheatcodes are processed or have some effect during stage 1:

pnpbios=	vga=	acpi=
mem=	ide2=	nopcmcia
pci=	nosmp	noapic
debug	nomce	noapm
nousb	nofirewire	expert
modules-disk	noscsi	fromhd
atapicd	knoppix_dir=	knoppix_name=
dma	nodma	

The most common problems seem to be issues with VGA settings, Direct Memory Access (DMA), power settings, and PNP BIOS. If you don't get to the stage 1 shell, reboot your machine and try booting with the following:

```
knoppix vga=normal nodma noapic noacpi pnpbios=off acpi=off ↵
   noapm debug -b 3
```

If that doesn't work, you can turn off a lot of options using the failsafe kernel label:

```
failsafe debug -b 3
```

Note

The boot command line has a limit of 256 characters.

Exploring Stage 2

To move on to stage 2, enter `exit` at the stage 1 shell prompt. A few lines of text messages appear, followed by this prompt:

```
bash-3.00#
```

The following cheatcodes are processed or have some effect during stage 2: `bootfrom=`, `tohd`, and `toram`.

Exploring Stage 3

To move on to stage 3, type `exit` at the stage 2 shell prompt. You'll then see a few lines of text messages followed by this prompt:

```
root@console (deleted)[/]#
```

No cheatcodes are processed when moving to stage 3. However, this does mark the end of the initial boot script, `/linuxrc`. When Knoppix leaves stage 3, `/linuxrc` is deleted and `/etc/init` takes over the boot process. Basically, `/UNIONFS` is set up in this stage.

Exploring Stage 4 (Emergency Mode)

Leave stage 3 by typing `exit`. You'll see the line "Starting the init process" followed by "Give root password for maintenance." Simply press the Enter key, and you will be in an emergency-mode shell. At this point, the `init` program (`/etc/init`) has taken over and begun processing `/etc/inittab`. The only cheatcode processed at this stage is `-b`, which causes `init` to boot directly into a single user shell without running any other startup scripts. This enables you to modify those startup scripts, change environment variables, or load/unload modules before continuing the boot process.

Tip

If you cannot get to the next stage, modify the file `/etc/init.d/knoppix-autoconfig` by placing a `set -x` command near the top. That commands tells Knoppix to display a lot of debugging information that may give you some clues as to why Knoppix does not successfully complete moving on to the next stage.

Exploring Stage 5 (Textmode Runlevel)

Move on to stage 5 by entering `exit`. Knoppix is then in textmode, specifically runlevel 3, in which you have a fully running Knoppix system. The big change between stages 4 and 5 is that the startup script `/etc/init.d/knoppix-autoconfig` ran, probing and configuring more of the hardware. Specifically, `knoppix-autoconfig` processes the following cheatcodes (some with examples):

myconf=/dev/sda1	myconf=scan
config=scan, myconfig=scan	floppyconfig, floppyconf
home=scan	splash
blind	brltty=type
port	table
alsa	alsa=es1938
lang=bg|be|ch|cn|cs|cz|da| de|dk|es|fi|fr|ie|it|ja|nl| pl|ru|sk|tr|tw|uk|us	keyboard=us, xkeyboard=us
testcd	desktop=fluxbox|icewm|kde|larswm|twm| wmaker|xfce
gmt|utc	tz
nohwsetup	noaudio
noagp	noswap
dma	nofstab
swap	config
nodhcp	

knoppix-autoconfig also calls some auxiliary scripts that generate a number of configuration files, most notably all the files in /etc/sysconfig/.

Virtual Consoles
While you are in textmode, you should become familiar with switching between the four virtual consoles (VCs). You can tell which VC you are in by looking at the shell prompt. When you boot into textmode level, you are in the first VC by default. The first VC has a prompt with tty1. The second VC has a prompt with tty2, and so on. In addition, each VC is associated with one of the function keys F1 through F4, respectively. To switch to the second VC, press the key combination Ctrl+Alt+F2. To switch back to the first VC, press Ctrl+Alt+F1. The same is true for the other virtual consoles: press Ctrl+Alt+F3 for the third VC, and Ctrl+Alt+F4 for the fourth.

Runlevels
One other task that you should be familiar with is changing runlevels. A Linux runlevel is similar to Windows' safe mode. You can tell which runlevel you are in by entering the command runlevel, which displays two numbers: the previous runlevel and your current one. Knoppix comes predefined with seven runlevels, numbered 0 through 6. By default, Knoppix boots into number 5 (more on this in the next section). You can specify a different runlevel at the boot prompt. For example, earlier you specified runlevel 3 by entering knoppix 3 at the boot prompt.

Depending on the runlevel, different features or services are enabled or disabled. In Knoppix, the runlevels are divvied up this way: four for textmode, one for graphics mode, and two that power down the computer. In runlevel 1, Knoppix starts up in textmode level with only one VC. In runlevel 2, Knoppix starts up in textmode with four VCs. Runlevels 2, 3, and 4 act identically. Runlevel 5 is the graphics mode (more on this in the next section). Runlevels 0 and 6 are, respectively, for powering down or rebooting the machine. To change runlevels once Knoppix is running, use the `init` command. For example, to change to runlevel 1, enter `init 1`. To change back to runlevel 3, enter `init 3`.

Examining the Graphics Phase

To start the graphics phase of the boot process, enter `init 5` from any virtual console. Of course, you could also get here by explicitly entering `knoppix 5` at the boot prompt or by simply pressing the Enter key at the boot prompt because runlevel 5 (graphics mode, which displays the KDE desktop) is the default for Knoppix.

To start the graphics environment, `/etc/init` ran the script `/etc/init.d/xsessions`, which processed the following cheatcodes by default:

`xserver=XFree86|XF86_SVGA`	`xkeyboard=us`
`xmodule=ati|radeon|fbdev|vesa|` `savage|s3|nv|i810|mga|svga|tseng`	`desktop=fluxbox|icewm|kde|` `larswm|twm|wmaker|xfce`
`nowheelmouse`	`wheelmouse`
`screen=1280x1024`	`xhrefresh=80 or hsync=80`
`xvrefresh=60 or vsync=60`	

From within graphics mode, you also can switch virtual consoles. To switch to the second VC, press Ctrl+Alt+F2. To return to the graphics virtual console, the fifth VC, press Ctrl+Alt+F5. You can also change runlevels by opening the K menu and selecting Run Command, and then typing `sudo init 3` to change to runlevel 3, for example. You can also do this by first switching to a text VC and then entering `init 3`. To return to runlevel 5, enter `init 5`.

You can cycle between different graphics modes using Ctrl+Alt+Shift+= and Ctrl+Alt+-. In addition, you can restart the X server by typing Ctrl+Alt+Backspace.

Examining the Shutdown Phase

To begin shutdown from graphics mode, open the K menu and select Logout, and then click either Turn Off Computer or Restart Computer, depending on whether you want to power off or reboot the machine. You can also shut down from a virtual console by entering `poweroff` or `reboot`. During the shutdown phase, Knoppix goes through two more stages before finally powering off. To proceed from one stage to the next, simply enter `exit` at the command line.

Cheatcodes processed during this phase are `noeject` and `noprompt`. Because of the way the scripts are currently written, if you specify `noprompt` (which instructs Knoppix not to prompt you to remove the CD and press Enter), you must also specify `noeject`. (which tells Knoppix not to eject the CD). If you specify only `noprompt`, Knoppix hangs just before rebooting.

Tips, Tricks, and Troubleshooting

The following sections contain a collection of tips and tricks that you can use to troubleshoot the boot process or to customize your Knoppix environment.

Blank Screen: Now What?

Remember the scenario described in the opening paragraph of this appendix? Your CD worked just fine on a friend's computer, yet when you put the same CD in your machine all you see is a blank screen. What's going on?

There could be a number of reasons why you're getting a blank screen, but they depend on where in the process you get it. To determine that, boot with this command:

```
knoppix vga=0 debug -b 3
```

Do you get to the bootloader phase? If not, you may want to explore some of the options mentioned in the section "Examining the Bootloader Phase," earlier in the appendix. If you get past the bootloader phase, how far do you get into the text phase? If you do not get to stage 1, the most common problems seem to be issues with VGA settings, power settings, and PNP BIOS, as mentioned earlier. Reboot your machine and try booting with this command:

```
knoppix vga=normal noapic noacpi pnpbios=off acpi=off noapm ⤵
    debug -b 3
```

If that doesn't work, then, as mentioned before, you can turn off several more options using

```
failsafe debug -b 3
```

Once you get to a shell prompt, enter `cat /proc/cmdline` to see the text of the successful boot command line. You can optimize your boot command by methodically removing the cheatcodes that `failsafe` uses:

`atapicd`	`nosound`	`noapic`
`noacpi`	`pnpbios=off`	`acpi=off`
`nofstab`	`noscsi`	`nodma`
`noapm`	`nousb`	`nopcmcia`
`nofirewire`	`noagp`	`nomce`
and `nodhcp`.		

Once you get into textmode, try getting into graphics mode by changing the runlevel using this command:

```
init 5
```

Are you able to get into graphics mode? If not, there are a couple of things to try. First, get back into text mode by pressing Ctrl+Alt+F1 to get to virtual console 1 and then enter `init 3`. You may have to press Enter once or twice before the prompt appears. The most common problem seems to be that Knoppix guesses the wrong video driver. You can tell what driver Knoppix will try by entering the following:

```
grep -i ^x /etc/sysconfig/knoppix
```

If for some reason the driver specified by the XMODULE= line does not allow the xserver to start, Knoppix tries the vesa driver followed by the fbdev driver before giving up. If you don't want Knoppix to guess, you can explicitly tell Knoppix to use a different driver. To do that, simply reboot and specify the driver at the boot prompt, like this:

```
boot: knoppix xmodule=fbdev
```

In addition to the xmodule= cheatcode, you may want to try out other cheatcodes that take effect in the graphics phase.

If you still have trouble booting Knoppix, you might have very new hardware, very old hardware, or very esoteric hardware. If so, post your question as well as a description of your hardware (using a command such as lspci) to the Knoppix forums, which can be accessed at www.knoppix.net/forum/.

Testing Various xmodule= Cheatcodes Quickly

You don't have to reboot to try out different xmodules. You can simply change runlevels and make adjustments to /etc/sysconfig/knoppix. To try this out, press Enter at the boot prompt to boot Knoppix using the defaults. When Knoppix finishes booting, change to VC 1 with Ctrl+Alt+F1 and enter runlevel 3 with init 3. To see what driver Knoppix used, type:

```
grep -i driver /etc/X11/XF86Config-4
```

Let's say that Knoppix chose "savage" as the driver, but you want Knoppix to use the fbdev driver. To do so, type these commands:

```
echo 'XMODULE="fbdev"' >> /etc/sysconfig/knoppix
rm /etc/X11/XF86Config-4
mkxf86config
init 5
```

Knoppix will now try the fbdev driver. To try another driver, change to VC 1 with Ctrl+Alt+F1, and repeat the steps. Once you find one that works better than what Knoppix guessed, you can use it at the boot prompt like so:

```
knoppix xmodule=fbdev
```

Rebooting Quickly . . . Very Quickly

Want Knoppix to reboot quickly? Just press Alt+SysRq+B (SysRq is the same key as the PrintScr key). This key combination is effectively the same as pressing the reset button on the machine. That is, your system reboots immediately without flushing the cache or unmounting the disks. Unless you tell Knoppix otherwise, it doesn't try to mount any drives until after stage 4 in the text phase. Until then, using Alt+SysRq+B is quite safe. After that stage, however, you need to be sure that you don't have any disks mounted. If you are not sure, do not use Atl+SysRq+B.

Testing Various vga= Cheatcodes Quickly

While vga=0 or vga=normal always works, your video card may be able to do more. You can test these extended video modes fairly quickly with the vga= and debug cheatcodes shown in the following table:

Colors	640x480	800x600	1024x768	1280x1024
256	769	771	773	775
32k	784	787	790	793
60k	785	788	791	794
16M	786	789	792	795

For example, to test out 800 × 600 with 256 colors, boot with

```
failsafe debug vga=771
```

If the screen goes black, press Alt+SysRq+B to quickly reboot the machine and try another value for vga=. Conversely, if you get to stage 1 of the text phase and like what you see, simply enter exit to continue the boot process. If you want to try other vga= codes, just press Alt+SysRq+B to reboot the machine (but remember not to use that command if your machine has mounted disks).

Quickly Changing Desktop Managers

If you've already booted into a desktop such as KDE, you can change desktops by changing to a text virtual console (such as Ctrl+Alt+F1) and issuing these commands:

```
init 3
echo 'DESKTOP="icewm"' >> /etc/sysconfig/desktop
init 5
```

This example changes your desktop to the Ice Window Manager.

Using Multiple Persistent Disk Images

Suppose you have two persistent disk images (which you learned to make in the Introduction to this book) on `/dev/hda2` — knoppix.java.img and knoppix.lamp.img, and you want to boot using the Java image. Here's what to do:

```
knoppix -b
```

When Knoppix enters stage 4 (emergency mode) in the text phase, enter the following:

```
rebuildfstab
mount /mnt/hda2
ln /mnt/hda2/knoppix.java.img /mnt/hda2/knoppix.img
umount /mnt/hda2
exit
```

When booting continues, confirm that you want to activate the image at `/dev/hda2/knoppix.img` by selecting OK.

If you want to use the lamp image when you reboot, repeat the same steps as before, but substitute the lamp image for the Java image:

```
ln /mnt/hda2/knoppix.lamp.img /mnt/hda2/knoppix.img
```

If `/dev/hda2` happens to be a vfat partition or some other filesystem that does not support linking, substitute the `cp` command for the `ln` command.

Playing DVDs or Audio CDs with Only One CD/DVD-ROM Drive

It's hard having only one CD/DVD drive if you want to play a DVD or audio CD while you're working with Knoppix. Here's a great workaround if you have Windows on `/dev/hda1`: Boot into Windows and download a copy of the Knoppix ISO to your `C:\` drive, name it `C:\knx.iso`, and reboot with the Knoppix CD generated from that same ISO. At the boot prompt, enter

```
knoppix bootfrom=/dev/hda1/knx.iso
```

Once Knoppix boots, you can remove the CD from the CD/DVD-ROM drive and happily insert your CD/DVD.

If you have more than one gigabyte of RAM, you could use `toram`:

```
knoppix toram
```

This copies the ISO into RAM and then continues the boot process from the image that's in RAM, enabling you to eject the CD.

This tip works as long as `/dev/hda1` contains a supported filesystem: ext2, ext3, reiserfs, vfat, or ntfs. If you have a vfat or ext2 partition, you also can use the `tohd=` cheatcode:

```
knoppix tohd=/dev/hda1/
```

It does a "poor-man's install" by copying all the files in the compressed image to the hard drive. After you've done this once, you can boot with this command:

```
knoppix fromhd=/dev/hda1/
```

Finding Undocumented Cheatcodes

There are basically three files that process cheatcodes:

- /linuxrc
- /etc/init.d/knoppix-autoconfig
- /etc/init.d/xsession

In each, grep for cmdline:

```
grep -i cmdline /etc/sysconfig/knoppix-autoconfig
```

or view the script with less:

```
less -iXS# 10 +/cmdline /etc/sysconfig/knoppix-autoconfig
```

If you want to explore the script /linuxrc, you have to copy it to /tmp/ before Knoppix leaves stage 3 of textmode. When Knoppix leaves stage 3, /linuxrc is deleted and less is not very functional until after stage 4. Alternatively, you can extract the script from the initial compressed ramdisk:

```
cd /tmp
mkdir /tmp/minirt
zcat /cdrom/boot/isolinux/minirt.gz➜minirt.img
mount -o loop minirt.img minirt
cp minirt/linuxrc .
umount minirt
```

Installing Knoppix to Your Hard Drive

Knoppix is a great way to try out Linux with no commitment and without modifying your hard drive. After using it a while, you may decide you want to install it to your computer so it is always readily available without your having to use the CD. This appendix explains how to prepare and install Knoppix to your hard drive.

The Good, the Bad, and the Ugly of Knoppix Hard Drive Installation

Knoppix is primarily geared for use from the CD-ROM, but there are some valid reasons to run Knoppix from your hard drive, including the following:

➤ Faster boot up

➤ Freeing up your CD drive for other uses

➤ Having a consistent, easily configurable Linux distribution without going through any extra steps required from the Live CD version

➤ Dual booting, so that you have a choice when you start your computer between Knoppix and another operating system on your PC, such as Windows 98, 2000, or XP

Be forewarned! You need to consider a few of the negative aspects of installing Knoppix to your hard drive instead of using one of the hard-drive–focused versions of Linux (such as Kanotix, Ubuntu/Kubuntu, and MEPIS) that also provide Live CDs to test drive:

➤ You aren't provided with the same level of granularity to choose what is going to be installed.

➤ If you install with some of the system types, you aren't afforded the standard security protections that come with most Linux distributions (security for the root account is open to any user on the live system, for example).

- The Knoppix system is designed to be run on any system, and some of the specialized hardware installed on most systems is treated generically, not taking full advantage of the hardware. In other words, your super-expensive video card may become, in the hands of Knoppix, the equivalent of an 8-year-old basic video card that outputs rudimentary VGA and not much else.

- Users have reported various levels of success upgrading their systems once Knoppix is installed. You may go through an install only to find that upgrading your system breaks things.

The reasons to *not* install Knoppix to your hard drive are significant and should be carefully considered prior to going through with the process.

 Note You can find out more about the other distros mentioned earlier in this section by pointing your Web browser at their home pages. You'll find Kanotix at www.kanotix.com, Ubuntu (a GNOME-based distro) at www.ubuntu.com, Kubuntu (the KDE-based brother of Ubuntu) at www.kubuntu.org, and MEPIS at www.mepis.org.

Preparing to Install

In addition to all the requirements for running Knoppix from the CD, you need the following to install it onto your hard drive (these are bare minimum requirements; as with most things involving computers, more is always better):

- 2GB or more of hard drive space to install the primary operating system
- 128MB of swap space (if you have less than 512MB of physical RAM).

You can set up partitions for these prior to starting the installation routine or you can wait until the install process and use QTParted.

Installing Knoppix

Open a console window by selecting Knoppix ➜ System ➜ Konsole. Enter su to switch to root, and then enter knoppix-installer at the # prompt, as shown in Figure B-1.

FIGURE B-1: Starting the knoppix-installer

After a few moments, the Knoppix Installation splash screen opens with a warning regarding the beta quality of the script and forfeiture of responsibility if the install causes data loss or hardware damage. Click OK if you agree to the terms.

Partitioning for Knoppix

If you do not have the proper partitions of at least 2GB for the software and at least 128MB for the swap space, the installer tells you (see Figure B-2 — if you created the partitions ahead of time, you will see the screen shown in Figure B-6).

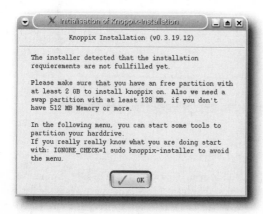

FIGURE B-2: Partition detection

Click OK, and the Partition Menu window opens (shown in Figure B-3). Here you choose to create the partitions (or quit without committing to the install).

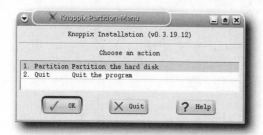

FIGURE B-3: Knoppix Partition Menu window

QTParted opens (see Figure B-4), providing you with a visual interface from which you can create and resize disk partitions.

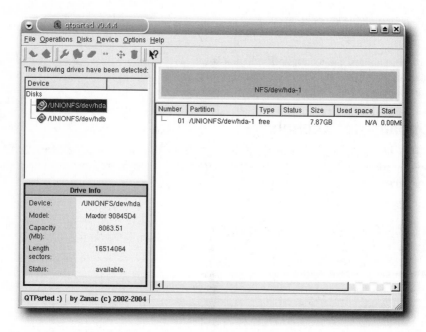

FIGURE B-4: QTParted

Refer to Chapters 4 and 5 for using QTParted to resize partitions. Make sure you have at least 2GB of space available for the software install and at least 128MB of space available for swapping, and commit the changes in QTParted. Write down the path to the partition (such as /dev/hda1) that is going to be used for installing Knoppix later in the process, and exit the program. The main menu for the installation displays, as shown in Figure B-5.

FIGURE B-5: Knoppix installer main menu

Configuring the Installation

You need to configure your installation, which is selected by default, so click OK. The installer asks you to choose a system type (see Figure B-6).

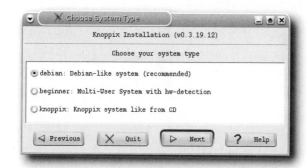

FIGURE B-6: Select a system type.

The three options are as follows:

- **Debian (recommended):** Installs a derivative of full-fledged Debian Linux (www. debian.org), which will behave like most regular hard-drive native Linux distributions. This is the preferred type.

- **Beginner:** Installs a multiple-user (more than one user on the same system) package with specialized hardware detection for the machine on which it's being installed.

- **Knoppix:** Installs the packages in such a way that the system behaves exactly as if you had booted off a CD.

Select the system type you want and click Next. Then choose the partition on which to install Knoppix (see Figure B-7).

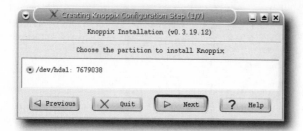

FIGURE B-7: Select a partition for the Knoppix installation.

In this example, there's only one large data partition, so that's the only choice. You may have several from which to choose. If you have a Windows partition, be very careful to enter the correct device, such as /dev/hda1, as noted earlier when using QTParted; otherwise, you may overwrite your data. Select the partition on which you want Knoppix and click Next. Then choose your filesystem type (see Figure B-8).

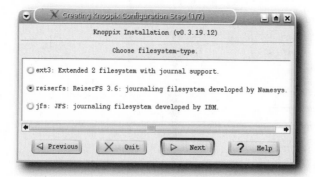

FIGURE B-8: Select a filesystem type.

The default filesystem is ReiserFS, but you can select JFS or ext3, if you prefer (the default is perfectly fine and will work beautifully for almost everyone). Make your choice and click Next. Enter your full name at the prompt (see Figure B-9), and click Next.

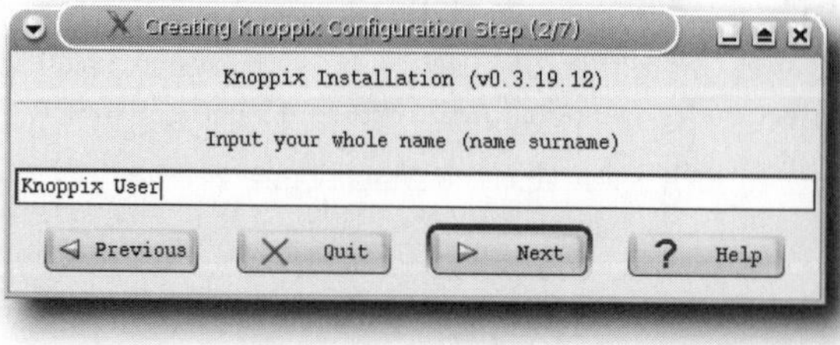

FIGURE B-9: Enter personal identification.

Knoppix uses the first letter of your first name and your full last name to create a username for you (see Figure B-10). You can change the username to whatever you'd like. You'll use it to log into the system both locally and remotely. When you're satisfied with your username, click Next.

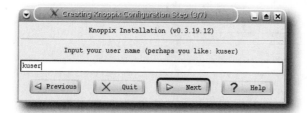

FIGURE B-10: Use the Knoppix-generated username or create your own.

Now create a password to go with your new username. Enter the password twice, as shown in Figure B-11, and click Next.

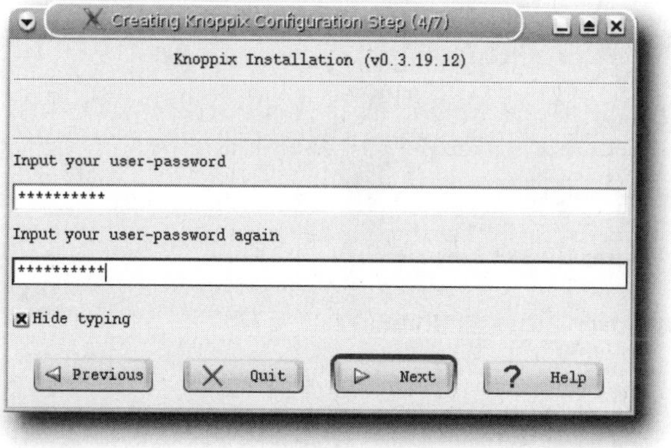

FIGURE B-11: Enter a user password.

The administration password (see Figure B-12) is not the user password you just created; it's not associated with your username at all. It is the all-important root or super-user account password that provides full access to the system. For security reasons, you should be especially careful to ensure that you use a strong password with a combination of alphanumeric and non-alphanumeric characters. Enter the password twice and click Next.

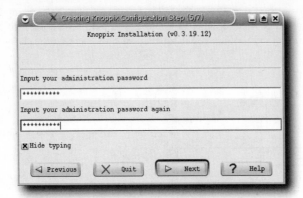

FIGURE B-12: Enter an administration (root) password.

You're prompted to provide your system hostname (see Figure B-13), which is the name by which you want to refer to your machine. The default is box, which should be changed to something more interesting and descriptive. After you've entered a name you like, click Next.

FIGURE B-13: Create a system hostname.

The boot loader (called GRUB, for grand unified boot loader) does the heavy work and starts the Knoppix operating system when you turn on your computer. It can be installed in the master boot record (MBR) or on the partition on which Knoppix will be installed (see Figure B-14). If you have multiple operating systems on the same computer and install GRUB in the MBR, you can use it to boot all your operating systems. If you are installing Knoppix on a computer with no other operating systems, you also probably want to choose the MBR option.

Later in the install process, you have the option to create a boot floppy disk. If you want to boot Knoppix only when you have the boot floppy installed and you normally operate the system without the diskette, you should select the partition option. Make your choice and then click Next.

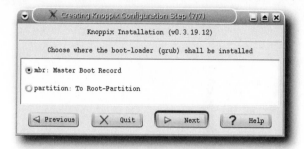

FIGURE B-14: Select the boot loader location.

Beginning the Install

You've finished the configuration part of the installation and are ready to start the Knoppix installation. Select Start Installation from the menu (see Figure B-15) and click OK.

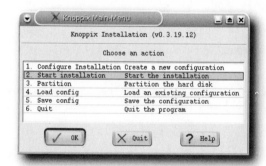

FIGURE B-15: Starting the installation from the main menu

The next screen summarizes the installation parameters associated with your choices, as shown in Figure B-16. Click Next to continue.

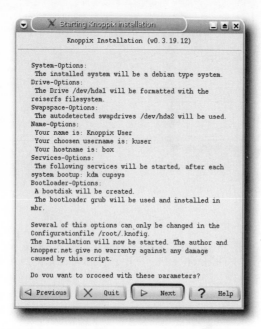

FIGURE B-16: Review the installation parameters.

The installation may take quite a while, depending on your system's speed, but the installer keeps you posted on its progress, as shown in Figure B-17.

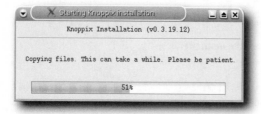

FIGURE B-17: Installation progress

After all the files have been installed, you are prompted to insert a floppy disk (see Figure B-18). The disk will enable you to boot your Linux partition if you installed the GRUB boot loader to the partition or enable you to boot if GRUB gets corrupted. You do not have to create the disk if you prefer not to or if you don't have a floppy drive; just click No and the installation will continue. To create the disk, click Yes and follow the prompts.

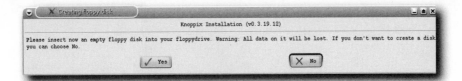

FIGURE B-18: Click yes to create a boot disk.

When everything's finished, the installer lets you know that the process was successful (see Figure B-19). (If it wasn't successful, you will encounter errors when starting the system, in which case you will need to reinstall.)

FIGURE B-19: Successful installation

Click OK, and reboot your system with the Knoppix CD removed. You can either start up your Windows partitions or your Linux partitions, depending on the setup of your system.

Hacking Knoppix

Index

SYMBOLS & NUMERICS

GNU General Public License

Version 2, June 1991

Copyright © 1989, 1991 Free Software Foundation, Inc.

675 Mass Ave, Cambridge, MA 02139, USA

Preamble

The licenses for most software are designed to take away your freedom to share and change it. By contrast, the GNU General Public License is intended to guarantee your freedom to share and change free software--to make sure the software is free for all its users. This General Public License applies to most of the Free Software Foundation's software and to any other program whose authors commit to using it. (Some other Free Software Foundation software is covered by the GNU Library General Public License instead.) You can apply it to your programs, too.

When we speak of free software, we are referring to freedom, not price. Our General Public Licenses are designed to make sure that you have the freedom to distribute copies of free software (and charge for this service if you wish), that you receive source code or can get it if you want it, that you can change the software or use pieces of it in new free programs; and that you know you can do these things.

To protect your rights, we need to make restrictions that forbid anyone to deny you these rights or to ask you to surrender the rights. These restrictions translate to certain responsibilities for you if you distribute copies of the software, or if you modify it.

For example, if you distribute copies of such a program, whether gratis or for a fee, you must give the recipients all the rights that you have. You must make sure that they, too, receive or can get the source code. And you must show them these terms so they know their rights.

We protect your rights with two steps: (1) copyright the software, and (2) offer you this license which gives you legal permission to copy, distribute and/or modify the software.

Also, for each author's protection and ours, we want to make certain that everyone understands that there is no warranty for this free software. If the software is modified by someone else and passed on, we want its recipients to know that what they have is not the original, so that any problems introduced by others will not reflect on the original authors' reputations.

Finally, any free program is threatened constantly by software patents. We wish to avoid the danger that redistributors of a free program will individually obtain patent licenses, in effect making the program proprietary. To prevent this, we have made it clear that any patent must be licensed for everyone's free use or not licensed at all.

The precise terms and conditions for copying, distribution and modification follow.

TERMS AND CONDITIONS FOR COPYING, DISTRIBUTION AND MODIFICATION

0. This License applies to any program or other work which contains a notice placed by the copyright holder saying it may be distributed under the terms of this General Public License. The "Program", below, refers to any such program or work, and a "work based on the Program" means either the Program or any derivative work under copyright law: that is to say, a work containing the Program or a portion of it, either verbatim or with modifications and/or translated into another language. (Hereinafter, translation is included without limitation in the term "modification".) Each licensee is addressed as "you".

   Activities other than copying, distribution and modification are not covered by this License; they are outside its scope. The act of running the Program is not restricted, and the output from the Program is covered only if its contents constitute a work based on the Program (independent of having been made by running the Program). Whether that is true depends on what the Program does.

1. You may copy and distribute verbatim copies of the Program's source code as you receive it, in any medium, provided that you conspicuously and appropriately publish on each copy an appropriate copyright notice and disclaimer of warranty; keep intact all the notices that refer to this License and to the absence of any warranty; and give any other recipients of the Program a copy of this License along with the Program.

   You may charge a fee for the physical act of transferring a copy, and you may at your option offer warranty protection in exchange for a fee.

2. You may modify your copy or copies of the Program or any portion of it, thus forming a work based on the Program, and copy and distribute such modifications or work under the terms of Section 1 above, provided that you also meet all of these conditions:

   a) You must cause the modified files to carry prominent notice stating that you changed the files and the date of any change.

   b) You must cause any work that you distribute or publish, that in whole or in part contains or is derived from the Program or any part thereof, to be licensed as a whole at no charge to all third parties under the terms of this License.

   c) If the modified program normally reads commands interactively when run, you must cause it, when started running for such interactive use in the most ordinary way, to print or display an announcement including an appropriate copyright notice and a notice that there is no warranty (or else, saying that you provide a warranty) and that users may redistribute the program under these conditions, and telling the user how to view a copy of this License. (Exception: if the Program itself is interactive but does not normally print such an announcement, your work based on the Program is not required to print an announcement.)

   These requirements apply to the modified work as a whole. If identifiable sections of that work are not derived from the Program, and can be reasonably considered independent and separate works in themselves, then this License, and its terms, do not apply to those sections when you distribute them as separate works. But when you distribute the same sections as part of a whole which is a work based on the Program, the distribution of the whole must be on the terms of this License, whose permissions for other licensees extend to the entire whole, and thus to each and every part regardless of who wrote it.

   Thus, it is not the intent of this section to claim rights or contest your rights to work written entirely by you; rather, the intent is to exercise the right to control the distribution of derivative or collective works based on the Program.

In addition, mere aggregation of another work not based on the Program with the Program (or with a work based on the Program) on a volume of a storage or distribution medium does not bring the other work under the scope of this License.

3. You may copy and distribute the Program (or a work based on it, under Section 2) in object code or executable form under the terms of Sections 1 and 2 above provided that you also do one of the following:

   a) Accompany it with the complete corresponding machine-readable source code, which must be distributed under the terms of Sections 1 and 2 above on a medium customarily used for software interchange; or,

   b) Accompany it with a written offer, valid for at least three years, to give any third party, for a charge no more than your cost of physically performing source distribution, a complete machine-readable copy of the corresponding source code, to be distributed under the terms of Sections 1 and 2 above on a medium customarily used for software interchange; or,

   c) Accompany it with the information you received as to the offer to distribute corresponding source code. (This alternative is allowed only for noncommercial distribution and only if you received the program in object code or executable form with such an offer, in accord with Subsection b above.)

The source code for a work means the preferred form of the work for making modifications to it. For an executable work, complete source code means all the source code for all modules it contains, plus any associated interface definition files, plus the scripts used to control compilation and installation of the executable. However, as a special exception, the source code distributed need not include anything that is normally distributed (in either source or binary form) with the major components (compiler, kernel, and so on) of the operating system on which the executable runs, unless that component itself accompanies the executable.

If distribution of executable or object code is made by offering access to copy from a designated place, then offering equivalent access to copy the source code from the same place counts as distribution of the source code, even though third parties are not compelled to copy the source along with the object code.

4. You may not copy, modify, sublicense, or distribute the Program except as expressly provided under this License. Any attempt otherwise to copy, modify, sublicense or distribute the Program is void, and will automatically terminate your rights under this License. However, parties who have received copies, or rights, from you under this License will not have their licenses terminated so long as such parties remain in full compliance.

5. You are not required to accept this License, since you have not signed it. However, nothing else grants you permission to modify or distribute the Program or its derivative works. These actions are prohibited by law if you do not accept this License. Therefore, by modifying or distributing the Program (or any work based on the Program), you indicate your acceptance of this License to do so, and all its terms and conditions for copying, distributing or modifying the Program or works based on it.

6. Each time you redistribute the Program (or any work based on the Program), the recipient automatically receives a license from the original licensor to copy, distribute or modify the Program subject to these terms and conditions. You may not impose any further restrictions on the recipients' exercise of the rights granted herein. You are not responsible for enforcing compliance by third parties to this License.

7. If, as a consequence of a court judgment or allegation of patent infringement or for any other reason (not limited to patent issues), conditions are imposed on you (whether by court order, agreement or otherwise) that contradict the conditions of this License, they do not excuse you from the conditions of this License. If you cannot distribute so as to satisfy simultaneously your obligations under this License and any other pertinent obligations, then as a consequence you may not distribute the Program at all. For example, if a patent license would not permit royalty-free redistribution of the Program by all those who receive copies directly or indirectly through you, then the only way you could satisfy both it and this License would be to refrain entirely from distribution of the Program.

   If any portion of this section is held invalid or unenforceable under any particular circumstance, the balance of the section is intended to apply and the section as a whole is intended to apply in other circumstances.

   It is not the purpose of this section to induce you to infringe any patents or other property right claims or to contest validity of any such claims; this section has the sole purpose of protecting the integrity of the free software distribution system, which is implemented by public license practices. Many people have made generous contributions to the wide range of software distributed through that system in reliance on consistent application of that system; it is up to the author/donor to decide if he or she is willing to distribute software through any other system and a licensee cannot impose that choice.

   This section is intended to make thoroughly clear what is believed to be a consequence of the rest of this License.

8. If the distribution and/or use of the Program is restricted in certain countries either by patents or by copyrighted interfaces, the original copyright holder who places the Program under this License may add an explicit geographical distribution limitation excluding those countries, so that distribution is permitted only in or among countries not thus excluded. In such case, this License incorporates the limitation as if written in the body of this License.

9. The Free Software Foundation may publish revised and/or new versions of the General Public License from time to time. Such new versions will be similar in spirit to the present version, but may differ in detail to address new problems or concerns.

   Each version is given a distinguishing version number. If the Program specifies a version number of this License which applies to it and "any later version", you have the option of following the terms and conditions either of that version or of any later version published by the Free Software Foundation. If the Program does not specify a version number of this License, you may choose any version ever published by the Free Software Foundation.

10. If you wish to incorporate parts of the Program into other free programs whose distribution conditions are different, write to the author to ask for permission. For software which is copyrighted by the Free Software Foundation, write to the Free Software Foundation; we sometimes make exceptions for this. Our decision will be guided by the two goals of preserving the free status of all derivatives of our free software and of promoting the sharing and reuse of software generally.

NO WARRANTY

11. BECAUSE THE PROGRAM IS LICENSED FREE OF CHARGE, THERE IS NO WAR-
RANTY FOR THE PROGRAM, TO THE EXTENT PERMITTED BY APPLICABLE
LAW. EXCEPT WHEN OTHERWISE STATED IN WRITING THE COPYRIGHT
HOLDERS AND/OR OTHER PARTIES PROVIDE THE PROGRAM "AS IS" WITHOUT
WARRANTY OF ANY KIND, EITHER EXPRESSED OR IMPLIED, INCLUDING, BUT
NOT LIMITED TO, THE IMPLIED WARRANTIES OF MERCHANTABILITY AND
FITNESS FOR A PARTICULAR PURPOSE. THE ENTIRE RISK AS TO THE QUALITY
AND PERFORMANCE OF THE PROGRAM IS WITH YOU. SHOULD THE PROGRAM
PROVE DEFECTIVE, YOU ASSUME THE COST OF ALL NECESSARY SERVICING,
REPAIR OR CORRECTION.

12. IN NO EVENT UNLESS REQUIRED BY APPLICABLE LAW OR AGREED TO IN
WRITING WILL ANY COPYRIGHT HOLDER, OR ANY OTHER PARTY WHO MAY
MODIFY AND/OR REDISTRIBUTE THE PROGRAM AS PERMITTED ABOVE, BE
LIABLE TO YOU FOR DAMAGES, INCLUDING ANY GENERAL, SPECIAL, INCIDEN-
TAL OR CONSEQUENTIAL DAMAGES ARISING OUT OF THE USE OR INABILITY
TO USE THE PROGRAM (INCLUDING BUT NOT LIMITED TO LOSS OF DATA OR
DATA BEING RENDERED INACCURATE OR LOSSES SUSTAINED BY YOU OR
THIRD PARTIES OR A FAILURE OF THE PROGRAM TO OPERATE WITH ANY
OTHER PROGRAMS), EVEN IF SUCH HOLDER OR OTHER PARTY HAS BEEN
ADVISED OF THE POSSIBILITY OF SUCH DAMAGES.

END OF TERMS AND CONDITIONS